FREUDIAN MYTHOLOGIES

Freudian Mythologies

Greek Tragedy and Modern Identities

RACHEL BOWLBY

UNIVERSITY PRESS

OXFORD
UNIVERSITY PRESS

Great Clarendon Street, Oxford OX2 6DP

Oxford University Press is a department of the University of Oxford.
It furthers the University's objective of excellence in research, scholarship,
and education by publishing worldwide in

Oxford New York

Auckland Cape Town Dar es Salaam Hong Kong Karachi
Kuala Lumpur Madrid Melbourne Mexico City Nairobi
New Delhi Shanghai Taipei Toronto

With offices in

Argentina Austria Brazil Chile Czech Republic France Greece
Guatemala Hungary Italy Japan Poland Portugal Singapore
South Korea Switzerland Thailand Turkey Ukraine Vietnam

Oxford is a registered trade mark of Oxford University Press
in the UK and in certain other countries

Published in the United States
by Oxford University Press Inc., New York

First published 2007

British Library Cataloguing in Publication Data
Data available

Library of Congress Cataloging in Publication Data
Data available

Typeset by Laserwords Private Limited, Chennai, India
Printed in Great Britain
on acid-free paper by
Biddles Ltd., King's Lynn, Norfolk

ISBN 978–0–19–927039–2

1 3 5 7 9 10 8 6 4 2

For Hellie, Jonathan, and Loulou

Acknowledgements

EARLIER versions of some chapters have appeared elsewhere. Parts of the Introduction and of Chapter 1, 'Freud's Classical Mythologies', contributed to 'Family Realisms: Freud and Greek Tragedy', given as the 2006 Bateson Lecture at Oxford; this appeared in *Essays in Criticism*, 56: 2 (April 2006). Parts of Chapter 2, 'Never Done, Never to Return', are adapted from the Introduction to the new Penguin translation of Freud and Breuer's *Studies in Hysteria*, published in 2004. Chapter 4, 'The Other Day', was published in *Sigmund Freud's 'The Interpretation of Dreams': New Interdisciplinary Essays*, edited by Laura Marcus (Manchester University Press, 1999). Chapter 5, 'A Freudian Curiosity', was in *Literature, Science, Psychoanalysis, 1830–1970: Essays in Honour of Gillian Beer*, edited by Helen Small and Trudi Tate (Oxford University Press, 2003). 'The Cronus Complex' (Chapter 6) is in *Laughing with Medusa*, edited by Vanda Zajko and Miriam Leonard (Oxford University Press, 2006). All previously published material is substantially different in the present volume.

Parts of the book were presented as papers at the universities of Bilkent, Cambridge, Edinburgh, London (Birkbeck, KCL, Queen Mary, and UCL), Manchester Metropolitan, Otago, Oxford, Paris 3 (the Sorbonne Nouvelle), Reading, and Texas A&M; I learned much from the discussions that followed. In 2004, the award of an AHRB (now AHRC) Research Leave Term enabled me to complete a first draft. I am most grateful for this support.

Many friends and colleagues contributed in many different ways. Thanks especially to Gillian Beer, Malcolm Bowie, Peter Brooks, Sara Crangle, Matthew Frost, Trevor Hope, Mary Jacobus, Ladislaus Löb, Raphael Lyne, Charles Martindale, Vicki Mahaffey, Barbara Melosh, Rod Mengham, Hillis Miller, Mary Ann O'Farrell, Jan Parker, Sandeep Parmar, David Shuttleton, Geoff Wall, and Vanda Zajko. I would also like to thank Margaret Dillon and Catherine Whiskin of the University of York Library, John Allen of UCL Library, and Keith Davies and Ivor Evans of the Freud Museum in London, who all went out of their way to help me find relevant materials.

Without Helena, Jonathan, and Louisa Dollimore, the book would not have been this one. The good bits are theirs.

Contents

Abbreviations, Texts, and Translations

GW Sigmund Freud, *Gesammelte Werke* (1951–87; Frankfurt am Main: Fischer Taschenbuch Verlag, 1999).

SE *The Standard Edition of the Complete Psychological Works of Sigmund Freud*, trans. James Strachey, 24 vols. (London: Hogarth Press, 1953–74).

Unless otherwise indicated, citations of Greek and Latin works are taken from the Oxford Classical Texts.

Translations into English not otherwise attributed are mine. In the case of Freud, although I discuss the new Penguin translations in Chapter 9, I refer throughout to James Strachey's translation in the *Standard Edition* (of which a substantial selection was reprinted in the first Penguin Freud series). This is partly because of its familiarity, completeness, and accessibility; and partly for the sake of consistency: being by different people, the new Penguin translations have no terminological homogeneity between volumes.

Introduction

A century after the arrival of Freud's Oedipus, it might seem that modern lives are very different from what they were then. Typical family formations and norms of sexual attachment have changed and are changing, while the conditions of sexual difference, both biologically and socially, have undergone far-reaching modifications. Today, it is possible to choose and live subjective stories that the first psychoanalytic patients could only dream of. Different troubles and enjoyments are speakable and unspeakable; different selves are rejected, discovered, or sought. Many kinds of hitherto unrepresented or unrepresentable identity have entered into the ordinary surrounding stories through which children and adults find their bearings in the world. Biographical narratives that would previously have seemed unthinkable or incredible—'a likely story!'—have acquired the straightforward plausibility of a likely story.

At the same time, normal patterns of behaviour that previously appeared as timelessly natural may now have the dated feel of the historical curiosity; they in their turn have come to verge on the incredible or the obsolete. This leads to a question about how or whether the fundamental determinations of identity have changed—or what, if any, they might be. How fixed are the myths or ideologies through which, consciously or unconsciously, people understand their place in their world? How do people change, or fail to change—both individually, and in the slow time of history through which characters and their typical stories come and go? Conversely, how do the stories change through which we grasp such characters, ourselves included—as individuals, as pairs, or as collectivities?

This book turns back to Freud to look at the ways in which he was himself engaged with such issues. In the light of present-day questions about new forms and conditions of life history, different emphases may show up or seem to be adumbrated in his writing, while others may now appear as striking omissions.[1] Freud's extraordinary interpretation of Sophocles' *Oedipus the King*—that its continuing force was due to its evocation of forgotten infantile impulses common to all—have turned attention away from aspects of the play which have a bearing on different issues of identity, family, and origin, many of them highly charged today. The same is true of other tragedies neglected by Freud in his concentration on Oedipus.

On the question of changing determinations of identity, Freud's own answer was a divided one. Sometimes there is one story and one only, and its primary name is Oedipus; at other times, there is movement and multiplicity and idiosyncrasy, both cultural and personal. In this connection, Freud often makes a distinction between ancient and modern registers, as between tragic universality and inevitability and realistic variation and particularity. But he is hesitant about the weight he grants to the contemporary side. On the one hand there are permanent ur-stories of identity, destined to get hold of every new arrival in the world, without historical differences or individual choice. On the other hand there are ongoing, contemporary stories or fantasies that are inherently impermanent, altering all the time according to the person's age and the changing world they are in. Freud even says that daydreams have something like a *Zeitmarke*, a date-stamp that both ties them specifically to their moment and marks in advance a limit to their useful narrative life; unlike dreams, they are wish-fulfilling in a realistic and contemporary mode.[2] In Freud's study of Wilhelm Jensen's novella *Gradiva*, the lightness and liveliness of the modern takes the form of a girl who mimics a statue to save the archaeologist hero from his absorption in the remains of Pompeii at the expense of any interest in the present, including herself. Here, the young man's preoccupation with the dead classical past ultimately yields to a contemporary revitalization, and the statue/girl's distinctive walk (in her stepping name, 'Gradiva') suggests a movement of mutual reanimation, past and present together.[3]

[1] For instance, when the Aids crisis emerged in the mid-1980s, the many references to sexually transmitted diseases in Freud's cases histories stood out in a new way. The issue of old age, on the other hand, is not visible in Freud's writing. Perhaps it is culturally prominent today because of the great increase in life expectancy; it was, however, a theme in Greek tragedy: in Sophocles' *Philoctetes* and *Oedipus at Colonus*, and several of Euripides' plays, including *Hecuba* and *Alcestis*.

[2] See further Ch. 4 below.

[3] See Freud, 'Delusions and Dreams in Jensen's *Gradiva*' (1907), *SE* ix. 7–95; 'Der Wahn und die Träume in W. Jensens *Gradiva*', *GW* vii. 31–125. On the interplay

This contrast between age-old and contemporary perspectives can be illustrated through the short essay known as 'Family Romances' (1909). Here Freud talks first about the successive, conscious fantasies that children make up at different ages about their origins. They imagine themselves to be adopted or stepchildren; they replace their real parents with preferable substitutes, invariably of a higher social class. Freud stresses that there is always a hook of realism: the stories will take their cue from 'actual experience [*wirklichen Erlebnißen*]' involving some chance encounter with a local dignitary.[4] If they live in the country it will be, according to the English version, someone like a 'Lord of the Manor'. Thus the stories will have, says Freud, using the technical literary term, some degree of 'verisimilitude [*Wahrscheinlichkeit*]', tying the fantasy down to local conditions.[5]

Then, as the child grows up, these semi-realistic stories encounter a different order of determination. At a later age, in the light of increasing sexual knowledge, the questioning of joint parental origins is replaced by a new kind of distinction between a mother and a father whereby one is ultra-certain or '*certissima*', while the other is 'always' uncertain. As if to underline the timelessness of this difference, Freud gives the Latin tag: *pater semper incertus est*; the mother remains earthily non-Latin, a *Mutter*.[6] From now on, Freud thinks, this is the founding and universal myth of identity that sets both limits and possibilities to the young

of classical and modern in Freud's text see Rachel Bowlby, 'One Foot in the Grave: Freud on Jensen's *Gradiva*', in *Still Crazy after All These Years: Women, Writing and Psychoanalysis* (London: Routledge, 1992), 157–82; Jennifer Wallace, *Digging the Dirt: The Archaeological Imagination* (London: Duckworth, 2004), 97–9; and Richard H. Armstrong, *A Compulsion for Antiquity: Freud and the Ancient World* (Ithaca, NY: Cornell University Press, 2005), 12–25.

[4] Freud, 'Family Romances', *SE* ix. 239; 'Der Familienroman der Neurotiker', *GW* vii. 229. I borrow the metaphor of a 'hook' of realism from Christopher Prendergast, *The Order of Mimesis: Balzac, Stendhal, Nerval, Flaubert* (Cambridge: Cambridge University Press, 1986).

[5] Freud, 'Family Romances', *SE* ix. 239; 'Der Familienroman', *GW* vii. 229. The 'Lord of the Manor' translates *Schloßherr*. We can sympathize here with the difficulties of cultural translation, more problematic the more specific the context. Freud goes on to provide a possible urban minor celebrity in the form of 'some member of the aristocracy if he lives in the town', 'der Fürstlichkeit in der Stadt'. It is interesting that he chooses the geographical difference of town and country as a marker of varying (but equivalent) fantasies; the distinction is not, for instance, in terms of sex as it is in the typical fantasies discussed in Ch. 4 below. Nor is the present social place of the parents a pointer to different levels or types of 'better parents'; upwards, though perhaps not much upwards, is the direction in which the dreaming takes place.

[6] Freud, 'Family Romances', *SE* ix. 239; 'Der Familienroman', *GW* vii. 229.

person's sexual curiosities and the stories that he or she invents to accompany them.

In later works, Freud links this revolution of infantile thought to the prehistoric change from a matriarchal to a patriarchal order that was postulated by nineteenth-century anthropologists. In this passage from *Moses and Monotheism*, the establishment of democratic justice at the end of Aeschylus' *Oresteia* is regarded as an ancient allusion to an already ancient mutation:

> [I]t came about that the matriarchal social order was succeeded by the patriarchal one—which, of course, involved a revolution in the juridical condition that had so far prevailed. An echo [*Nachklang*] of this revolution seems still to be audible in the *Oresteia* of Aeschylus. But this turning from the mother to the father points in addition to a victory of intellectuality over sensuality—that is, an advance in civilization [*Kulturfortschritt*], since maternity is proved by the evidence of the senses while paternity is a hypothesis, based on an inference and a premiss. Taking sides in this way with a thought-process in preference to a sense perception has proved to be a momentous step.[7]

Some swerves occur in the premises and inferences of *this* argument, too. A cultural revolution implies—'of course'—a change in its juridical procedures, and then a change in the forms of knowledge, as the movement from mother to father is represented as a privileging of logic (inference and premise) over the senses. Yet the difference between these two, juridically speaking, is the difference between conclusive evidence—'maternity is proved'—and circumstantial speculation: the idea that there must be some one father, and this is presumably him. Finally, the supersession is represented as a matter of neither logic nor justice (or injustice), but of 'preferring [*erhebt*]' and 'taking sides [*die Parteinahme*]'.

What is the *Oresteia* doing here? Matriarchal justice, it is suggested, means Clytaemnestra ganging up with her lover to murder her returning husband. Patriarchal justice is the exoneration of Orestes, in turn his mother's murderer and Agamemnon's avenger, by a proto-democratic court of law in Athens; he will not have to suffer endless pursuit by the (female) Erinyes, the Furies. The maternal order in this connection would be not so much sensual as violent. The new order is to do with mediation: with argument before attack, and the balancing of accusations where justice may not necessarily lie unequivocally on

[7] Freud, *Moses and Monotheism* (1939), *SE* xxiii. 113–14; *Der Mann Moses und die monotheistische Religion*, *GW* xvi. 221–2.

one side or the other. At the start of the Trojan War, Agamemnon had sacrificed his and Clytaemnestra's daughter Iphigenia to secure favourable winds for the Greek army's voyage. But that means that two out of three of the successive family atrocities in the story are committed by men, making it unclear how the transition to democratic justice should be associated or identified with the hypothetical transition from matriarchy to patriarchy. Yet it is always represented in Freud as *the* progressive move. Much earlier, in the 'Rat Man' case history of 1909: 'A great advance was made in civilization when men decided to put their inferences upon a level with the testimony of their senses and to make the step from matriarchy to patriarchy.'[8]

This linking of Greek tragedy to the move from one sexual and social state to another is exactly what happens, more prominently and pervasively, with Freud's general theory of human development. The Oedipus complex, derived from Sophocles' play, defines the crucial subjective revolution that sends a boy off into the adult, masculine world of culture, intellect, and reasonableness, leaving his mother behind him. Between the pseudo-historical (the purported real transition from matriarchy to patriarchy) and the individual development that is thought to repeat or resemble it, Greek tragedy provides Freud with a pivot that is authoritative in its apparent combination of the historical and the mythical. Greek tragedies had a real cultural existence, perhaps with some tangible connection to the posited ancient shift; and myth could harbour authentic and ancient human meanings.

Yet Freud's gesture in underwriting his cultural argument with tragedy was not in itself unusual: quite the contrary. Since Hegel's extensive use of Sophocles' *Antigone*, it had been almost standard practice for German philosophers to do this: Greek tragedy came naturally to hand as historical-literary matter for thinking with.[9] Freud's own Aeschylean example is in fact taken straight from the central German book for the sexual-cultural transformation, J. J. Bachofen's *Mutterrecht* (1861); Bachofen makes the same point too about the move from sensory to intellectual reasoning in relation to paternity.[10] But Freud goes for Oedipus over Orestes in forging his own tragedy-backed mythistory of

[8] Freud, 'Notes upon a Case of Obsessional Neurosis' ('The Rat Man'), *SE* x. 233; 'Bemerkungen über einen Fall von Zwangsneurose', *GW* vii. 450.

[9] See M. S. Silk and J. P. Stern, *Nietzsche on Tragedy* (Cambridge: Cambridge University Press, 1981), esp. chs. 1 and 9.

[10] See Rosalind Coward, *Patriarchal Precedents: Sexuality and Social Relations* (London: Routledge & Kegan Paul, 1983), 31–3.

how boys do better than girls. The *Oresteia* offers mother-murder rather than mother-love and father-murder; but the crucial difference is that the act is knowingly done (and motivated, as revenge). *Oedipus* gave Freud not just, perhaps not even primarily, the two crimes of incest and parricide, converted in his theory to universal infantile wishes; it also gave him the unconscious.[11]

Today, the specific sexual-familial set-up invoked in Bachofen and Freud may well be obsolescent, both biologically and socially. The age-old bedrock of parental dissymmetry—the sureness of mothers and the speculation about fathers—has lost its realistic basis. DNA testing makes paternity verifiable, while the new reproductive technologies of egg donation and surrogacy mean that maternity is now itself indeterminate. The woman who gives birth is not necessarily the genetic mother—or, to put it another way, a child can have two biological mothers, one the source of the egg and the other the one who was pregnant.[12] Socially, the kinds of parenting regarded as possible or ordinary have gone forth and multiplied, to the point that the previously normative and usual unit of a married heterosexual couple, both first-time partnered, who raise two or three children to adulthood may now seem not just not assumed but not even particularly common. Parents may be single by choice, or gay, or cohabiting but not married. The stigma of illegitimacy has all but gone, with the term 'single parent'—a man or a woman, and often post-married—bearing almost no ideological relation to the now obsolete and culturally meaningless 'unmarried mother'. Where previously the political and medical focus was on the right not to have a child, it is now, and not only for women, much more on the right and the positive wish to be a parent. The question of where that wish might come from, or how it might differ between women, or between men and women, is rarely mentioned in any kind of discourse; the assumption has shifted towards regarding all men and women as both workers

[11] See further Ch. 1, pp. 17–18, below.

[12] I discussed some implications of these changes in 'Frankenstein's Woman-to-be: Choice and the New Reproductive Technologies', in *Shopping with Freud* (London: Routledge, 1993), 82–93; see also Marilyn Strathern, *Reproducing the Future: Essays on Anthropology, Kinship and the New Reproductive Technologies* (Manchester: Manchester University Press, 1992). New research is also raising the possibility of two *genetic* mothers, when the nucleus of one woman's egg, containing all her genetic material, is injected into another 'donor' egg, empty of its nucleus but still with some individuating 'mitochondrial' DNA which would be passed on to the embryo. See Maxine Frith, 'Ban on scientists trying to create three-parent baby', *The Independent*, 14 October 2003, 10.

and parents, potentially, whose needs in performing both of these roles should be met as far as possible with the help of various kinds of enabling legislation, from longer maternity leave to flexible work-time. All these developments are related to another, equally prominent social change, which is the dramatic rise in serial families and, concomitantly, in the break-up of co-parenting relationships. No permanence in the parental couple is to be assumed—as it was before, when marriage was the parenting norm, and divorce was unusual.

All these changes diminish the force of hitherto fundamental premises of identity, which may only now show up as such: the theory, for instance, that a child is the child of two parents and two only, one of each of two sexes, fifty–fifty. Now that it is common for children to have more than two adults in past or present parental roles, that is no longer self-evident, either biologically or socially—insofar as it ever was. In 1897 Henry James's character Maisie was 'vaguely puzzled to suppose herself now with two fathers at once. Her researches had hitherto indicated that to incur a second parent of the same sex you had usually to lose the first.'[13] Nowadays, it is probable that she would not be puzzled at all.

In the myth of mythologizing that 'Family Romances' narrates, the lightweight, locally prompted fantasies of adoption are supplanted by fantasies tied to an immutable symbolic order differentiating between mothers and fathers. But the 'always' of *semper incertus* has now been kick-loosened by scientific developments as well as by social changes. The mutability, in fact, of that fixed order suggests that no Freudian mythology need or may be taken as final. Freud, at times, said the same thing himself; several chapters of this book explore his varying hypotheses on questions of changing stories or mythologies, both in personal lives and in cultural history.[14] There is a 'give' in the most seemingly unchanging conditions of identity, just as, on the other side, there may be a tenaciousness about the ideologies of identity—the likely stories of ordinary life—whose historical relativity seems more obvious.[15]

As well as referring to classical myths, my use of the term 'mythologies' is borrowed from structuralism, above all from Roland Barthes's

[13] Henry James, *What Maisie Knew* (1897; Harmondsworth: Penguin, 1982), 46.

[14] See esp. Chs. 1, 2, 3, 6, and 9, below.

[15] On how stories indicate their cultural plausibility, see Gérard Genette, 'Vraisemblance et motivation', in *Figures II* (1969; Paris: Seuil, 1979), 71–99.

Mythologies.[16] Rather than their obscuring a reality that might be free of fabrication, I am taking mythologies to be both inescapable and ubiquitous; they are the implicit explanatory stories through which we make sense of the world, and also the kinds of realistic or likely stories through which, at any one time, or in any particular culture, we experience and narrate our own and others' lives. Often, but not always, the words 'ideology' or 'theory' are interchangeable with 'mythology' in this sense. Freud sometimes used 'theory' in this way himself, for instance in relation to the 'Sexual Theories [*Sexualtheorien*]' of children, from the title of an essay of 1908 which describes the succession of typical stories that children come up with in relation to their changing questions about sexuality.[17] But I like 'mythologies' because, unlike 'ideology' or 'theory', the word implies a narrative movement of telling and retelling that at once sustains and changes the likely or fabulous ideas and stories in circulation. Conversely, a myth that makes sense to no one will fade away. It fails to *have a point*, to bite or hook with the pressure or claim of its relevance. This relevance may amount to no more than a common-sense obviousness, so that in the most extreme cases a myth may not emerge as such until the moment when it is superseded by a new reality and thus appears as mutable. Many such myths in the fields of sexuality and kinship are now newly open to question in this way—beginning with the two-parent theory mentioned above.

In the *Gorgias*, Plato's Socrates uses the exact word 'mythologizing', '*mythologôn*', speaking about someone making up a myth or story—in his case, to make a philosophical and psychological suggestion.[18] Freud himself used the word in this sense. 'The theory of the instincts is so to say our mythology': '*Die Trieblehre ist sozusagen unsere Mythologie.*'[19]

16 Roland Barthes, *Mythologies* (1957; Paris: Seuil, 1970); selection trans. Annette Lavers, *Mythologies* (1972; St Albans: Paladin, 1976).

17 Freud, 'On the Sexual Theories of Children' (1908), *SE* ix. 209–26; Über infantile Sexualtheorien', *GW* vii. 171–88. See further Ch. 5, below.

18 Plato, *Gorgias* 493a. In fact the mythologizer himself appears as part of a half-invented story; he is an unidentified 'clever [*kompsos*] man, a Sicilian maybe or an Italian', and his myth involves wordplay, '*paragôn tôi onomati*', as he likens the seat of human desires to a pitcher or *pithos*, which is *pithanon* or persuadable, and leaky in the case of fools (with further untranslatable puns). Socrates' associative logic here now appears to have another kind of likeness, as if it were a mythical anticipation of Freud's own myth or theory of the displacements of language in relation to repressed desires (see esp. *The Interpretation of Dreams* (1900), *The Psychopathlogy of Everyday Life* (1901), and *Jokes and their Relation to the Unconscious* (1905)).

19 Freud, 'Anxiety and Instinctual Life', Lecture XXXII, *New Introductory Lectures on Psycho-Analysis* (1933), *SE* xxii. 95; 'Angst und Triebleben', *Neue Folge der Vorlesungen*

My use of 'mythologies' is also meant to highlight the crossing between classical and modern stories that is one focus of the book: the differences and comparisons between the uses and significances of myths 'proper' and everyday 'myth'. At a further level, there is the question of how traditional myths have been and continue to be modified by their incorporation into literary and other works—from Greek epic, poetry, tragedy, and philosophy onwards—to Freud and beyond. Like almost all Greek tragedies, Sophocles' *Oedipus the King* is itself a retelling and thus an interpretation of a myth. Another, minor type of mythical mobility occurs in the many passing references to different myths that occur within individual tragedies. Mythical allusions are commonly used as analogy to and commentary on the present action of the play; in the comparison both the accessory myth and the myth that is the subject of the tragedy may be differently illuminated, their stories subtly modified, myth to myth.

Myths also alter their possible or likely meanings according to the changing cultural contexts in which they are retold. In the light of present-day Western experience of the undoing or mutation of family forms, the stories of some ancient Greek tragedies can seem strangely contemporary: step-parents, single parents, step-siblings, half-siblings, second families, and adoption are everywhere to be found—the last three in *Oedipus the King* alone. Yet despite his interest elsewhere in what he takes to be the universal children's fantasy of being adopted, Freud never mentions that this in fact is Oedipus's reality. Oedipus's adoption fantasies, if they followed the Freudian rules, could only have been true: he really was originally the son of other parents, and royal ones too.[20] He has two mothers and two fathers, his birth and adoptive parents, as well as having been rescued and given a second life through the initiative and care of servants, not of his past or future parents. And he was adopted

zur Einführung in die Psychoanalyse, *GW* xv. 101. In 'Why War?' too, from the same year, Freud refers to 'Our mythological theory of instincts', having previously said: 'It may perhaps seem to you as though our theories are a kind of mythology and, in the present case, not even an agreeable one. But does not every science come in the end to a kind of mythology like this?' (*SE* xxii. 212, 211; *GW* xvi. 23, 22).

[20] Oedipus was also brought up in a royal family. In 'Family Romances', Freud does not consider the case of aristocratic, let alone princely daydreams, where there is no higher place to go; in particular, he does not consider a possible posh boy's downwards daydream of originating from nowhere—or slumming it. He is, however, interested in how the story told of Moses differs from the usual myth of the hero's origins in that he was originally of humble, not royal birth; he discusses this in connection with Otto Rank's *Der Mythus von der Geburt des Helden* (*The Myth of the Birth of the Hero*) (1909), in *Moses and Monotheism* (1939), *SE* xxii. 10–14; *Der Mann Moses*, *GW* xvi. 106–11.

across the borders of two countries, from Thebes to Corinth, so has no one place of origin, familially or culturally; or rather, he has two, and even a third in the intermediate place of Mount Cithaeron where he was exposed and to which he 'returns' in a speech at the end of the play. With the rise, since the 1990s, in transnational adoption as well as the marginalization of mid-twentieth-century nuclear family forms, the play may now speak to the undoing of stories of single origins.[21] '*Tis kai pothen*?'—'Who are you and where do you come from?' To that question always put to the new arrival, the stranger or foreigner, in Greek epic and tragedy, there is not necessarily, now, a single or knowable answer.

Yet it is also possible to see how Freud's own distillation of the Greek myth into the 'nuclear' Oedipal family of father, mother, and child projected a social reality that, in his own time, was yet to be. The theory anticipates a specifically twentieth-century historical moment in which, for the first and perhaps the last time in human history, the typical reproductive pattern in Western industrialized societies involved a lifelong parental couple with a limited number of children, and no additional family members living with them. In the middle decades of the twentieth century, contraception had become acceptable and available; divorce had not yet become frequent; life expectancy was rapidly increasing. The tendency is to think of second marriages and serial families as characteristically contemporary phenomena. But prior to the mid-century nuclear moment of marital and spousal longevity, the frequency of early death, often as a result of childbirth,[22] meant that more than one marriage was commonplace, as it is now. There were the accompanying complexities, again as today, of step-parents and half- and step-sibling relationships. Freud himself was the son of his father's second wife, the first having died in childbirth, and had two elder half-brothers who were around twenty years his senior.[23] The one crucial difference between the periods before and after the heyday of the nuclear family is that children then acquired step-parents only, or almost always, after the death of the birth parent—which is why Maisie would have been puzzled then, but wouldn't be puzzled now.

[21] See further Ch. 7 below.

[22] It is testimony to the change that has taken place that the 'maternal mortality rate', registering the number of women dying as a result of childbirth, is no longer significant enough to be commonly quoted.

[23] On Freud's complex position in his birth family and its relation to his own theories of generational differences, see Chs. 6 and 9 below.

In its focus on a myth of the nuclear family, Freud's model of development thus departed from his own origins yet preceded a new but temporary social norm and typical reality. There is a further way in which Freud's theory proved to be prescient about new social and psychological realities, which is its categorical separation of sexuality from reproduction. In the twentieth century, the increasing availability of reliable contraception made that a practical fact for the first time in history. At the same time, the increasing acceptance, in some cases normalization, of multiple and mutable 'sexualities' weakened the force of the straight-sex paradigm—two bodies, two sexes, and sexual activity directed towards the discharge of semen in the vagina—whose naturalness Freud had challenged in his *Three Essays on the Theory of Sexuality* (1905). Socially, the diversity of sexuality is no longer seen as inherently disruptive as it was in Freud's time.[24]

Finally, the place of women in the social order has changed quite radically in the past century. In this context, some of Freud's larger claims for the persistence of patriarchal structures in the imagining of identity now seem to be anachronistic. In particular, his account of the skewed relationship of women to the Oedipus and castration complexes posited for boys may have lost its explanatory force when women are no longer excluded from professional and public life (and when men may take on domestic and childcaring roles that were formerly thought of as women's alone).

This book explores Freud's elaboration of myths of human identity in relation to their possible mutability, juxtaposing a 'then' of Freud's references to ancient sources as markers, usually, of permanence, with the 'nows' both of his own historical moment and of the present time, when the circumstances and possibilities of personal identity and stories of origin are in many ways very different from what they were for Freud.[25] Chapter 1, 'Freud's Classical Mythologies', considers various

[24] And if contraception separated sexuality from reproduction, technologies like IVF (and before that, donor insemination) go one stage further by separating reproduction from sexuality: babies are conceived without a two-body sexual act.

[25] As a feminist reinterpretation of Freud and his use of classical culture, my project has much in common with Page duBois's in *Sowing the Body: Psychoanalysis and Ancient Representations of Women* (Chicago: University of Chicago Press, 1988). DuBois argues that 'we must use psychoanalysis to analyze our position in the present but, at the same time, refuse its claims on the future' (p.3). I share this resistance to the universalizing tendencies of Freud's phallocentric model of development, but I also think that there are other tendencies which go against them and do not rule out such future changes (see

backgrounds to Freud's extraordinary adaptations of classical stories in his modern mythmaking. The focus of Chapter 2, 'Never Done, Never to Return', is the *Studies on Hysteria*, in which there is an opposition between symptoms that 'vanish', once and for all, and a more low-key, undramatic, and ongoing approach to therapy as 'never done'. I also consider the ways in which hysteria itself has figured in various myths to do with the history of psychoanalysis. Chapter 3, 'Fifty–Fifty', turns to the Danaids, relatively obscure mythological characters who surface momentarily and allusively in the *Studies on Hysteria* only to be mysteriously lost in English translation. I look at various versions of their sensational and multi-faceted story, beginning with Aeschylus' *Suppliants*, and compare it with Freud's very different myth of a protesting female subjectivity. In Chapter 4, 'The Other Day', I consider Freud's different treatments of dreams and daydreams in relation to an implied separation on his part between the timeless force of the dreaming unconscious and the constantly changing, conscious fantasies associated with modern life and a modern novel. The next two chapters, 'A Freudian Curiosity' and 'The Cronus Complex', are concerned with Freud's accounts of children's myths of origin and his theory of the asymmetrical development of the sexes as powerful myths in their time; both examine some of the assumptions that now, in the light of the changed situation of women, appear to serve no useful explanatory purpose. Chapter 6, 'The Cronus Complex', also explores Freud's use of Greek mythology and his recourse to tragic plot structures in his own theories of human development. Chapters 7 and 8 concentrate on particular Greek tragedies—the one Freud made into the key to all mythologies, and another he ignored but which has many points of fruitful comparison with *Oedipus*. As described above, *Oedipus the King* is considered in terms of its plurality of families and origins. Euripides' *Ion*, on the surface a play which happily ends in the forming of a nuclear family, also highlights the secrecy and contradictions that may underlie or undermine it.

The final chapter looks at the idea of significant reinterpretation or retranslation—changing stories—that is part of Freud's theory of psychoanalytic therapy. This is also, I argue, a structure through which to understand changing stories and issues of human identity: as constantly being grasped and remoulded and passed on in new ways—constantly

esp. Chs. 2 and 4 below). It is when he goes Greek that Freud is most stuck to the single unchanging stories.

in motion. (And stories whose interest has ceased are just 'dropped', neither picked up nor handed on.) Throughout the book I seek to think about the theories of Freudian psychoanalysis and related classical texts in relation to future possibilities—to how those stories, past and present, are always, however imperceptibly, moving on, and open to new developments.

1

Freud's Classical Mythologies

Starting with a famous few pages in *The Interpretation of Dreams*, Freud made the myth of a single Greek tragedy into a universal pattern of human experience: *the* story. The Oedipus complex became the cornerstone of psychoanalytic theory, its paradigmatic account of the typical emotional configurations of early childhood, supposedly echoing events in the ancient history of humanity. Oedipus was not exceptional; every single human being is destined to live through the beginnings of a comparable story in early life, and has had no choice in it: 'It is the fate of all of us, perhaps [*Uns allen vielleicht war es beschieden*] to direct our first sexual impulse towards our mother and our first hatred and our first murderous wish against our father.'[1]

Freud drastically reinterpreted the Oedipus legend, making it into a common pattern in which each individual can and has to 'recognize' a guilty, long-suppressed part of themselves:

> Here is one in whom these primaeval [*urzeitliche*] wishes of our childhood have been fulfilled, and we shrink back from him [*schaudern wir zurück*] with the whole force of the repression by which those wishes have since that time been held down within us [*in unserem Innern*]. While the poet, as he unravels the past, brings to light the guilt of Oedipus, he is at the same time compelling us to recognize our own inner minds [*nötigt er uns zur Erkenntnis unseres eigenen Innern*], in which those same impulses, though suppressed, are still to be found.[2]

Oedipus' tragedy is 'ours'. As his guilt is gradually revealed to the light, so are the impulses up till then concealed in our innermost feelings (*Innern*). But the recognition is not straightforward or complete. It appears to operate by the double movement of exposure and

[1] Freud, *The Interpretation of Dreams* (1900), *SE* iv. 262; *Die Traumdeutung, GW* ii–iii. 269. In the German, 'it *was* fated', in the past tense, adds to the sense of an ancient doom, as with the curse on Laius' family in the Oedipus legend.

[2] Freud, *Interpretation, SE* iv. 262–3; *Die Traumdeutung, GW* ii–iii. 269.

withdrawal (the shrinking back); it is conflicted, and forced. Recognition—*anagnôrisis*—is one of the components of tragic plots in Aristotle's definition in the *Poetics*. Here it is not confined to the interior of the drama; it is forced upon 'us' the audience—or readers of Freud. In Freud's 'tragedy', every human being is in the position of a dramatic character who must recognize their part in a long-buried past of which they were previously unaware.

Oedipal recognition has a further dimension, to do with the theory itself. Freud's hypothesis about the earliest childhood emotions is initially offered as an independent finding which the legend then validates:

> This discovery is confirmed by a legend that has come down to us from classical antiquity: a legend whose profound and universal power to move [*durchgreifende und allgemeingültige Wirksamkeit*] can only be understood if the hypothesis I have put forward in regard to the psychology of children has an equally universal validity [*Allgemeingültigkeit*]. What I have in mind is the legend of King Oedipus and Sophocles' drama which bears his name.[3]

The 'discovery', however, is actually another 'recognition' (*Erkenntnis*). More literally, the translation of the first sentence would read: 'Antiquity has handed down to us a piece of legendary material [*ein Sagenstoff*] in support of this recognition'. Modern audiences (are compelled to) 'recognize' the relationship of their childhood impulses to Oedipus's destiny, and Freud presents his own hypothesis not as a new theory but as something that must itself be recognized as a 'universal' truth. As Terence Cave argues, there are many questionable moves in Freud's argument.[4] Everything is subsumed under a single covering story that stretches from Freud to Sophocles, who is implicitly credited with having been the first Freudian (even if, like Oedipus, he did not know what he was doing at the time). All intervening interpreters are eliminated as though superseded; Oedipus becomes Oedipal and psychoanalytic, just as Sophocles, seemingly honoured, is in another way relegated to

[3] Freud, *Interpretation*, *SE* iv. 261; *Die Traumdeutung*, *GW* ii–iii. 267.

[4] Terence Cave, *Recognitions: A Study in Poetics* (Oxford: Oxford University Press, 1988), 162–7. In *A Compulsion for Antiquity: Freud and the Ancient World* (Ithaca, NY: Cornell University Press, 2005), Richard H. Armstrong gives a more sympathetic account of Freud's universalization of the Oedipus story: 'the [contemporary] audience reaction proves the relevance of this ancient material to his very modern psychological concerns, while the great antiquity of the myth reinforces the notion that something primeval, deeply human, and universally true must be contained in the plot, something he will then unpack effectively for the first time in history' (p. 48).

the secondary role of evidential 'confirmation' for Freud's own theory, represented as a recognition not a hypothesis.[5]

Freud's proclaimed intellectual achievement suggests another significant motif of the Oedipus legend, one not mentioned in the *Interpretation* passage, which is Oedipus' rescue of the city of Thebes from plague through his answering of the Sphinx's riddle. In his 'recognition' of the legend's meaning, Freud answers that riddle of human existence in a new way himself, and claims to do so once and for all, past, present, and future. His identification with Oedipus as an intellectual and cultural hero seems to be a powerful element in his attraction to the story. Ernest Jones, in his biography of Freud, told the story of Freud's reaction when, for his fiftieth birthday in 1906, he was presented with a medallion inscribed with a line from *Oedipus* about his solution of the riddle. Freud, so *this* legend goes, was disturbed by this because as a young man he had fantasized about being one day commemorated by a bust inscribed with the very same phrase: '*hos ta klein' ainigmat' êdei kai kratistos ên anêr*'—'Who knew the famous riddle and was the most powerful of men'.[6] The words occur five lines from the end of the play; after the denouement in which Oedipus has lost his power and been revealed as ignorant, the chorus is making a general point about the vicissitudes of human fortune.

Freud quotes this line with several others from the final Chorus, saying that their point 'strikes as a warning [*Mahnung*] at ourselves and our pride'.[7] In his view, the force of the story does not derive from its suggestion of the mutabilities of human fortunes, nor from a general and comparatively abstract tension between (inevitable) destiny and (powerless) individual wills, but rather from the supposedly idiosyncratic

[5] In *The Psychoanalytic Theory of Greek Tragedy* (New Haven: Yale University Press, 1992), C. Fred Alford expands the range of tragic source-texts by comparing the models of ethical subjectivity to be found in tragedies with those in various different types of psychoanalysis (including existential, object-relations, and Lacanian). Alford rightly identifies the priority of familial ties to individual agency in tragedy, seeing this as an emphasis shared with most psychoanalytical theory. But his elaboration of the tragic—and human—situation as one of 'responsibility without freedom' re-establishes a focus on the isolated self ('we must meet our lives, and our deaths, alone', p. 183) as well as implying a transhistorical sameness of subjectivity (the question for Alford is whether either tragedy or psychoanalysis 'got it right').

[6] Ernest Jones, *Sigmund Freud: Life and Work*, ii (London: Hogarth Press, 1956), 15; on the story as itself a 'psychoanalytic parable', see Peter L. Rudnytsky, *Freud and Oedipus* (New York: Columbia University Press, 1987), 4–6.

[7] Freud, *Interpretation*, iv. 263; *Die Traumdeutung*, ii–iii. 270.

and scandalous stuff of Oedipus's own turbulent history: incest and parricide. Once again, 'recognition' is invoked as confirmation:

If King Oedipus can shake up [*erschüttern*] a modern audience no less than he did the contemporary Greek one, the explanation can only be that the effect of the Greek tragedy does not lie in the contrast between destiny and human will, but is to be looked for in the particular nature of the material [*in der Besonderheit des Stoffes*] on which that contrast is exemplified.[8]

Freud mentions *Hamlet* as a supporting example in which 'the changed treatment of the same material [*des nämlichen Stoffes*] reveals the whole difference in the mental life of these two widely separated epochs of civilization: the secular advance of repression in the emotional life of mankind.'[9]

Leaving aside the particular interpretation of the Shakespeare play (that Hamlet's inability to avenge his father's death arises from an unconscious identification with the uncle who in marrying his mother has done what he would have liked to do himself), this appears at first sight to offer a model of historical variation, albeit in terms of a rather grand and unidirectional narrative: 'the secular advance of repression in the emotional life of mankind'. But in reality the example only serves to reinforce the claim for the universality of the Oedipus complex, clearly 'brought into the open [*am Licht gezogen*]' in *Oedipus*, whereas 'in *Hamlet* it remains repressed'.[10] The ancient Greek period becomes the childhood of civilization, in the Renaissance grown to repressed maturity—and at the present time, as Freud would argue elsewhere, to over-repressed modernity.[11] It will take psychoanalysis to unpick the layers of repression or mystification and reveal the underlying Oedipal reality: the myth is true. The two hypotheses then come to overlay one another, as the 'advance [*Fortschreiten*]' of repression historically is matched in the individual's life story by a primitive period: 'Here is one in whom these primaeval wishes of our childhood

[8] Freud, *Interpretation*, *SE* iv. 262, tr. mod.; *Die Traumdeutung*, *GW* ii–iii. 269. In Strachey's version, it is *Oedipus Rex*, the play, that 'moves [*erschüttern*]' the audience, but in the German it is at this point 'König Ödipus', the character.

[9] Freud, *Interpretation*, *SE* iv. 264; *Die Traumdeutung*, *GW* ii–iii. 271; '*säkulare*' is translated as 'secular' in the sense of 'through the ages'.

[10] Freud, *Interpretation*, *SE* iv. 264; *Die Traumdeutung*, *GW* ii–iii. 271.

[11] See Freud, '"Civilized" Sexual Morality and Modern Nervous Illness' (1908), *SE* ix. 181–204; 'Die "kulturelle" Sexualmoral und die moderne Nervosität', *GW* vii. 143–67.

have been fulfilled.' The implied narrative of the difference between Sophocles' world and Shakespeare's also initiates a new psychoanalytic concept—repression—as the single motor of cultural development, operating on 'the same material' of basic Oedipal wishes; grounding this more explicitly, Freud says that *Hamlet* 'has its roots in the same soil [*Auf demselben Boden*] as *Oedipus Rex*'.[12]

It is worth pointing out that the contrast between the two plays in terms of the degree of repression is not as clear as Freud says. In *Hamlet*, the hero is consciously plotting the murder of a close relative; Oedipus never plans to murder anyone. The closer Greek antecedents, and the better examples for his present argument, would have been the three plays about Orestes' murder of Clytaemnestra: Aeschylus' *Libation Bearers* and the *Electras* of Sophocles and Euripides. Here a son kills a parent and her lover to avenge the murder of the other parent and does it deliberately; in fact he has wished to do it since infancy. In reality it is the unconsciousness of Oedipus, his not knowing who he is and his consequent discovery of a different meaning to past events and relationships in his life, that qualifies Sophocles' play for Freud's demonstrative purpose. The 'repression' is precisely what makes it proto-psychoanalytic.[13]

The strategy in this passage of making a would-be historical argument to affirm the transhistorical validity of psychoanalytic dynamics anticipates Freud's theoretical transposition of the Oedipus complex from individual biography to human development in general. This is what he did explicitly in *Totem and Taboo* (1913). A footnote added to the 1914 edition of the *Interpretation* says that 'Later studies have shown that the "Oedipus complex", which was touched on for the first time in the above paragraphs ... throws a light of undreamt-of importance [*ungeahnt große Bedeutung*] on the history of the human race and the evolution of religion and morality.'[14] Beyond the dreams of the dream book, in *Totem and Taboo*, Freud claimed that a real act of parricide, carried out not by an individual like Oedipus but by a group of brothers, brought about the first significant change of social regime. The ousting of the tyrant in favour of a fraternal collectivity adumbrates the transition to more advanced and more psychologically complex forms of organization.

[12] Freud, *Interpretation*, *SE* iv. 264; *Die Traumdeutung*, *GW* ii–iii. 271.

[13] On Freud's use of *Oedipus* rather than Aeschylus' *Oresteia* trilogy as his paradigm text, see further Introduction, pp. 4–6.

[14] Freud, *Interpretation*, *SE* iv. 263; *Die Traumdeutung*, *GW* ii–iii. 270.

For this argument, too, Freud makes an analogy with Greek tragedy, here at its postulated earliest stage of development—its own prehistory, prior to the addition of more actors at the time of Aeschylus and Sophocles:

I have in mind the situation of the most ancient Greek tragedy. A company of individuals, named and dressed alike, surrounded a single figure, all hanging upon his words and deeds: they were the Chorus and the impersonator of the Hero. He was originally the only actor. Later, a second and third actor were added, to play as counterpart to the Hero and as characters split off [*Abspaltungen*] from him; but the character of the Hero himself and his relation to the Chorus remained unaltered.[15]

Freud then goes on to interpret the hero's '"tragic guilt"' as a 'systematic distortion' of the reality, in which the Chorus had in fact committed, against him, the crimes for which he is now held guilty; the Chorus's sympathy shows 'a refined hypocrisy': 'In the remote reality it had actually been the members of the Chorus who caused the Hero's suffering; now, however, they exhausted themselves with sympathy and regret and it was the Hero himself who was responsible [*schuld*] for his own sufferings.'[16]

Immediately after this passage on tragedy Freud moves to his summary, which is as categorical in its even wider claim as the statement from the *Interpretation*:

At the conclusion, then, of this exceedingly condensed inquiry, I should like to insist that its outcome shows that the beginnings of religion, morals, society and art converge in the Oedipus complex. This is in complete agreement with the psycho-analytic finding [*Feststellung*] that the same complex constitutes the nucleus [*Kern*] of all neuroses, so far as our present knowledge goes. It seems to me a most surprising discovery [*eine große Überraschung*] that the problems of social psychology, too, should prove soluble on the basis of one single concrete point [*einem einzigen konkreten Punkte*]—man's relation to his father.[17]

Even before (Sophocles') Oedipus, the story is Oedipal. And just as *Hamlet* presented a distorted later version of an Oedipus complex, so

[15] Freud, *Totem and Taboo* (1913), *SE* xiii. 155–6; *Totem und Tabu*, *GW* ix. 187.

[16] Freud, *Totem and Taboo*, *SE* xiii. 156; *Totem und Tabu*, *GW* ix. 187. In German the 'tragic guilt' is qualified by 'so-called' as well as by the inverted commas that also appear in the English: 'die sogennante *"tragische Schuld"*'.

[17] Freud, *Totem and Taboo*, *SE* xiii. 156–7; *Totem und Tabu*, *GW* ix. 188. Again, Strachey's translation has a 'surprising discovery' where there is no discovery in the German—rather, 'a great surprise'.

archaic tragedy, prior to Sophocles, has its own characteristic disguises of what remains always the same primary material, here given in the 'nucleus' of the neuroses and the 'single concrete point' of the inter-generational conflict between fathers and sons. The more specific and focused the Oedipus complex becomes, the more its reach is extended outwards to encompass nothing less than the entirety of 'religion, morals, society and art'. And it is notable that at this point the over-connection to the mother has disappeared from view; in the analogy between individual and collective history, the myth itself becomes one that refers exclusively to male characters and their mutual relations. As in the *Interpretation* passage, here too a finding is stretched about as far as it could conceivably go, from (every man's) individual psychology, the scope of the dream book, to the entire cultural history of mankind. One story fits all, and its pure form is to be found in Greek tragedy, in particular in just one Greek tragedy.

Yet even in connection with the allegedly universal occurrence of Oedipal impulses, there is an occasional suggestion that a more localized reality may be shaping the child's feelings—indeed a reality coming from the parents themselves. In his *Introductory Lectures on Psycho-Analysis*, Freud says: 'Incidentally, children often react in their Oedipus complex to a stimulus [*Anregung*] coming from their parents, who are frequently led in their preferences by difference of sex, so that the father will choose his daughter and the mother her son as a favourite, or, in the case of a cooling-off [*Erkaltung*] in the marriage, as a substitute for a love-object that has lost its value [*zum Ersatz für das entwertete Liebesobjekt*].'[18] Here it is the parents' own heterosexual partialities, or perhaps the fragile state of their relationship, which spurs the complex into existence; it arises in contingent and realistically motivated circumstances. The same point is made in Lecture XXI: 'We must not omit to add that the parents themselves often exercise a determining influence on the awakening of a child's Oedipus attitude by themselves obeying the pull of sexual attraction, and that where there are several children the father will give the plainest evidence of his greater affection for his little daughter and the mother for her son.'[19] This passage goes so far as to allow a

[18] Freud, Lecture XIII, 'The Archaic Features and Infantilism of Dreams', *Introductory Lectures on Psycho-Analysis* (1915–17), *SE* xv. 207; 'Archaische Züge und Infantilismus des Traumes', *Vorlesungen zur Einführung in die Psychoanalyse*, *GW* xi. 212.

[19] Freud, Lecture XXI, 'The Development of the Libido and the Sexual Organizations', *Introductory Lectures*, *SE* xvi. 333; 'Libidoentwicklung und Sexualorganisationen', *Vorlesungen*, *GW* xi. 345–6. Here 'obeying the pull of sexual attraction' elides Freud's

possibly 'determining [*entscheidenden*]' influence, before then pulling back from it in the next sentence: 'But the spontaneous nature of the Oedipus complex in children cannot be seriously shaken [*erschüttert*] even by this factor.' 'Even' ('*einmal*') seems to maintain the doubt. And *erschüttern* is the very verb that Freud uses to describe the way that the tragedy of Oedipus 'moves' or 'shakes up' its audience.[20] In the present passage, perhaps what must not be shaken is the belief in the spontaneity and universality of the Oedipus complex itself; the realistic contingencies of an individual family setting must not be allowed to make a significant difference. It is important, too, that the impetus here comes from the top down, not the other way around: it is the parents who are doing the instigating. Keeping the desires, for the most part, on the infantile side reinforces Freud's claim for their quasi-innateness: no worldly influences can be said to have intervened to promote their development.

TRAGEDY AND THERAPY

Apart from the themes of incest and parricide, dwindling to just the 'single' focus of father–son relations in *Totem and Taboo*, there is another, quite different reason that Freud gives in *The Interpretation of Dreams* for focusing on Sophocles' *Oedipus*. The very movement of this drama, he says, in its gradual build-up and 'cunning delays' before the end, can be 'likened to the work of a psycho-analysis'.[21] The comparison occurs only in passing, at the end of Freud's plot summary of the history of Oedipus prior to the action that takes place in Sophocles' play. But it is worth dwelling on, since it is suggestive in a number of ways.

First, as a formal element of tragedy, the quick-fire 'stichomythia', in which two characters speak one line each, alternately, is particularly well suited to set up a verbal denouement. Freud himself uses a version

point about heterosexuality: 'sie selbst der geschlechtlichen Anziehung folgen', 'they themselves follow the gender-differentiated attraction'.

20 Freud, *Interpretation*, *SE* iv. 262; *Die Traumdeutung*, *GW* ii–iii. 269; see above, p. 17.

21 Freud, *Interpretation*, *SE* iv. 262; *Die Traumdeutung*, *GW*: ii–iii. 268. The translation speaks of 'cunning delays and ever-mounting excitement' but actually, there is no 'excitement' in the German; 'der schrittweise gesteigerten und kunstvoll verzögerten Enthüllung' is literally 'the gradually built up and artfully delayed uncovering' of the fact that Oedipus is Laius' murderer and his son.

of this in his own reporting of case histories, reproducing the build-up towards the ending that is his point of comparison between analysis and tragedy.[22] Second, both tragedy and therapy involve formal conventions. There are fairly rigid time-spans in each case: therapeutic sessions came to be scheduled for what is conventionally called an 'hour', usually fifty minutes long; tragedies, roughly an hour and a half long in performance time, are supposed to deal with an action that takes place in a single day. Another point is that both the actors in a tragedy and the participants in a therapeutic session play parts, in a context that is set apart from that of their real lives. This is scripted and relatively straightforward in the case of the drama; with psychoanalysis, it involves the patient's replaying of familiar roles when faced with the analyst's non-part of consciously not 'being'—acting as—their own everyday self (or any other character). Ideally, the patient comes to understand their default ways of relating to others by seeing the parts they spontaneously play in relation to this undefined interlocutor.

Both tragedy and therapy involve higher emotional levels than those that are normally experienced in ordinary life, but both exclude what in other contexts would be understood as real action. Therapy consists of words and their accompanying emotions; there is no other action. In Greek tragedy: violent acts are generally not presented on the stage, but reported to characters elsewhere and afterwards by witnesses (the 'messenger speech'). Words can take on strong roles, as fifth-century Greek citizens were well aware. Characters in tragedy comment themselves on the power of language to achieve good or bad effects. In a positive way, words may be represented as a substitute for war or a fairer way to settle a dispute. The theatre, which most adult male citizens attended for one or both of the two annual dramatic festivals in which tragedies were performed, was akin to the lawcourts and the political assembly as a forum in which speech-making was seen as a particular kind of skill.[23] Tragic characters are rhetoricians and politicians, just as

[22] See e.g. the case of 'Miss Lucy R.', Freud, *Studies on Hysteria*, *SE* ii. 114–15; *Studien über Hysterie*, *GW* i. 172–3. Conversely, stichomythia can be used therapeutically within tragedy. In Euripides' *Bacchae* Cadmus, line by line, restores his daughter Agaue to reality, bringing her to recognize that the slaughtered head she is triumphantly holding up is not an animal's but that of her own son, Pentheus (ll. 1263–1300).

[23] There is an unresolved and probably unresolvable argument about whether women, who were not citizens in democratic Athens, attended tragic performances. (All performers on the stage were male.) The question is important not only in terms of the history of women, but also because it makes a difference to our understanding of the many intelligent and complex female characters in tragedy if we know that, as well as being

legal advocates and military or civic leaders would themselves make use of the dramatic techniques they picked up from their tragic expertise as regular spectators.

In therapy, as in drama, words have palpable effects in that a two-person conversation in the present can transform the patient's perception of who they are and have been, or the significance of their past actions and experiences. This is also precisely what happens in *Oedipus*. Through dialogue alone, a man's identity and history are revealed to be quite different from what he had believed. Right before the comparison with psychoanalytic practice, Freud quotes two lines—the only quotation he makes in the course of his initial summary of the story—which indicate this other similarity without making it explicit. He describes the situation at the start of the play when the information is given (by 'messengers', says Freud; in fact, in the play, by Creon) that the murderer, many years ago, of King Laius must be found in order for the plague afflicting the city of Thebes to cease: 'Where shall now be found the footprint, hard to trace, of the ancient guilt?'[24] *Oedipus*, like a psychoanalysis, goes back over the ground of long-forgotten stories, or of marks whose meanings may now be conjectured and put into words for the first time. No other surviving Greek tragedy does anything like this.

men's inventions, they were only seen and heard by men. See Simon Goldhill, 'The Audience of Athenian Tragedy', in P. E. Easterling (ed.), *The Cambridge Companion to Greek Tragedy* (Cambridge: Cambridge University Press, 1997), 54–68.

[24] Sophocles, *Oedipus the King*, ll. 109–10. Freud quotes only this; the *Standard Edition* adds the preceding half-line and thereby introduces an error. The translation, attributed there to Lewis Campbell, reads 'But he, where is he? Who shall now read | The fading record of this ancient guilt? (*Interpretation*, *SE* iv. 261). But in the Greek it is not yet a question of a single suspect. Oedipus answers Creon's saying that the oracle commands that Laius' murderers (in the plural) must be punished. Later in the play, the sole surviving witness at one point claims that 'robbers', more than one, did the deed. This discrepancy, never resolved, is forgotten under the weight of evidence that points by the end to the likelihood that the murderer was Oedipus (alone). See further Jonathan Culler, 'Story and Discourse in the Analysis of Narrative', in *The Pursuit of Signs: Semiotics, Literature, Deconstruction* (London: Routledge & Kegan Paul, 1981), 169–87, and Frederick Ahl, *Sophocles' Oedipus: Evidence and Self-Conviction* (Ithaca, NY: Cornell University Press, 1991). Ahl argues that Oedipus's guilt is not proven on many different grounds; in effect he comes to believe he is Laius' and Jocasta's son through the dubious power of 'hearsay'. It is perhaps part of Sophocles' brilliant ingenuity to have left open this possibility (as well as the contrary possibility, sometimes mooted, that Oedipus or Jocasta knew the truth all along). Ahl warns against remaining 'oblivious to the pluralism' of the play (p. 265), and it is in that spirit that, in Ch. 7, I look more closely at the minor roles of the mothers and the servants.

REWRITING MYTHS

Sophocles' *Oedipus* is unique in its enactment of an investigation into a past event and its retrieval of an old story which now transforms the understanding of the present situation. But this Oedipal distinctiveness draws attention to a different feature common to all Greek tragedies, which is that they are always, supposedly, re-enactments of legendary stories already familiar to their audiences (and not original to their authors). Tragic audiences knew in advance what story to expect; the interest was in the particular interpretation that the dramatist would put on it. Aristotle defined tragedy as the representation or imitation (*mimêsis*) of an action. In formal terms, tragedy is always a representation of a representation—of a *mythos*: story or myth—and thus at two removes from a hypothetical original action.

In one way, this is very different from what happens in modern forms of literature, where the expectation is precisely that the story will be unfamiliar or 'novel'. Whereas in tragedy the same stories are recycled again and again, here it is assumed that the events, and probably the characters too, are being represented for the first time. Yet in other respects, the difference is not so great. Literary works tend to stay within recognizable generic forms in which certain kinds of language, plot structure, or psychological plausibility are deployed: at a given time, readers (or audiences) know roughly what they are getting under a particular heading. And there is one kind of contemporary fictional representation in which the convergence with tragedy is in some respects quite close. British TV soap operas are probably the nearest equivalent to Athenian tragedy in terms of their significance as public dramas watched by a high proportion of the population at the same time; soap events are widely shared and discussed. In the past few years, it has become the practice to announce the story-lines in advance, with promotional write-ups in women's magazines and daily newspapers. Like the spectators of tragedy, viewers know more or less what is going to happen; the point of watching is to see the details of how the already known story is played out.[25]

[25] There are other points of similarity. For instance soaps, like tragedies, are full of transgressive actions, notably involving violence and illicit sex; the 'Who's the father?' plot-line, which is a part of the Oedipus story too, is a staple (and continues to be post-DNA, when the test can function as a moment of truth). Also, soaps tend to have

In tragedians' new versions of the ancient legends, different elements of a given story could be brought forward or backgrounded, added or suppressed. This means, of course, that over time, and across the variations of different cultures and specific retellings, the sense of the basic myth that was being reworked might itself, retrospectively, be changed. Once again, this involves a familiar pattern of psychoanalytic interpretation. A story about the past that has meaning to an individual or to a culture in their present situations may have little or even nothing in common with its distant beginnings as a story for another culture or another, earlier time of someone's life. John Gould spoke of the 'multivalency of myth, as well as its universal currency'.[26] Tragedy was a notably self-conscious arena for mythical mobility, with dramatists making subtle or startling changes to the existing versions, cutting or supplementing or inventing.

Of the three tragedians by whom complete plays survive it is in general Euripides who most frequently and provocatively *plays* with the

a chorus equivalent. Characters gossip about what is happening to other characters, or throw in their sententious thoughts about human life in the light of what has been going on. Pub scenes are standard for this (even though in reality most of the population stays at home in the evening watching the soaps, in soaps they don't, because otherwise there would be no occasion for chorus-like commentary).

The differences between tragedies and soap operas are equally suggestive. They are diametrically opposed in the gender weighting of their audiences, since it is likely that women were not permitted to watch tragedy at all, while soaps are watched more by women than by men. Then soaps, unlike tragedies, have different relationships to real time. The action of most tragedies, lasting an hour and a half or so, is confined to a single day. But when a soap character finds she is pregnant, it really will be six or seven months before she gives birth—time for plenty of wondering about whether the father really is the father. Similarly, there is an approximate correspondence to the days of the week and the seasons of the year outside the box (soaps do Christmas, even if they don't do general elections). Soaps also contain a large element of everyday life, with the representation of ordinary goings-on in the home and the workplace and the pub; as a result, they often appear as bizarre amalgams of the melodramatic and the realistic. Thus, given the utterly unlikely story of a middle-aged woman who was married to a serial killer, who murdered a number of neighbours before fortunately he drowned, that isn't the end of the story, as it would be in a tragedy; what follows—realistically—is months and years of her saying periodically that 'We've all been through such a lot', and talking about going into therapy. The partial realism of soaps is related to one more difference, which is the ordinariness of their characters. In tragedy, the protagonists are royal or heroic, in accordance with their legendary status; this gives rise to situations and arguments relating to larger political topics such as war and immigration of a kind which are never raised in soaps.

[26] John Gould, 'Myth, Memory, and the Chorus: "Tragic Rationality"' (1999), in *Myth, Ritual, Memory, and Exchange: Essays in Greek Literature and Culture* (Oxford: Oxford University Press, 2001), 410.

characters' stories. He goes so far as to alter their life cycles or have them turn out to have been phantoms standing in for their real selves all along. So Helen, in the play of that name, is discovered to have been in Egypt throughout the Trojan War (it was a surrogate Helen who went to Troy with Paris). In the *Phoenician Women*, we find Oedipus' wife and mother Jocasta living on many years after the time when in Sophocles' play, as in other versions of the legend, she commits suicide after Oedipus' real identity as her son has become apparent to her. In Euripides' prologue, Jocasta offers a distinctive spin on the story of Oedipus' birth. She mentions long years of childlessness as having prompted her husband Laius' consultation of the oracle, which delivered back the news that any son born to the pair would murder his father. After that prognosis, fertility ceased to be the issue, it is implied, since they had been advised not to have a baby at all: 'Don't sow the child-bearing furrow against the will of the gods' (l. 18). But Oedipus was then conceived by accident—when Laius 'abandoned himself to pleasure and got drunk' (l. 21), Jocasta says. Further on, Jocasta tells a new version of the story of Oedipus' adoption (a story of which the Jocasta in Sophocles' *Oedipus* would have been unaware in any form, given that at the start of that play she does not yet know what happened to her baby). Instead of the Corinthian herdsman giving the infant abandoned by Laius and Jocasta to both Polybus and Merope, the childless Corinthian royal couple, now he gives him to Merope alone, and she convinces her husband that she has just given birth herself (ll. 30–2). The scope for such permutations and reconstructions is limitless.[27] It is also one means by which old stories can be remade to suit or to act upon the changing circumstances and pressures of their culture.

THE THEBAN LEGEND

All three tragic authors wrote plays based on the Theban cycle of legends, and examples survive by each of them, as many as three in Sophocles' case (*Oedipus the King*, *Antigone*, and *Oedipus at Colonus*). Aeschylus' *Seven Against Thebes*, like Euripides' *Phoenician Women*, is about the

[27] As Jan Bremmer puts it, this is the means of 'staying in business' for myth-tellers, tragedians among them. Jan N. Bremmer, entry on 'Mythology', *Oxford Classical Dictionary*, 3rd edn., ed. Simon Hornblower and Antony Spawforth (Oxford: Oxford University Press, 1996), 1019. The phrase is in inverted commas in Bremmer's article.

battle between Oedipus' and Jocasta's two sons, Polynices and Eteocles, the brother enemies, who were cursed to kill one another by their father; it formed part of a trilogy in which it was accompanied by plays called *Laius* and *Oedipus*. Sophocles' *Antigone* and Euripides' *Suppliant Women* concern the aftermath of the siege on Thebes, as a sister (Antigone) in one play and a group of Argive mothers in the other seek the right to bury their dead. According to Léopold Constans, the author of a late nineteenth-century book on the Oedipus legend, this part of the myth—the brothers' story—is actually the oldest element; the history of Oedipus, Laius, and Jocasta was a subsequent arrival on this narrative scene, its object being to explain the animosity between father and sons: 'It was only later that a moral explanation was sought for such strange facts: the rivalry between two powerful people, two brothers' struggle for the throne, did not seem sufficient reasons; the immediate origin of these implacable hatreds was attributed to the paternal curse, and it was alleged that the sons bore the sentence for the involuntary crimes committed by their father.'[28] This interpretation may appear to be the reverse of Freud's in *Totem and Taboo*, where the sons blame the father in order to cover up their own collective murder of him. But here too, in another sense, in the beginning was the battle of the brothers—rather than, as Freud's use of the Oedipus story normally suggests, the struggle between father and son.[29]

[28] L. Constans, *La légende d'Œdipe, étudiée dans l'Antiquité, au Moyen-Âge et dans les temps modernes, en particulier dans 'Le Roman de Thèbes'* (Paris: Maisonneuve, 1881), 11. Constans was a medievalist who published an edition of the twelfth-century *Roman de Thèbes*.

[29] Recent psychoanalytic work has begun to give attention to sibling and lateral relationships as opposed to intergenerational ones. See in particular Juliet Mitchell, *Mad Men and Medusas: Reclaiming Hysteria and the Effects of Sibling Relations on the Human Condition* (London: Allen Lane, 2000); and *Siblings* (Cambridge: Polity Press, 2003).

In Freud, there are father–son and brother–brother relationships in the big theories of human sociality. Mothers and sisters have no strong roles to play, mothers coming to feature negatively as she-who-must-be-abandoned (for boys) or she-who-comes-to-be-rejected (for girls); becoming a mother is at best a compensatory destination for women deprived of masculine potential. Sisters figure in the background of Little Hans's and the Wolf Man's childhood stories, but their relationship to other siblings or to brothers or sisters specifically is not addressed as such. In Greek tragedy, on the other hand, mothers and sisters are prominent. Childlessness is a frequent theme—in relation to women (and men) unable to have children, and to mothers whose sons or daughters have died, most often in connection with war. The Danaids, discussed in Ch. 3 below, are a spectacular fifty-strong sorority. Most often, siblings come in significant pairs, bonded or hostile or alternately both, and often more important than other couples in which either participates. Antigone's first loyalty is to her dead brother Polynices; she argues with their sister who is not, initially, so willing to contravene the law and she ignores

Like Euripides' *Phoenician Women*, Aeschylus' *Seven Against Thebes* also mentions the conception of Oedipus as an act of rashness in the face of a warning oracle. This time it is not Jocasta but the chorus who speak the lines. Laius 'conquered by love's thoughtlessness [literally, 'lack of planning', *aboulian*]' engendered 'the father-killer Oedipus', who in turn sowed children in the 'holy field where he had grown himself'; 'madness brought about this crazed coupling' (ll. 750–7). Aeschylus juxtaposes the two men as both engaging in acts of sexual folly; as in Euripides' version of the story, Oedipus' conception is Laius' fault, and Aeschylus makes this disobedience of the oracle the reason for the curse on his family (ll. 742–9). Thus Euripides and Aeschylus both include an element of sexual excess or madness in the background to Oedipus' story (Laius' 'drunkenness' in Euripides' play is a *baccheia*, a Bacchic frenzy). From one point of view, this story seems perverse in making conjugal intercourse the source of endless evil. But both Aeschylus' and Euripides' versions stress that the sex is nonetheless transgressive—against the god's orders, and the result of a moment of madness. In this connection, it is striking that sexual desire is quite absent as a subject from Sophocles' version of the Oedipus and Jocasta story,[30] the one from which Freud would take the cue for his new theory of human sexuality in its unacknowledged pervasiveness.

Going back a stage further still in the chronology of the myth, another layer was added on at some point which gave a different reason for there being a curse on Laius' family, the Labdacids. This story was treated in a missing play by Euripides called *Chrysippus*. Chrysippus was a young boy whom Laius raped when staying with his father, Pelops; he then committed suicide and his father cursed Laius' family in retaliation. Euripides is supposed to have represented Laius as the

her fiancé Haemon, who dies for her and with her in defiance of his own father. There is also the case of Electra. In both Sophocles' and Euripides' plays about her, Electra's bond with her younger brother Orestes is like an indissoluble contract: he has been raised by his sister as a mother-murderer who must avenge Clytaemnestra's murder of their father.

30 A point made by Martha C. Nussbaum: 'the play itself is not very much concerned with sexual desire as such, or with deep-hidden sexual urges toward one parent, combined with aggressive wishes toward one's parental rival'; 'Finally, the whole question of erotic desire does not appear to be salient in the play's treatment of the marriage to Jocasta—Eros is mentioned frequently in Sophocles, but not in this play' ('*Oedipus Rex* and the Ancient Unconscious', in Peter L. Rudnytsky and Ellen Handler Spitz (eds.), *Freud and Forbidden Knowledge* (New York: New York University Press, 1994), 43, 44).

first to engage in what Constans calls this '*amour honteux*'—'shameful love'.[31] Although Freud was to argue that homosexuality is no less (or more) natural than heterosexuality, he never refers to this myth that is tucked away behind the central Oedipus story. Unlike the open-ended dispositions that Freud first discusses in the *Three Essays on the Theory of Sexuality* (1905), the part of the Oedipus story extracted in Sophocles' play is wholly concerned with heterosexual couples—Laius and Jocasta, Polybus and Merope, Oedipus and Jocasta. But in his later theories of female development, Freud added other permutations, considering not only the girl's attachment to her father but also the same-sex attachments between girl and mother or boy and father. So the nuclear Sophoclean Oedipus story was expanded in Freud's own version. And he drew on a different classical myth for his presentation of homosexuality as natural in the *Three Essays*, alluding to the tale told by Aristophanes in Plato's *Symposium*.[32]

MYTHOLOGICAL DEVELOPMENT

Freud, it is clear, read Constans's book about the Oedipus legend; his copy is in the Freud Museum in London and marked up in his hand. It is not known when he read it, but the indications are that it would have been after, not before, he first decided on the centrality of the Oedipus story, in a famous letter to Wilhelm Fliess of October, 1897. It was several months later, the following March, in another letter sketching out the plan of the book on dreams that he was then in the middle of writing, that Freud declared: 'I first must read up on the Oedipus legend—do not yet know where [*Vorher muß ich über die Ödipussage*

31 Constans, *La légende*, 18.

32 Freud also referred to this myth in *Beyond the Pleasure Principle* (1920), where it is used to illustrate or corroborate the hypothesis that the sexual instincts are linked to 'a need to restore an earlier state of things' (*SE* xviii. 57–8; *Jenseits des Lustprinzips*, *GW* xiii. 62). In the *Three Essays* (*SE* vii. 136; *Drei Abhandlungen zur Sexualtheorie*, *GW* v. 34), he actually misremembers the story (misremembering rather than reinterpreting, since here the 'myth' is fixed as a written text, not a tale told in many evolving versions). In his eagerness to make the scandalous point about the naturalness of homosexual dispositions, he forgets that Plato's Aristophanes implicitly makes precisely that point himself, instead quoting him as the counter-argument. See Rachel Bowlby, 'Walking, Women and Writing', in *Still Crazy after All These Years: Women, Writing and Psychoanalysis* (London: Routledge, 1993), 1–3.

nachlesen, weiß noch nicht wo]';[33] and here Jeffrey Masson, the editor of these letters, provides a footnote suggesting Constans's book as having likely served the purpose.

Before turning to consider the book's contents, it is worth pausing on what Freud is saying at this stage about where his theories come from. Clearly the issue of how much and when to read is on his mind, since he writes in the next letter, just over a week later:

> I do not at all think of this version as final. First I want to put my own ideas [*mein Eigentum*] into shape, then study the literature in detail, and thereafter insert or revise where this is indicated by my reading. I cannot do the reading until I have finished what I myself have to say, and I can compose the details only in the process of writing.[34]

To call this the issue of 'secondary' or 'background' reading is to beg the question. Freud is saying that his ideas, which in fact he calls something more like 'my property', '*mein Eigentum*', can and must be shaped prior to the back-up or cross-checking that supplementary scholarly reading will provide. Such reading, in the meantime, would interfere with the process of shaping his 'own' work. What he writes is based on ideas independently formed—both generated and shaped by himself, without either confirmation, challenge, or complication from relevant reading. But at the same time, Freud begins by saying that the present version is subject to change in the light of the reading not yet undertaken; it is not just not definitely final but emphatically 'not at all ... final [*überhaupt nicht ... definitive*]'.

In the case of the Oedipus legend, the versions found in the 15 October 1897 letter to Fliess and the book, published two years later,[35] are not substantially different; no secondary reading seems to have intervened either to reinforce or to undermine the outline:

> A single idea of general [*allgemeinen*] value dawned on me. I have found, in my own case too, being in love with my mother and jealous of my father, and I now consider it a universal [*allgemeines*] event in early childhood, even

[33] Freud, Letter of 15 March 1898, in *The Complete Letters of Sigmund Freud to Wilhelm Fliess, 1887–1904*, trans. and ed. Jeffrey Moussaieff Masson (Cambridge, MA: Harvard University Press, 1985), 304; Sigmund Freud, *Aus den Anfängen der Psychanalyse: Briefe an Wilhelm Fliess, Abhandlungen und Notizen aus den Jahren 1887–1902* (London: Imago, 1950), 264.

[34] Freud, letter of 24 March 1898, *Letters*, 305; *Briefe*, 265.

[35] The first edition of *The Interpretation of Dreams* appeared in late 1899, but with its publication date printed as 1900—as if to mark its intended significance in the new century.

> if not so early as in children who have been made hysterical. (Similar to the invention of parentage in paranoia—heroes, founders of religion.) If this is so, we can understand the gripping power [*die packende Macht*] of *Oedipus Rex*, in spite of all the objections that reason [*der Verstand*] raises against the presupposition of fate; and we can understand why the later 'drama of fate' [*Schicksalsdrama*] was bound to fail so miserably. Our feelings rise [*bäumt sich unsere Empfindung*] against any arbitrary individual compulsion, such as is presupposed in [Grillparzer's] *Die Ahnfrau* and the like; but the Greek legend seizes upon a compulsion which everyone recognizes [*jeder anerkennt*] because he senses its existence within himself. Everyone in the audience was once a budding Oedipus in fantasy and each recoils in horror [*schaudert jeder zurück*] from the dream fulfillment here transplanted into reality, with the full quantity of repression which separates his infantile state from his present one.[36]

The letter provides a capsule version of what remains, in *The Interpretation of Dreams*, a few pages devoted to a very big idea. Here, the paradigmatic Oedipus is first embodied in Freud himself who in the course of his ongoing self-analysis has found Oedipal impulses of his own and then generalized them as 'universal'. There is the same ambivalent recognition involving a 'shrinking back': 'recoils in horror' in the letter translates the same verb as the *Interpretation*'s 'we shrink back from him'. As in the later text, Freud also goes on to bring up *Hamlet*—'Fleetingly the thought passed through my mind that the same thing might be at the bottom of *Hamlet* as well'—just as he would in the *Interpretation*; both texts also cite the same nineteenth-century *Schicksalsdrama* by the Austrian dramatist Franz Grillparzer, *Die Ahnfrau* (*The Ancestress*) (1817), as a counter-example meant to emphasize the uniqueness of the Oedipal story in its universal power to disturb. Freud argues that it is the particular material (the child's love and hate in relation to the two parents) that moves the audience, not the contrast between an arbitrarily predetermined fate and an individual powerless to resist it. It also seems likely that the contrast of ancient and modern adds its weight here. In the letter as in the book, Freud's argument is that the power of *Oedipus* is in its evocation, over against their 'repression', of wishes already present in the minds of its audience. The recognition ('everyone recognizes') is dependent on the assumed pre-existence of long-forgotten experience, and the distance between the 'infantile state and the present one' has its parallel in the distance that separates Sophocles' play from the allegedly ineffective imitation

[36] Freud, letter of 15 October 1897, *Letters*, 272; *Briefe*, 238.

'tragedy of destiny'.[37] Freud does not make his negative comparison with some other Greek tragedy from the fifth century BCE.

It is likely, then, that Freud did not do his projected secondary reading in the interval between the letters to Fliess and the final (first) version of *The Interpretation of Dreams*.[38] Yet he certainly read Constans's book, as the markings show, and in several ways, not all of them directly related to the Oedipus legend, its argument is relevant to the development of Freud's thinking around the turn of the century. In his footnote about the book, Jeffrey Masson notes that Freud marked the passages about incest in a particular section. So he did. But there are also several other features of Constans's argument which directly or indirectly bear on psychoanalytic ideas.

Constans's work is a contribution to the study of comparative mythology, a discipline whose history and recent developments, culminating in the work of Max Müller, he summarizes in the first few pages of the book. He then homes in on a specific controversy about the origins of one strand of the Oedipus myth: the hero's contest with the Sphinx. In the recent stand-off he outlines between a French and an Italian scholar, Michel Bréal and Domenico Comparetti, there are two related issues.[39]

One concerns the age of different elements of the myth, the other their generality. Tying the two questions together is a dispute about the universality of cultural development: whether the same stories arise, as if by nature, in all cultures at a comparable stage of development; and whether, correlatively, it is reasonable to postulate similar, parallel stages of development that would apply equally to the history of any and every local community.

Bréal, the 'naturalist', had argued that the Sphinx myth (Oedipus' conquest of the monster plaguing Thebes) goes back in origin to the very early proto-story of a struggle between the sun and the clouds found in diverse mythologies relative to diverse heroes; in one Oedipal

[37] Grillparzer's plays were all written in classical metres; many were rewritings of classical dramas or stories, such as that of Medea in the trilogy *Das goldene Vliess* (*The Golden Fleece*) (1821). Like the French novelist Alphonse Daudet (see Ch. 4), he wrote a *Sappho* (1817).

[38] Freud added substantially to *The Interpretation* in subsequent editions; the eighth was published as late as 1934.

[39] Bréal, a professor of comparative grammar in Paris, was actually the inventor of semantics; he coined the word, in the title of his 1895 *Essai de sémantique (science des significations)*. He also invented the modern marathon for the relaunched Olympic Games. Comparetti wrote an influential study translated into English as *Vergil in the Middle Ages*.

example, 'Oedipus has killed the Sphinx' was a proverbial expression for rain (the Sphinx falling from her rock is like a cloudburst). For Bréal, Laius, etymologically 'the enemy', was to be identified with the Sphinx; his murder (not yet of a father) was simply a new version of Oedipus' victory over the monster. Bréal also links Oedipus' blinding to a primitive idea of the disappearance of the sun; likewise, the 'swelling' present etymologically in his name, and usually related to the injury to his feet when he was exposed, is for Bréal derived from the setting sun's apparent increase in volume. The elements of parricide and incest, on the other hand, would be developments from a later period intended to give the myth religious and moral significance. Comparetti's counter-argument insisted on the separation of the Sphinx myth (which, he agreed with Bréal, was primitive) from Oedipus; the Sphinx episode was added to the Oedipus story to provide a plausible explanation for the incest. Thus the early solar myth is subsumed into a later Oedipus legend, but with a quite different significance, 'after the feeling of the primitive meaning had been extinguished'; 'The popular imagination not only transformed the primitive data, but created from scratch new fables to fit the new situation of people's minds, and a formulation which, at its origin, had served to express natural phenomena, could serve to express something quite different later on, in other words the phenomena of the moral world.'[40] Freud did not underline or otherwise mark this particular sentence (though he did mark several passages in the section on Bréal and Comparetti). With his classical training and interests, he was no doubt very familiar with these kinds of argument about mythology; indeed they fit exactly with the model of children's mental and mythical development that he would himself adopt.

First in the *Three Essays*, successive stages or phases of mental orientation—oral, anal, and genital—push the child along a certain evolutionary path that corresponds also to the growing complexity of characterization that is said to accompany the myths of developing early humanity. In the particular genealogical story inscribed as part of Greek mythology, there is a progression from the primitive copulating and consuming entities like Earth (Gê or Gaia) and Heaven (Uranus), barely differentiated as separate from one another, through the crudely devouring, murderous activities of Uranus and Cronus, and then on to the mature phase of identifiably human characters, like Oedipus himself, with 'moral' motivations and social and familial dimensions

40 Constans, *La légende* (summarizing Comparetti), 8, 9.

to their behaviour.[41] In later writings, Freud's theories of children's sexual researches and 'primal fantasies' go a stage further in stressing the story-making or myth-forming aspect of psychical development. The primal fantasies raise and provisionally respond to what Freud posits as being the fundamental sexual questions—indeed the child's fundamental questions, *tout court*.[42] These are about the origin of babies, the nature of the sexual act, and the difference between the sexes, and to each corresponds a particular psychical reality, a way of imagining and experiencing the world and the relationships that take place in it. It would seem that comparative mythology provided Freud with the framework for theorizing this narrative mental evolution of the child, apparently recapitulating the mythmaking history of humanity.[43]

Unlike the supposed supersession of each developmental stage by the next in Darwin's evolutionary theory, the contemporary mythological model allowed for different elements being retained and reused as they were incorporated into the new paradigm. In the 'Dora' case, for instance, Freud associates the penis with the nipple, claiming that the fantasy of fellatio 'is a new version of what may be described as a prehistoric impression of sucking at the mother's or nurse's breast', and that: 'It ... needs very little expenditure of creative power [*kein großer Aufwand von schöpferischer Kraft*] to substitute the sexual object of the moment [*das aktuelle Sexualobjekt*] (the penis) for the original object'.[44] In a common Freudian pattern, an ancient reality is reworked into a contemporary fantasy, here with great efficiency—minimum creative expenditure—by the minor mythmaker that is each fantasizing individual.

The argument about whether the struggle with the Sphinx represents the oldest stratum of the Oedipus myth or whether it is a later development is connected to another chronological question to do with the arrival of the incest theme. Constans argues for its lateness with some confidence, speaking of the absence of this particular threat from some records of the oracle given to Laius: '[incest] was probably not part

[41] See further Ch. 6, below, on the pre-Olympian gods in their relation to Freud's mythologies of the Oedipus and castration complexes.

[42] On the child's first sexual questions, see Ch. 5, below.

[43] On recapitulation, see further Ch. 9, below. Recapitulation theory, including its application in the supposed repetition of the history of mythology in each individual, is itself one of Freud's mythologies, shaping his own way of imagining both constancy and change.

[44] Freud, *Fragment of an Analysis of a Case of Hysteria* (1905), *SE* vii. 52; *Bruchstück einer Hysterie-Analyse*, *GW* v. 212; tr. mod.

of the primitive legend'.[45] This ambiguity is present in Sophocles' play, where sometimes it is reported that the oracle said only that Laius' and Jocasta's child would kill his father and sometimes the marrying of his mother is mentioned too. The crime against Pelops (meaning primarily Laius' sexual assault on his son) is, however, mentioned in the version of the oracle cited by Constans as not mentioning incest, and marked in the margin by Freud. From this point of view, heterosexual incest replaces a homosexual injury as the source of subsequent ills. In both cases, there is a suicide (Chrysippus' or Jocasta's) and in both a profound violation of domestic relationships: through the kinship confusions of incest, and through Laius' infraction of the laws of hospitality, since he was Pelops' guest.

There is, however, an important difference of another kind between Laius' alleged crime and the incest between Oedipus and Jocasta. Laius' transgressions are voluntary (he knew what he was doing, and to whom); Oedipus's and Jocasta's are not. At just one point in a book of nearly 400 pages, Freud put a wavy line to underscore a passage. Constans is summarizing one commentator's endorsement of a version of the myth in which Oedipus does not blind himself, on the grounds that he 'could not have been so stupid as to punish himself for a crime for which he was in no way responsible'.[46] Freud would appear to be indicating his scorn for the stupidity of this very idea. Early in the book, Constans explains the Greek view of *atê* or destruction that pursues wrongdoers irrespective of whether they knew or intended what they did.[47] He is elaborating on a quotation from Comparetti's book, just given: 'A fatal combination can lead someone to commit the greatest crimes, independently of their will; without wishing or knowing it, a man can be guilty, and subject to all the consequences of his wrongdoing.'[48] This passage too was marked by Freud; it is a strikingly clear formulation of the power of unconscious guilt (and the separation of the sense of guilt from intention or actual crime) that would be central to his own psychological theories. Freud's own 'legend' includes an element of ancient guilty intentions. In the childhood version of the Oedipus story that he creates in the *Interpretation*, the child is indeed the subject of criminal wishes that have subsequently been shamefully repressed.

[45] Constans, *La légende*, 24. [46] Ibid. 39. [47] Ibid. 7.

[48] Ibid. 6. On ancient Greek psychology and conceptions of madness and punishment, see E. R. Dodds, *The Greeks and the Irrational* (1951; Berkeley: University of California Press, 1973); Ruth Padel, *In and Out of the Mind* (Princeton: Princeton University Press, 1992) and *Whom Gods Destroy* (Princeton: Princeton University Press, 1995).

The tragic Oedipus has no wish or intention to do what he does (but subsequently takes on the responsibility); the grown-up Oedipal child did once wish to do what he then could not and did not do, and 'recoils' from the revival of such thoughts.

CHRYSIPPUS AND LAIUS

Freud was evidently interested by the Chrysippus story, since he marks up all Constans's references to it. In terms of narrative logic it is not incompatible with the incest story. Laius' crime is the reason for Pelops' curse (and the oracle's back-up of this); the mistaken marriage of Jocasta and Oedipus is part of the punishment. Freud gives a rare double line in the margin to Constans's summary of one version of the myth, in which the Sphinx was sent from Ethiopia to plague the Thebans because they had not punished Laius for his double crime against Pelops (abusing his son and thereby his hospitality).[49] Yet despite its compatibility with other parts of the story, and its additional motivation for both the curse on Laius' family and the presence of the Sphinx, the Chrysippus story found no place in Sophocles' version of the myth—and *a fortiori*, it is tempting to put it, in Freud's. For he is faithful, in his account of the Oedipus legend, to Sophocles—even though, as the markings in his copy of Constans's book show, he was (or later became) familiar with the other possibilities.

It was in the *Three Essays* that Freud turned his attention specifically to questions of infantile and non-heterosexual sexuality, arguing for instance against the idea of homosexuality as either a later acquisition or a separate nature in the development of individuals. In that context, as mentioned above, he draws indirectly on another classical source, Plato's *Symposium*. But in all his writings on sexuality and fantasy over the next few decades, he never refers to the Chrysippus story, despite the fact that it obviously attracted his attention when he did read up on the Oedipus legend.

NIETZSCHE

Freud's remark in the letter to Fliess about doing his reading of 'the literature' only after he has got his own ideas written down may well

[49] See Constans, *La légende*, 26.

be relevant in relation to another story about the interpretation of the Sphinx. Nietzsche's highly influential book *The Birth of Tragedy* was published in 1872. Its argument that the true spirit of Greek tragedy was wild and pre-classical, rather than serenely civilized, was scandalous, and meant to be. Only a few decades later, Freud would make a comparable gesture. What he did was not to alter the prevailing valorization of Greek culture, but rather to subvert the assumptions of culture in general by using of all writers Sophocles—not just a classical Greek writer but by general agreement the most 'civilized' of the three tragedians—to make his case for the universality of murderous and incestuous impulses in humankind.

Was Freud at some level trying to out-Nietzsche Nietzsche? Nietzsche's primary tragic hero is Prometheus, not Oedipus. When Freud writes, in one short late essay, about the Prometheus myth, he does not mention Nietzsche.[50] When he writes about the Oedipus legend, he does not mention Nietzsche's own take on it, which highlights the Sphinx episode in such a way as to link it both with the question of knowledge and with the violation of nature implied by the motif of incest, 'against nature'. Here is the passage from *The Birth of Tragedy*:

Oedipus his father's murderer, his mother's husband, Oedipus who solved the riddle of the Sphinx! What can we learn from the cryptic trinity of these fateful deeds? There is an ancient folk belief, particularly prevalent in Persia, that a wise magus can be born only from incest: our immediate interpretation of this, with reference to Oedipus the riddle-solver and suitor of his own mother, is that for clairvoyant and magical powers to have broken the spell of the present and the future, the rigid law of individuation and the true magic of nature itself, the cause must have been a monstrous crime against nature—incest in this case; for how could nature be forced to offer up her secrets if not by being triumphantly resisted—by unnatural acts [*durch das Unnatürliche*]? I see this insight as quite clearly present in the terrible trinity that shapes Oedipus' fate: the man who solves the riddle of nature—of the dual-natured Sphinx—must also, as his father's murderer and his mother's lover, transgress the sacred codes of nature. Indeed, what the myth seems to whisper to us is that wisdom, and Dionysiac wisdom in particular, is an abominable crime against nature [*ein naturwidriger Greuel*].[51]

[50] See Freud, 'The Acquisition and Control of Fire' (1932), *SE* xxii. 187–93; 'Zur Gewinnung des Feuers', *GW* xvi. 3–9.

[51] Friedrich Nietzsche, *The Birth of Tragedy* (1872), trans. Shaun Whiteside (London: Penguin, 1993), 47; *Das Geburt der Tragödie*, in *Werke*, ed. Karl Schlechta (Darmstadt: Wissenschaftliche Buchgesellschaft, 1958), i. 57.

Nietzsche too draws on comparative mythology in his reference to Persian narratives. What is particularly interesting here is the priority his interpretation gives to Oedipus' human triumph (this is also the focus of his discussion of Prometheus, which follows immediately). The violation of nature is narratively subordinate to the intellectual victory; but that triumph itself becomes identified, scandalously, as 'an abominable crime against nature'. And of the 'unnatural acts' it is incest which takes priority over parricide: incest three times stands alone without mention of the father's murder as a sufficient crime—the Persian myth, the 'suitor of his own mother', and 'a monstrous crime, against nature—incest in this case'. The intellectual victory is Freud's own point of identification with Oedipus in the story about the plaque presented on his fiftieth birthday, but it is the least weighted strand of the 'terrible trinity' in his theoretical uses of Oedipus. It does not appear directly in the section on Oedipus in *The Interpretation of Dreams*. When he comes to explore the phenomenon of human curiosity and a possible 'instinct for research', Freud hesitates about whether to allot it a separate status or whether to tie it definitively to the sexual instincts and their derivatives.[52] But in this context he never makes a connection with Oedipus, for whom sexual and intellectual prowess are fatefully intertwined. Is that because this was Nietzsche's territory?

Freud sometimes claimed not to have read Nietzsche's work in case it should interfere with his own; he said the same of Schopenhauer, another obvious candidate for intellectual precedence, and the argument is reminiscent of the letter to Fliess in which ideas are said to come before reading up on the subject. In *On the History of the Psycho-Analytic Movement* (1914), the two philosophers are juxtaposed in a passage that is double-edged in numerous ways. Freud is discussing his theory of repression which 'quite certainly came to me independently of any other source', until Otto Rank pointed out to him a passage in Schopenhauer:

> What he says about the struggle against accepting a distressing piece of reality coincides with my concept of repression so completely that once again I owe the chance of making a discovery to my not being well-read [*ich wieder einmal meiner Unbelesenheit für die Ermöglichung einer Entdeckung verpflichtet sein durfte*]. Yet others have read the passage and passed it by without making this discovery, and perhaps the same would have happened to me if in my young days I had had more taste [*Geschmack*] for reading philosophical works. In later years I have denied myself the very great pleasure of reading the works of

[52] On the relationship between intellectual curiosity and sexuality, see Ch. 5, below.

Nietzsche, with the deliberate object of not being hampered in working out the impressions received in psycho-analysis by any sort of anticipatory ideas.[53]

Originality, 'making a discovery', is dependent on not reading (*Unbelesenheit*), although it takes maturity (and perhaps more?) to see what is there to be seen. Reading philosophy was something for which the young Freud had little 'taste', though now, implicitly, things have changed. Not to read Nietzsche is to forgo a 'very great pleasure' which would, however, be likely to create obstacles to clear thinking and inventiveness in relation to clinical experience (as opposed to books). In any case, as Jacques Le Rider among others has documented, it seems hardly credible that Freud was really as unfamiliar as he claims with Nietzsche's writing; at the very least, he was certainly involved, especially in his formative student years, in social and intellectual circles where that work was being keenly debated (and the denial of reading Nietzsche is not a denial of familiarity with his ideas).[54]

EMPEDOCLES

It seems that one advantage of ancient Greek authors was that the temporal distance removed any sense of rivalry. No Oedipal or post-Oedipal sibling or father–son battles needed to be fought with long-gone progenitors, whose ideas lent an ancient authority rather than detracting from present originality. This is the way that Freud presents his use of Sophocles in *The Interpretation of Dreams*: as *support*, presumably by virtue of age and established value, for a new but hence also an old idea. Ancient philosophers give him much less trouble than recent or contemporary ones. Plato's Aristophanic myth appears in the same role in *Beyond the Pleasure Principle* as well as in the *Three Essays*; Aristotle is behind the conception of the 'cathartic method' of Breuer and Freud's *Studies on Hysteria*. In 'Analysis Terminable and Interminable', Freud refers to the pre-Socratic philosopher Empedocles as having anticipated his own theory, at the end of his life, of the permanent human struggle between Eros and the death instinct:

[53] Freud, *On the History of the Psycho-Analytic Movement* (1914), *SE* xiv. 15–16; *Zur Geschichte der psychoanalytischen Bewegung*, *GW* x. 53.

[54] See Jacques Le Rider, *Freud, de l'Acropole au Sinaï: Le retour à l'Antique des Modernes viennois* (Paris: PUF, 2002), esp. 158–61.

> I am well aware that the dualistic theory according to which an instinct of death or of destruction or aggression claims equal rights as a partner [*als gleichberechtigten Partner*] with Eros as manifested in the libido, has found little sympathy and has not really been accepted even among psychoanalysts. This made me all the more pleased when not long ago I came upon this theory of mine in the writings of one of the great thinkers of ancient Greece. I am very ready to give up the prestige of originality for such a confirmation [*Bestätigung*].[55]

Ancient authority ostensibly makes up for losing '*das Prestige der Originalität*' and for the unenthusiastic or sceptical contemporaries as well. But what Freud does not say is that ancient authority is also so ancient that while it remains authoritative, it does not really detract from that prestige of originality at all, at the same time as its longevity reinforces a sense of permanently valid truth. Freud next launches into a paragraph describing Empedocles' multifarious talents ('an investigator and a thinker, a prophet and a magician, a politician, a philanthropist, and a physician with a knowledge of natural science'[56]). Like Leonardo, his polymathic qualities make him an object of admiring identification for the Freud whose own skills and knowledges move between the sciences and the humanities, and between theory and therapeutic practice.[57] The point of correspondence between Empedocles and Freud is then elaborated, with Empedocles' hypothesis of a constant and universal tension between *neikos* and *philia* (conflict and love) being almost identical, Freud says, to his own theory by this point of the permanent struggle between the death instincts and Eros.

THE LOVE OF GREEK

Ancient Greece offered Freud a source of pedagogical authority and focus for admiration that was much less complicated in its engagements than nearer cultural relations. In *Group Psychology and the Analysis of the Ego* he makes, or rather borrows, a joke on this very point. He is discussing the way in which pedagogical relationships often outlast overtly romantic ones because the erotic element is sublimated; from this point of view, the teacher and the student may well be the happiest of couples:

[55] Freud, 'Analysis Terminable and Interminable' (1937), *SE* xxiii. 244–5; 'Die endliche und die unendliche Analyse', *GW* xvi. 90.

[56] Freud, 'Analysis', *SE* xxiii. 245; 'Die endliche', *GW* xvi. 91.

[57] On Freud's interpretation of Leonardo, see Ch. 5, below.

It is well known how easily erotic wishes develop out of emotional relations of a friendly character, based upon appreciation and admiration (compare Molière's 'Kiss me for the love of Greek'), between a master and a pupil, between a performer and a delighted listener, and especially in the case of women.[58]

In the German text, Molière is quoted (in fact slightly misquoted) only in the original French. In the English Freud, Molière is in English in the main text, and the French is (accurately) provided in a footnote, together with the name of the play, *Les femmes savantes* (*The Clever Women*) (1672), which Freud does not give himself. Freud's quick parenthesis assumes that his readers will understand the French and recognize both the quotation and the play; Strachey's English readers are not assumed to have such knowledge. In the modern relations between German, French, and English there is thus an issue about whether translation from an esteemed foreign literature (French in this case) is necessary for the presumably educated readers of Freud.

The linguistic politics of the passing citation beautifully re-enacts the joke itself. In Molière's comedy, 'the love of Greek' does indeed supersede love in other forms. The *femmes savantes*, mother and daughter, try to dissuade Henriette, daughter of one and sister of the other, from abandoning the intellectual cause by getting married to a young man remote from their literary and philosophical passions; they plan to form an academy for the reform of the French language. In the passage from which Freud quotes, a certain M. Vadius is presented to them as supremely attractive by virtue of his knowledge of Greek:

TRISSOTIN He is fully conversant with the old authors, and knows Greek, Madame, as well as any man in France.
PHILAMINTE Greek! Oh gosh, Greek! He knows Greek, sister!
BÉLISE Ah! Niece, Greek!
ARMANDE Greek! How lovely!
PHILAMINTE What? Monsieur knows Greek? Ah! Monsieur, for the love of Greek, do let us kiss you.
[*He kisses them all, up to Henriette, who refuses him.*]
HENRIETTE I apologize, Monsieur—I don't know Greek.[59]

The shared Greek kiss is all the romance the women want; they do not know Greek themselves but they know its (grand) meaning to them (the distinction which Henriette's pointed refusal makes clear).

[58] Freud, *Group Psychology and the Analysis of the Ego* (1921), *SE* xviii. 139; *Massenpsychologie und Ich-analyse*, *GW* xiii. 156.

[59] Molière, *Les femmes savantes* (1672), *Théâtre complet de Molière*, ii (Paris: Garnier, 1958), Act III, Scene ii, l. 719.

In Freud's light quotation, the cultural politics of classical education is not uppermost in his mind; in the play itself, the Greek-knowing Vadius is no object of envy but a pedant.[60] Ancient Greek is a very rare acquisition in seventeenth-century Paris, Molière implies. For Freud, growing up in nineteenth-century Vienna, it was certainly impressive but it was not exceptional. He benefited from a remarkable moment in Austrian educational history when some gifted male students were given an advanced-level secondary state education in both scientific and arts subjects, with a strong focus on Latin and Greek at the core of the arts curriculum. For several years, Freud studied Greek and Latin intensively at school. About two-fifths of the weekly teaching time was allocated to these two subjects, both compulsory; 15 per cent of the total was given to Greek.[61] As part of his final examinations, Freud was set the task of translating a passage from the beginning of Sophocles' *Oedipus the King*: lines 14 to 57, the speech in which the chorus of Theban elders asks for King Oedipus's help against the plague afflicting their city.[62]

It would not have to follow from their prominence in the élite secondary-school curriculum that classical studies were a thriving or influential intellectual field elsewhere. But in Freud's time and culture, arguments derived from the academic discipline of philology were not confined to it and could play a part in many forms of public debate, in Austria as in other European countries; Nietzsche, for instance, was a university philologist by profession. At the same time, the educational appropriateness of classical studies to the modern world was being both challenged and ardently defended.[63] Before Freud made the meaning of Sophocles' *Oedipus* into a quintessentially modern

[60] Vadius was based on Gilles Ménage (1613–92), tutor and close friend to the novelist Madame de Lafayette. In *The Penguin Companion to Literature*, ii, *European Literature*, ed. Anthony Thorlby (Harmondsworth: Penguin, 1969), he is described by W. G. Moore as 'a man less pedantic than his reputation' (p. 452). He was in fact the author (in Latin) of a guide to women intellectuals from the ancient world. This has appeared for the first time in French as *Histoire des femmes philosophes*, trans. Manuella Vaney (Paris: Arléa, 2003).

[61] See Le Rider, *Freud*, 41–68. Le Rider describes the Prussian educational policies initiated by Wilhelm von Humboldt at the start of the nineteenth century, on which the Austrian system was based. It was only in Austria (not in Prussia where it originated) that the *Realgymnasium* of the type that Freud attended, combining scientific and humanistic studies, included Greek as well as Latin. See also Hugo Knoepfmacher, 'Sigmund Freud in High School', *American Imago*, 36: 3 (1979), 287–99.

[62] See Rudnytsky, *Freud and Oedipus*, 12.

[63] See Le Rider, *Freud*; and for comparable arguments in Britain at the time, Christopher Stray, *Classics Transformed: Schools, Universities, and Society in England, 1830–1960* (Oxford: Clarendon Press, 1998), and Simon Goldhill, *Who Needs Greek?*

question, Nietzsche had done something comparable in his affirmation of Dionysian authenticity as a source of German identity in *The Birth of Tragedy*. For Freud, Greek carried an authority which bolstered the force of present originality.[64]

Freud kept up his reading in classical subjects throughout his life; far from representing a rote-learned school subject quickly left behind, it was a passionate source of intellectual interest and inspiration. His knowledge of Greek and Roman archaeology provided one rich strand of metaphorical models for his thinking about the structures of mind and memory.[65] He had an extensive collection of classical *objets*, many of them on display in his consulting room.[66] Both Rome and Athens were places of great significance to him because of their classical histories. 'A Disturbance of Memory on the Acropolis', a public letter to the poet Romain Rolland written late in Freud's life, recalls the complex emotional significance of a visit to Athens with his brother, many years before. It involves a buried inter-generational story: the son's mixture of guilt and pride at the achievement of having 'gone further than' an uneducated father to whom classical Greece meant nothing.[67]

JACOB BERNAYS

In Freud's adult life, classics was close to home; it was even in the family. Jacob Bernays, one of the most significant German-speaking

Contests in the Cultural History of Hellenism (Cambridge: Cambridge University Press, 2002).

[64] For a critical account of Freud's exploitation of his knowledge of Greek, see Sarah Winter, *Freud and the Institution of Psychoanalytic Knowledge* (Stanford, CA: Stanford University Press, 1999). Winter considers that Freud's study of Greek at school is inseparable from a particular kind of professional ambition which duly marked his later life: 'Freud could only have encountered Sophocles' play as freighted with the prestige of its canonical status and the promise of professional social advancement that classical learning held out' (p. 47).

[65] See Malcolm Bowie, *Freud, Proust and Lacan: Theory as Fiction* (Cambridge: Cambridge University Press, 1987), 18–37. Richard H. Armstrong's *A Compulsion for Antiquity* (see n. 4, above) is an extensive engagement with the question of how the ancient world in its various manifestations or representations, both academic and antiquarian, actively shaped the forms taken by Freud's psychoanalysis.

[66] See Lynn Gamwell and Richard Wells, *Sigmund Freud and Art: His Personal Collection of Antiquities* (London: Thames and Hudson, 1989).

[67] Freud, 'A Disturbance of Memory on the Acropolis: An Open Letter to Romain Rolland on the Occasion of his Seventieth Birthday' (1936), *SE* xxii. 239–48; 'Brief an Romain Rolland (Eine Erinnerungsstörung auf der Akropolis)', *GW* xvi. 250–7.

Greek scholars in the second half of the nineteenth century, was the uncle of Freud's wife, Martha Bernays. In 1857 Bernays had written a much-debated essay on Aristotle's notion of catharsis, challenging the contemporary understanding of it as primarily a spiritual or moral concept referring to the audience's moral edification through the experience of tragedy. In Bernays's version, catharsis works therapeutically; a small, controlled arousal of distressing feelings through watching a tragedy enables spectators to be freed from them.[68] Mind and body were not separate in this quasi-medical model of inoculation, and Bernays's slide from the spiritual to the physical could be seen as itself a kind of tragic turnaround, bringing the exalted literature and philosophy of classical Greece down to the level of bodily human beings. Bernays's argument and the controversy it elicited found a place in Nietzsche's differently iconoclastic revision of the Enlightenment view of tragedy when he spoke of 'that pathological discharge, catharsis, which philosophers are uncertain whether to class among the medical or the moral phenomena'.[69] The broad influence of Bernays's work anticipates the classificatory confusion that would soon be instigated by psychoanalysis. Enter first the 'cathartic method' of treatment for hysteria put forward by Freud and Breuer, extending the therapeutic suggestion of Bernays's thesis into the field of medical practice itself. Bernays had added a therapeutic component to the philosophy of tragedy; Freud and Breuer offered a medical cure based on a literary theory. And a few years later, in *The Interpretation of Dreams*, Aristotle's own choice of the exemplary tragedy—*Oedipus the King*—would become the central 'proof' of Freud's new psychology of the mind and its development.

Tragedy itself moves on and changes its appearance in the powerful new philosophies and theories that seek to grasp it in the period leading up to Freud's turn-of-the-century appropriation of Oedipus. Challenging modern adaptations and performances of Greek tragedy also formed part of the background to the psychoanalytic Oedipus. Freud had

[68] The first past of Bernays's trenchant and witty essay, 'Grundzüge der verlorenen Abhandlung des Aristoteles über Wirkung der Tragödie', is translated by Jennifer Barnes as 'Aristotle on the Effect of Tragedy', in Andrew Laird (ed.), *Ancient Literary Criticism* (Oxford: Oxford University Press, 2006), 159–75. On the arguments about Aristotle that would have impinged upon Freud's thinking, see Le Rider, *Freud*, 177–89. On Bernays see also Ch. 2, below.

[69] Nietzsche, *Birth*, 107.

been much affected when he saw the role of Oedipus performed by Mounet-Sully during his time in Paris in the mid-1880s.[70] In the early 1900s the Austrian Hugo von Hofmannsthal's translations of plays such as Sophocles' *Electra* were performed across Europe; they focused especially on the psychology of the heroines. As well as being familiar with contemporary studies in anthropology and mythology, Hofmannsthal had read Freud. The *Studies on Hysteria* influenced his version of *Electra*, and *The Interpretation of Dreams* made its way into his interpretation of Oedipus, as the Delphic oracle becomes a dream-reader.[71] As early as this, psychoanalysis was itself already starting to change the literature that it took as its model for an unchanging, timeless pattern of the human mind; ironically, it was even adopting the role of philology as itself a source of interpretative authority.

But the new Freudian interpretation of tragedy claimed to have discovered an ancient and unchanging meaning in Sophocles' play. Even as he was transforming the understanding of tragedy, Freud insisted that that meaning had been there all the time. Greek tragedy offered the monumental associations of a phenomenon fixed for all time but also invested with the temporally distant dignity of an ancient culture. As discussed in Chapter 4, Freud varied in his views about whether or not the typical stories of human experience were subject to significant change, both for the individual and in terms of the larger evolutions that he took to be shared across different human cultures; and the tension between those two conceptions was mapped onto an opposition between ancient and modern literature. Two models of historical and personal change are tied to this pair, and they are co-present in much of Freud's writing.

A hundred years on from Freud's initial discovery, or recognition, or invention, the psychoanalytic version of Oedipus is itself subject to a host of new questions and possible reinterpretations—some derived from the influence exercised by psychoanalysis itself and some, as discussed in the Introduction, from the changing forms and conditions of personal and familial identity that have developed since then. In 1954 T. B. L. Webster wrote in his essay on 'Greek Tragedy' for *Fifty Years of Classical Scholarship* that 'the discussion goes on and on, and will continue to

[70] Jones, *Sigmund Freud: Life and Work*, i (London: Hogarth Press, 1953), 194.

[71] On Hofmannsthal see Goldhill, *Who Needs Greek?*, 108–76, and Le Rider, *Freud*, 201–15.

go on as long as we ask new questions based on our own experience of art and life.'[72] A further fifty years on from *that* statement, we may continue to take our cue from its invitation and exhortation to ask new questions of Greek tragedy and to use it to think about issues of contemporary life and identity. That is what Freud did, too.

[72] T. B. L. Webster, 'Greek Tragedy', in *Fifty Years of Classical Scholarship*, ed. Maurice Platnauer (Oxford: Basil Blackwell, 1954), 92.

2

Never Done, Never to Return: Hysteria and After

Near the start of the *Studies on Hysteria* (1895), Freud and Breuer describe what they have newly understood to be the sequence by which hysterical symptoms are cured:

> The psychical process which originally took place must be repeated as vividly as possible; it must be brought back to its *status nascendi* and then 'spoken out'. Where what we are dealing with are phenomena involving stimuli (spasms, neuralgias and hallucinations)—these re-appear once again with the fullest intensity and then vanish for ever [*schwinden dann für immer*].[1]

The order outlined here involves three stages: a return to a point of origin, a repetition or re-reaction, and a final ending. Past, present, and future interfere with one another and reconnect; a return of or to a painful past moment, resurrected and relived, makes possible a future 'for ever' free of the symptom that has taken the place until now of an

[1] Freud and Josef Breuer, 'On the Psychical Mechanism of Hysterical Phenomena: Preliminary Communication' (1893), *Studies on Hysteria* (1895), *SE* ii. 6–7; 'Über den psychischen Mechanismus hysterischer Phänomene: Vorläufige Mitteilung', *Studien über Hysterie*, *GW* i. 85. Breuer's two individual contributions to the *Studies*, the 'Anna O.' case history and the chapter entitled 'Theoretical', appear in the supplementary volume to Freud's *Gesammelte Werke*, *Nachtragsband: Texte aus den Jahren 1885 bis 1938* (1999), henceforth cited as *GW Nachtragsband*. Apart from the co-written 'Preliminary Communication', all other parts of the *Studies*—four further case histories and 'On the Psychotherapy of Hysteria'—are by Freud.

In the present passage, Strachey's translation of '*ausgesprochen*' as 'given verbal utterance' seems too abstract; 'spoken out' or simply 'uttered' might be closer. The inverted commas, dropped by Strachey, signal the colloquiality, as with the 'talking cure' that makes its début later in the book. At other points Strachey does bring out the conversational tone. In the 'Anna O.' case, for instance, Breuer says—again with inverted commas—how his patient habitually 'talked away' her symptoms; here the German word is *wegerzählt*, literally 'narrated away'; and 'talked away' is also the translation for '*abgesprochen*' ('talked off'), also in inverted commas, two pages later (Breuer, *Studies*, *SE* ii. 35, 37; *GW Nachtragsband*, 233, 235).

unhappy memory, and kept it out of the way of conscious knowledge. 'Hysterics suffer mainly from reminiscences', in Breuer and Freud's resonant phrase;[2] for their suffering to be relieved, the sore past must be allowed to emerge into the present, its pressure relieved.

What happens in this is dramatic. A performer makes a final appearance, a reprise for one last time, charged with the built-up emotion ('with the fullest intensity') of the finale. A rebirth (going back to the *status nascendi*) is followed by sudden death. This is a drama of two times, made up of the patient's retrospective telling or reliving during the therapeutic conversation, and the past history, brought out again to be seen for what it was or is: for its subsequent painful significance. This double timing anticipates what was to be the future role in psychoanalysis of an actual play, Sophocles' *Oedipus the King*, likened by Freud to a psychoanalysis in its dialogic discovery of a past history previously out of mind.[3]

The theatrical language of Breuer and Freud's exposition points to both its connection with and its departure from the treatment of hysteria at the time—when hysteria was as prevalent, as multifarious, and as enigmatic an illness as depression is today. Defined as bodily symptoms with no organic basis, hysteria could refer to anything from a headache to a paralysed limb; it could be mildly inconvenient or incapacitating. It was associated with 'attacks' involving involuntary contractions or else, in its slighter manifestations, with ordinary daydreaming. It was almost exclusively associated with women, as the word's etymology from the Greek *hystera*—'womb'—suggested.[4] In the mid-1880s, Freud had spent six months in Paris following the work of Charcot, the renowned psychiatrist who gave presentations of his hysterical patients at the Salpêtrière hospital. The patients were exhibited before an audience; their illness was seen in the form of a repeatable performance, in the four characteristic 'phases' of a hysterical attack. Charcot used hypnosis to induce hysterical acts and attacks as a means of demonstrating their typical features. In Breuer and Freud's treatment, by contrast, the stress fell on the auditory rather than the visual; not on the patient as a bodily

[2] Freud and Breuer, *Studies*, *SE* ii. 7; *Studien*, *GW* i. 86.

[3] On the dramatic parallel between *Oedipus* and psychoanalysis, see Ch. 1, pp. 21–3.

[4] On the history of hysteria see Ilza Veith, *Hysteria: The History of a Disease* (Chicago: University of Chicago Press, 1965), and Helen King, 'Once Upon a Text: Hysteria from Hippocrates', in Sander L. Gilman, Helen King, Roy Porter, G. S. Rousseau, and Elaine Showalter, *Hysteria Beyond Freud* (Berkeley: University of California Press, 1993), 3–90. As King shows, *contra* Veith and others, the noun 'hysteria' is not itself a Greek word, though the adjective *hysterikos* is used in contexts implying uterine illness.

spectacle for assembled observers, but on her words to a single trusted interlocutor. Here the rehearsal of the symptoms is not didactic (for an audience) but therapeutic (for the patient). The theatre, as in the first quotation, is no longer like a real one, with symptoms induced to appear, but an analogical one in which they spontaneously perform for one last time.[5]

The move from the real to the analogical theatre is also a passage from public to private space. In one of her many striking verbal inventions, Breuer's patient 'Anna O.' speaks of her 'private theatre [*Privattheater*]'.[6] She is referring to the sometimes painful daydreaming through which she drifts away from the here and now into what the text calls her 'absences'.[7] Anna O. got into the habit of describing the scenes she saw to Breuer, and the one-woman show changed its register, becoming a form of communication and release. The dramatic analogy is used in other cases too. Each of the traumatizing incidents in the past that returned, eventually, to 'Miss Lucy R.' is described by Freud as a 'scene [*Szene*]'.[8] When the scenes have appeared to her one by one, and she has reported on them to Freud, she is freed of their accumulated weight. She becomes the spectator and critic of these extracts from her history that, in being represented, can be both recognized and set at a distance; speaking them out in words was a way of becoming free of them. Another patient, 'Frau Emmy von N.', on one occasion produced a whole set of parallel memories 'in a single sentence and in such rapid succession that they might have been a single episode [*Ereignis*] in four acts'.[9] It was Anna O. herself who, famously, named this performative process the 'talking cure',[10] surely the mother of all soundbites, and as telling a catchphrase for what was not yet psychoanalysis as anyone could have dreamt up.

With its combination of a palindrome and a big circle, the name 'Anna O.' might seem to have been invented expressly to serve as the alpha and omega, the *fons et origo* of the new therapeutic method. Hers is

[5] On the visual emphasis of Charcot's practice, see Georges Didi-Huberman, *Invention de l'hystérie: Charcot et l'iconographie photographique de la Salpêtrière* (Paris: Macula, 1982).

[6] Breuer, *Studies*, *SE* ii. 22; *GW Nachtragsband*, 222.

[7] Breuer, *Studies*, *SE* ii. 24, 26; *GW Nachtragsband*, 224, 225.

[8] See e.g. Freud, *Studies*, *SE* ii. 123; *Studien*, *GW* i. 182.

[9] Freud, *Studies*, *SE* ii. 57; *Studien*, *GW* i. 109.

[10] Breuer, *Studies*, *SE* ii. 30; *GW Nachtragsband*, 229.

the first of the five case histories presented in the *Studies in Hysteria* as they appeared in 1895; she had been a patient of Breuer's some years before that, at the start of the 1880s. Later on, Breuer had lengthy conversations about the case with his much younger friend and colleague Sigmund Freud, who persuaded him to write it up. In 1893 the two men published a joint article on hysteria which then became the 'Preliminary Communication' to the book of 1895; and the rest is psychoanalytic history.

Anna O. in one way never did exist in that indeterminate sphere known as real life: she is a character in Breuer's story, and later a character in the history of psychoanalysis. Like all the other heroines of the book, she was given a pseudonym to protect the identity of the woman now known to have been Bertha Pappenheim, who subsequently became well known in her own right. After her treatment by Breuer, and some later mental troubles, she went on to live an exceptional and fruitful life as a social worker, feminist, and Jewish activist. Meanwhile Anna O.'s story, and her inventions, as told and interpreted by herself and by Breuer and Freud, went on to have a life of their own independent of Bertha Pappenheim's. It was Anna O., not Bertha Pappenheim, who would come to figure for psychoanalysis, as its ambiguous ghost or largely forgotten mother.[11]

The Anna O. case became a focal point for Freud's later returns, in works like *On the History of the Psycho-Analytic Movement* (1914) and *An Autobiographical Study* (1925), to the moment of the *Studies*, now retrospectively seen as that of the origin or birth of psychoanalysis. In looking back at Anna O., and at the other case histories of the volume, Freud was also looking back at and reinterpreting the partnership with Breuer that was not to last. Initially, psychoanalysis had (at least) two fathers. But already by the time of the second edition of the *Studies*, in 1908, Breuer's preface clearly marks his distance from what what had by then become firmly established as Freudian psychoanalysis.

Though Breuer records her phrase in his case history, Freud and Breuer together gave their own name to what Anna O. called the 'talking cure'. The 'cathartic method [*kathartischen Methode*]', with inverted commas this time given to highlight its novelty, is named on the opening page of the joint Preface to the first edition of the *Studies*.[12] The

[11] For Bertha Pappenheim's life story, see Lisa Appignanesi and John Forrester, *Freud's Women* (1992; 2nd edn. London: Penguin, 2000), ch. 3.

[12] Freud and Breuer, *Studies*, *SE* ii. p. xxix; *Studien*, *GW* i. 77–8.

new term seals the dramatic analogy, in that the idea of catharsis comes originally from Aristotle's theory of Greek tragedy. The phrase also translates Anna's words into a different kind of language, more formal and technical. And it shifts the perspective from the patient, the one who talking-cures herself, to the physician, who applies a particular method of treatment. The medical term points to several issues of translation and alteration in the *Studies on Hysteria*. What are the implications of moving from one linguistic register to another—between a specialist vocabulary and ordinary speech? What is the right kind of language for talking about psychological matters, when the patients' own words are the medium of the treatment? How do feelings get carried over as if from mind to body, or in the other direction?

It happens that the phrase *talking cure* was first uttered in English, although Anna O.'s first language was German. Breuer's German text quotes the English phrase, and the foreign expression in the middle of the sentence, just like the 'foreign body' (*Fremdkörper*) to which Breuer, and Freud initially, likened the hysterical symptom, is noticeably at odds with its environment.[13] In the story of Anna O.'s treatment, the English phrase comes out of a moment when she was compulsively speaking in languages other than her native German. Languages are multiplied, set alongside one another, as if to exhibit their separate meanings for the speaker; there is a constant movement across boundaries between different languages and between language and other domains. In another case, that of Freud's patient Frau Emmy von N., bodily symptoms are said to 'join in the conversation', reacting to the memories that the patient is coming up with.[14] It follows from this that words are far from being just a neutral tool for stating a fact, or communicating a message.

[13] The 'foreign body' is mentioned early in the 'Preliminary Communication' of 1893: 'We must presume rather that the psychical trauma—or rather the memory of the trauma—acts like a foreign body which long after its entry must continue to be regarded as an agent that is still at work' (Freud and Breuer, *Studies, SE* ii. 6; *Studien, GW* i. 85).

[14] Freud, *Studies, SE* ii. 148; *Studien, GW* i. 212. *Mitzusprechen* is put in inverted commas, highlighting the choice of a conversational rather than abstract expression for what is literally a conversational idea. And later, in Freud's closing essay, this single example is granted the dignity of theoretical generality: 'Among the tasks presented by analysis is that of [the] getting rid of [*Beseitigung*] symptoms which are capable of increasing in intensity or of returning ... While we are working at one of these symptoms we come across the interesting and not undesired phenomenon of "joining in the conversation [*Mitsprechens*]".' A page later, the inverted commas have gone, and we have a paragraph beginning: '*Das Phänomen des Mitsprechens des hysterischen Symptoms*'—'The phenomenon of hysterical symptoms joining in the conversation' (*SE* ii. 296, 297; *GW* i. 301, 303).

Like weapons they may hit and hurt (and it is by the same logic that they can also heal). Here Freud is speaking about 'Frau Cäcilie M.', who was treated by both him and Breuer: 'She described a conversation which she had had with him [her husband] and a remark of his which she had felt as a bitter insult. Suddenly she put her hand to her cheek, gave a loud cry of pain, and said: "It was like a slap in the face." With this both her pain and her attack were at an end.'[15] Without her being aware of it, the body has translated the patient's identification of verbal and physical injury by 'symbolization' (*Symbolisierung*). Once Frau Cäcilie has recognized her own unconscious connection—it was *like* a slap in the face—she is free of its painful effects; once again, the sequence here involves a revived, relived event which is followed by a definitive ending.

In the dominant account of the formation of hysterical symptoms in the *Studies*, an unwelcome thought or memory is split off from consciousness and 'converted' by unknown means into a physical ailment which may be trivial or, on the contrary, quite debilitating. This symptom may (but need not) have some discernible relationship to the precipitating event—in Frau Emmy von M.'s case, the clacking sound that came out just when she was trying to stay quiet at her sick daughter's bedside; in Miss Lucy R.'s, the hallucinated smell of burnt pudding associated with the distress of a moment when that smell had been really there. For Freud, the forgetting occurs because the perception is unbearable; it is associated with something the patient cannot *admit* to herself: cannot allow into her conscious mind. The person does not want to know, and so the memory subsists in the altered, 'converted' form of the symptom, translated from a mental to a physical status, and kept well away from conscious awareness. It was Miss Lucy who gave Freud what he praises as the perfect formulation of this phenomenon: 'I didn't know—or rather I didn't want to know [*Ich wußte es ja nicht oder besser, ich wollte es nicht wissen*].'[16]

The Greek word *cathartic* adopted to name the new therapeutic treatment carries the connotation of a (good) riddance of bodily or emotional matter that would otherwise clog or interfere with a person's health. It is evocative of high drama, being derived from Aristotle's *Poetics*, where the word is used to describe the emotional effect of tragedy. Its

[15] Freud, *Studies*, *SE* ii. 178; *Studien*, *GW* i. 247.
[16] Freud, *Studies*, *SE* ii. 117; *Studien*, *GW* i. 175.

meaning has been endlessly contested over the centuries, and though they do not say this—they do not, in fact, discuss their choice of the term at all—Breuer and Freud's 'cathartic' method is mediated through the latest developments in the history of the text's interpretation by classical scholars. In the key sentence of Aristotle's text, tragedy is given a definition which ends with an affective function: 'through pity and fear achieving the catharsis of such emotions [*pathêmatôn*]'.[17] Jacob Bernays's influential work in the mid-nineteenth century had countered the prevailing post-Enlightenment view of a spiritual or aesthetic effect of 'purification', taking a passage from the end of the *Politics* as an amplification of the meaning of catharsis in the *Poetics*.[18] In it, Aristotle describes a process of musical therapy to modify extremes of emotion; there is an inoculatory use of (moderately) heightened feeling to cure (pathologically) heightened feeling.[19]

It is from this interpretation of Aristotelian catharsis that Freud and Breuer's 'cathartic treatment [*kathartische Behandlung*]' takes its cue,

[17] The full sentence reads (in a translation which is necessarily tendentious, having to make some of the significant interpretative choices): 'So tragedy is an imitation [*mimêsis*] of a serious and complete action [*praxeôs*] of a certain magnitude, with language embellished by each kind [of embellishment] in the separate sections, in acted not narrative form, through pity and fear achieving the catharsis of such emotions' (Aristotle, *Poetics* 1449b).

[18] See Aristotle, *Politics* 1341b–1342a; on Jacob Bernays see also Ch. 1, pp. 43–4, above.

[19] In 1957, exactly a century after Bernays, a compendiously argued case was made by Gerald F. Else, against the homeopathic understanding of the operation of catharsis: 'The reason why the notion of pity and fear being purged by pity and fear has persisted is that no other agency has been visible in the sentence through which the catharsis could be brought about' (*Aristotle's Poetics: The Argument* (Cambridge, MA: Harvard University Press, 1957), 228); Else found that missing agency earlier in the sentence, wanting the *pathêmata* of the last clause to refer to the events or 'things experienced' of the earlier 'action'. The catharsis would then refer not to the audience's emotions, but to the hero's deeds, cleansed or purified of their polluting qualities by his not doing them deliberately (the theory applies best to accidental murderers—like Oedipus, or Deianira in Sophocles' *Women of Trachis*). By shifting the focus away from the audience (now reduced to the role of acknowledging the rightness of the character being cleared), Else was partly depathologizing them, Bernays and his psychotherapeutic descendants now having become the 'traditional' view of catharsis and often represented in a caricatural form. A. J. A. Waldock, for instance (*Sophocles the Dramatist* (Cambridge: Cambridge University Press, 1951), 42) had said that 'medicinal' interpretations 'assume that a theatregoer is a person on the brink of hysteria': where once the consulting room was a private theatre, now the real theatre is being parodically imagined as an emergency consulting room. It is interesting in this connection that long after the term 'cathartic' had ceased to be used by Freud, a version of the homeopathic model survived in the theory of transference, in which a small-scale version of an existing pathology is induced in controlled conditions, so as to effect a general cure.

transposing Aristotelian artistic function, whether primarily physical or mental, to a new psychiatric practice. Freud and Breuer thus took a term from literary criticism and moved it into a medical context. Their adoption of 'catharsis' also blurred the modern boundary between the scientific and the aesthetic by offering a cure by dramatic enactment and story: literary medicine.[20]

Arguments over the notion of catharsis have frequently involved a tension between tragic grandeur and bodily bathos, between higher and lower species of human event: in Greek, catharsis can be associated with the periodic purgation of bowel movements. So the 'high' term of catharsis chosen to name the new treatment itself contains a division similar to the one in which catharsis appears as more elevated than Anna O.'s colloquial talking cure. And as well as speaking in newly forged technical terms of 'cathartic' treatment and 'abreaction', Freud and Breuer also use ordinary words for clearing away or cleaning up, like *Ausräumung* or *Reinigung*. *Reinigung* was in fact the usual word chosen in the nineteenth century to translate the Greek *catharsis* into German; its associations could range from the moral purification implied by Lessing and Schiller to the quasi-physiological purgation of Bernays.[21] The existence of the *Politics* passage strengthens the position of critics who argue for a non-intellectual component in catharsis (where the intellectual is taken to be non-bodily and non-emotional). But it also tends to polarize the distinction between the two hypothetical orders. This is the effect that A. D. Nuttall illustrates in his argument about the meaning of catharsis with Martha C. Nussbaum.[22] Yet both senses, of a primarily intellectual 'clarification' (Nussbaum's word) and a bodily 'purgation' (Nuttall's preference, based on the *Politics* passage) come

[20] The *Politics* passage also makes the point that there is a continuum, not a qualitative distinction, between different orders of affliction: 'The emotion [*pathos*] that affects some minds strongly exists in all minds, with more or less strength—pity and fear, for instance, but also excitement [*enthousiasmos*]' (1341a). At the stage of the *Studies*, Freud separated the structures he and Breuer had identified in hysterical mental functioning from those of non-hysterical people, but later, the existence of unconscious ideas, centred on the repression of a multifariously 'perverse' sexuality, would not be confined to one class of patients but would form the core of his model of all minds—beginning, in *The Interpretation of Dreams*, with his own.

[21] On the history of German versions of 'catharsis' in the century before Freud, see Jacques Le Rider, *Freud, de l'Acropole au Sinaï: Le retour à l'Antique des Modernes viennois* (Paris: PUF, 2002), 177–86.

[22] See A. D. Nuttall, *Why Does Tragedy Give Pleasure?* (Oxford: Clarendon Press, 1996), 11–14, and Martha C. Nussbaum, *The Fragility of Goodness: Luck and Ethics in Greek Tragedy and Philosophy* (Cambridge: Cambridge University Press, 1986), 388–91.

together in Freud and Breuer's version of cathartic therapy, even though they do not explicitly make the Aristotelian connection themselves.[23]

Another fruitful disturbance arises from the uncertainty of roles and agency in relation to tragic catharsis. Catharsis is most often taken to apply to the spectators of tragedy, but it can also be thought to refer to the characters on stage, ultimately 'cleansed' of their crimes, or even to the purified spirit of the play's creator.[24] In *Oedipus the King*, Aristotle's own exemplary play, the roles of the investigator and the one under investigation become switched and confused. Oedipus begins as the person in authority, seeking the cause of a 'plague [*loimos*]' (28), which is infecting the city. The oracle has declared that the remedy lies in discovering who murdered King Laius, many years before, and ultimately Oedipus finds that he is unwittingly the object of his own judicial inquiry. One effect of this is to complicate the position of the investigator, who is not situated securely outside the problem. In a related way, the one-to-one dialogue between patient and doctor comes to rest on a premise of both active direction and potential vulnerability on both sides that is very different from the clear separation of functions in which patients are presented, by the doctor, as exhibits before an audience. In the cathartic treatment, the patient is meant to relive her own sufferings from a newly conscious perspective; actor and spectator merge and change position, as she becomes the comprehending, interpreting audience of her own past experiences and is released from the weight of painful emotions that they have left behind. From this point of view, the question of 'audience or characters?' would cease to matter: the catharsis applies to a patient who is both.[25]

[23] Jonathan Lear has drawn out the therapeutic combination of both empathetic reliving and conscious understanding that the *Studies on Hysteria* develop, in *Love and Its Place in Nature: A Philosophical Interpretation of Freudian Psychoanalysis* (New York: Farrar, Straus, & Giroux, 1990), 29–68.

[24] Goethe posited an aesthetic 'purification' of the passions (of the characters, and thereby of the audience) effected by the genius of the poet.

[25] In the essay 'Psychopathic Characters on the Stage', Freud does give a view of Aristotelian catharsis, though without naming it as such. 'If, as has been assumed since the time of Aristotle, the purpose of drama is to arouse "terror and pity" and so "to purge the emotions", we can describe that purpose in rather more detail by saying that it is a question of opening up sources of pleasure or enjoyment in our emotional life [*die Eröffnung von Lust- oder Genußquellen aus unserem Affektleben*]' (*SE* vii. 305; 'Psychopathische Personen auf der Bühne', *GW Nachtragsband*, 656). The word for the purging of the emotions is '*Reinigung*', the usual German translation of (tragic) *catharsis* (in the *Studies*, Freud and Breuer use the transliterated adjective *kathartische*). Freud goes on to explain this as a form of safe identification: the pleasure is because we can both be and not be

Repeatedly, Breuer and Freud stress not only the active collaboration of their patients in the therapeutic process, but also their own contributions to the development of the new method of treatment. Proclaiming the intelligence of their patients went against the prevailing wisdom of the time that hysterics were weak-minded and tended to inherit the 'degenerate' tendencies of other members of their family. This doxa was partly a mistaken inference from social circumstances: the thousands of patients confined in the Salpêtrière hospital where Charcot worked were almost all poor and uneducated. But with the exception of 'Katharina', the down-to-earth working girl who follows Freud up a mountain to ask his advice and take her lofty place in psychoanalytic history, Breuer and Freud's experience, as they point out themselves at the outset, is with 'private practice in an educated and literate social class'.[26] They insist, against the dominant view, that hysterics may be exceptionally gifted. Fräulein Anna O.'s 'powerful intellect' is praised at length;[27] it is also suggested that, as a woman, her sufferings are partly due to her not having received an education commensurate with her intellectual capacities. In relation to their joint patient, Frau Cäcilie M., mentioned intermittently throughout the book, Freud in particular expresses fulsome admiration for her exceptional talents, from chess-playing to poetry-writing.

Freud never rejected heredity as irrelevant, but he consistently spoke against the view that it was the sole or even the dominant factor in the development of mental illness. He and Breuer stress the significance of traumatic experiences, including but not restricted to early sexual abuse. In the *Studies*, the 'reminiscences' from which hysterics suffer range from the real sexual advances of close male relatives in adolescence and early adulthood to unacknowledged romantic love for a sister's husband. Quite modest kinds of traumatic event or 'determining process [*veranlassende Vorgang*]' are to be found in the common experiences of grief and longing, love lost or unrequited, that filled the lives of middle-class women at the time.[28] Breuer identifies 'being in love and sick-nursing [*der Verliebtheit und der Krankenpflege*]'—as 'the two great

the hero, who is a hero but suffers. In the *Studies*, a similar kind of pleasure and release is implied; it is as though the patient's cure gives her an audience's relative exteriority, so that she is able now to see her suffering—and performing—self at a distance.

[26] Freud, *Studies*, *SE* ii. p. xxix; *Studien*, *GW* i. 77.

[27] Breuer, *Studies*, *SE* ii. 21; *GW Nachtragsband*, 221.

[28] Freud and Breuer, *Studies*, *SE* ii. 7; *Studien*, *GW* i. 86. On the first page of this 'Preliminary Communication', the same phrase '*veranlassende Vorgang*' is used, but translated by Strachey as 'precipitating event' (*SE* ii. 3; *GW* i. 81). The German allows

pathogenic factors' in hysteria.[29] They are linked by the concentration on a loved one and a kind of unreality. The lover's '"rapt" state of mind ["*Entrückung*"]' will 'cause his real environment to grow dim'.[30] Literally, the phrase refers to the 'twilighting of surrounding reality [*das Verdümmern der umgebenden Realität*]', linking it to the 'twilight states [*Dämmerzustand*]' of the bedside vigil just mentioned.[31] The lights go down.

Together with its theatrical overtones, the quotation at the start of this chapter also carries the suggestion of magic, as mysterious symptoms emerge one last time before disappearing forever. Freud often returns to this semi-supernatural phenomenon: 'a recollection [*Reminiszenz*] never returns a second time once it has been dealt with [*erledigt*]; an image that has been "talked away" never returns again.'[32] Elsewhere, the last moment is described as the end of a haunting: 'the image vanishes as a rescued spirit is laid to rest.'[33]

Later, as will appear, Freud would be less confident of the finality of analytic finishings and vanishings.[34] Yet this image of a magical vanishing also seems strangely to apply to broader hysterical phenomena: to the hypothetical 'end' of hysteria as a disease, and to the supersession of the *Studies on Hysteria* by later psychoanalytic theory. In both cases, it would seem—the illness and the theory—hysteria apparently disappears, but disappears only to reappear. It vanishes, and it returns.

From later perspectives, hysteria has frequently come to acquire a second, and secondary, significance. Whether it is being considered primarily either as a past diagnostic category or as a historical product of

for both the single distressing incident and the drawn-out causation suggested by the examples here.

[29] Breuer, *Studies*, *SE* ii. 219; *GW Nachtragsband*, 278. [30] Ibid.

[31] Breuer. *Studies*, *SE* ii. 218; *GW Nachtragsband*, 277.

[32] Freud, *Studies*, *SE* ii. 296; *Studien*, *GW* i. 301. Literally, the image 'is never seen again', '*ist nicht wieder zu sehen*'. '*Abgesprochen*', translated by 'talked away', is not in inverted commas in the German text.

[33] Freud, *Studies*, *SE* ii. 281, tr. mod.; *Studien*, *GW* i. 283.

[34] In 'Observations on Transference-Love' (1915), the emerging ghost is treated very differently. It would be 'senseless', Freud says, to leave at that a patient's admission of erotic attachment; 'It would be just as though, after summoning up a spirit from the underworld by cunning spells, one were to send him down again without having asked him a single question' (*SE* xii. 164; 'Bemerkungen über die Übertragungsliebe', *GW* x. 312). Like Odysseus or Aeneas, patient and analyst will now seek further knowledge from the returning spirit, to take them forward into the future; there is no immediate vanishing—no quick-fix cure. The change measures the importance that the notion of transference had acquired in the twenty years since the *Studies*.

its Victorian times, hysteria tends to figure as merely the backcloth to or warm-up act for the full production of psychoanalysis. It appears as the dress rehearsal, in colourful late nineteenth-century costume, for a settled performance that was to run and run through the twentieth century. Yet there have been constant changes of cast and direction, some more fundamental than others, and there have been revivals and reinventions of concepts and practices that had been discarded long before, some more apparent than others. Far from having definitely gone away, hysteria has kept on making comebacks. During the 1990s, in particular, it was the subject of a strong reprise, a century after Breuer and Freud's book and its previous *fin-de-siècle* flourishing and decline. The focus is sometimes more clinical, sometimes cultural, with each involving a notion of *return*—going back to hysteria, or hysteria itself coming back.

At the start of the twenty-first century, hysteria is still, or once again, out and about, both as a questionable and potent name for forms of contemporary malaise, and as a topic for historical research that may also have a bearing on issues of today. Some contemporary writers about hysteria adopt the ambiguous label 'new hysteria studies', indicating the double return both to, and of, hysteria. Reinterpretation of the pivotal nineteenth-century moment of the phenomenon is combined with questions about its persistence or resurgence in the present. It is as though hysteria were always surrounded by the question of its putative disappearance and possible return or remaining, perhaps in unrecognized forms. Elaine Showalter's book *Hystories*, for instance, explored contemporary parallels to, or manifestations of, hysterical imitation, in large-scale outbreaks of illnesses like Gulf War Syndrome, multiple personality disorder, or ME. Psychoanalysts such as Christopher Bollas and Juliet Mitchell have questioned the fading away of this most protean, amorphous of illnesses as a diagnostic category, and so help to bring it back by giving it a place in present discussions. In *Why Psychoanalysis?* Elisabeth Roudinesco argues that depression is the present-day cultural equivalent of hysteria in the nineteenth century. But its habitual treatment only by drugs indicates a refusal of Breuer and Freud's initial insights. Modern depression, like old hysteria, derives not primarily, or not only, from a chemical imbalance, but rather from conflicts of the mind whose disabling effects on the body might be freed up through an active process of thinking and talking.[35]

[35] Elaine Showalter, *Hystories: Hysterical Epidemics and Modern Culture* (London: Picador, 1997); Christopher Bollas, *Hysteria* (London: Routledge, 2000); Juliet Mitchell,

This centennial phenomenon appears itself to be re-enacting the ritual anniversary commemorations and revivals of past events described in the *Studies on Hysteria* more than a hundred years ago. Anna O. relives the period of her father's final illness exactly a year after it took place, as though to complete an event from which, through her own illness, she had been both physically and psychologically absent at the time. At another point, Freud draws a connection between the striking anniversary re-stagings on the part of hysterics and other ways of suffering from reminiscences, by knowingly living simultaneously in the past and the present. In one of the vignette accounts of other cases that are interspersed with discussions of the five principal patients, he gives a detailed description of how a woman he knows has been able to deal with the many deaths in her family in part by reviving and reliving the days of their dying as anniversaries and memorials. The difference from Anna O., what make this patient other than hysterical, as Freud is careful to underline, is that the remembering is conducted quite consciously, as a deliberate ritual enterprise of bringing back and laying to rest.[36]

Anniversaries both mark and make meanings. This return to and return of hysteria, the sleeping beauty awakened again after a hundred years, seems uncannily to be occurring like an enlarged version of the conscious and unconscious anniversary rites of Breuer and Freud's women of a past century. Related to this return, however, is another sense of hysteria as second: not now as repetition or return, but as occupying a secondary, subordinate place. In this context, hysteria and the cathartic method are seen as decidedly pre-psychoanalytic, the before of an achieved after.

Hysteria preceded analysis; it was something else and it also opened the way towards psychoanalysis. But in the light of a more fully developed analytic doctrine, hysteria—the illness itself and the experiments in its treatment—was overlaid and relegated to a preliminary status. Where Breuer and Freud, to return once again to the opening quotation,

Mad Men and Medusas: Reclaiming Hysteria and the Effects of Sibling Relations on the Human Condition (London: Allen Lane, 2000); Elisabeth Roudinesco, *Why Psychoanalysis?* (1999), trans. Rachel Bowlby (New York: Columbia University Press, 2001). See also Elisabeth Bronfen, *The Knotted Subject: Hysteria and its Discontents* (Princeton: Princeton University Press, 1998) and Mark S. Micale, *Approaching Hysteria* (Princeton: Princeton University Press, 1994), as well as Sander L. Gilman et al., *Hysteria Beyond Freud* (see n. 4, above).

36 The woman is not given a name; she is introduced as 'a highly gifted woman of my acquaintance', Freud, *Studies*, *SE* ii. 164; *Studien*, *GW* i. 229–31.

speak of going back to the *status nascendi* of a symptom, so hysteria itself becomes, subsequently, the embryonic moment of psychoanalysis. Without hysteria, without Anna O., without the collaboration of Breuer and Freud and the publication of the *Studies*, there would have been no psychoanalysis. But all that was superseded when Freudian psychoanalysis became a settled institution, practice, and theory. A century on, it is hard not to read the *Studies on Hysteria* as intermediate, a twilight or dawning state between a pre-psychoanalytic darkness and the new ways of thinking that psychoanalysis opened up for those treating and those undergoing mental suffering. When we look back with psychoanalytically-anchored attention, we seem to encounter the hazy dream or daydream of the theory that was yet to develop the firm lines that it established in the first decades of the twentieth century.

We may also perceive as out of place many descriptive or explanatory features that came to be rejected as superfluous or superstitious or simply wrong in the subsequent elaboration of psychoanalysis. Freud himself cannot resist, when he rereads the text for a later edition, adding the occasional almost embarrassed footnote—here at the end of the first of his case histories in the volume, that of Frau Emmy von N.:

> I am aware that no analyst can read this case history to-day without a smile of pity. But it should be borne in mind that this was the first case in which I employed the cathartic procedure to a large extent. For this reason I shall leave the report in its original form. I shall not bring forward any of the criticisms which can so easily be made on it to-day, nor shall I attempt to fill in any of the numerous gaps in it.[37]

'No analyst': Freud coyly pretends to forget that without himself or the now pitiable *Studies on Hysteria*, the profession would not exist. It is the subsequent development of psychoanalytic theory that has produced the 'numerous gaps' that can now be closed: literally, the passage speaks of their 'later filling', '*nachträglichen Ausfüllung*'.[38] This model of a delayed fulfilment and a changing relation to past events evokes a temporal and interpretative structure which, by the time of the belated footnote itself, applied both to the psychoanalytic theory of a life story and, as here, to the history of psychoanalysis as a practice. In psychoanalysis as a whole (as with other disciplines), apparent advances in knowledge will retrospectively reveal gaps in the notions of an earlier

[37] Freud, *Studies*, *SE* ii. 105; *Studien*, *GW* i. 162.

[38] Strachey's translation omits the word *nachträglichen*.

moment. But later developments can also bring out anticipations as well as absences in the earlier theory. According to Freud's 'afterwards' logic, old events are newly translated, take on a different significance, at a later point. In the same way, it is as though we have never quite done with hysteria: once again it is felt to be necessary or fruitful to return to it, to see what it lacked or promised.

Rereading the *Studies* in this way, we find that the two-time structure is already identified in the case of 'Fraülein Elisabeth von R.', for whom an earlier, forgotten scene turns out to have laid the foundations for her distress at a second event which is unconsciously recognized as comparable. The first moment now appears as a forerunner and first instance of the second, in relation to which its meaning is established. Or a memory of a traumatic event may cause, at this subsequent time, its rejection (and hysterical conversion): 'the pains—the products of conversion—did not occur while the patient was experiencing the impression of the first period, but only after the event [*nachträglich*], that is, in the second period.'[39] In such contexts Freud often uses the archaeological analogy that he would continue to deploy for the process of analysis: 'This procedure was one of clearing away [*Ausräumung*] the pathogenic psychical material layer by layer, and we liked to compare it with the technique of excavating a buried city.'[40] The *Studies* themselves become the buried beginnings and foundations of the fully elaborated theories and therapy of psychoanalysis. In reading the book, we can spot many 'germs' ('*Keime*'), as Freud calls them in the Preface to the Second Edition, of the later plague or plant that would come to establish itself in so many parts of the world in the course of the twentieth century.[41]

In some instances, what had first been seen as neurotic features of hysterical behaviour made their way into psychoanalytic accounts of subjectivity in general. After Anna O.'s 'private theatre' and double consciousness, the strange 'second' states of hypnosis and reverie, Freud proceeded, over the following years, to develop the theory of the unconscious as a universal feature of human minds. The division of conscious and unconscious, with the obscure pressures and deflections of inadmissible thoughts, became in his theory the pattern for human psychology in general, not just for the hysterical patients who had first pointed it out to him: 'I didn't know—or rather I didn't want

[39] Freud, *Studies*, *SE* ii. 168; *Studien*, *GW* i. 236.
[40] Freud, *Studies*, *SE* ii. 139; *Studien*, *GW* i. 201.
[41] Freud, *Studies*, *SE* ii. p. xxxi; *Studien*, *GW* i. 79.

to know.'[42] A related move from (neurotic) exception to (normal) generality, or ordinary neurosis, takes place with the notion of psychical conflict. In the *Studies*, this conception is more Freud's than Breuer's, and its deployment by the end of the book anticipates the parting of their ways. Where Breuer keeps to the idea of a missing reaction, an experience that has not been properly dealt with, Freud increasingly adopts the idea of a dynamic rejection from consciousness of what is incompatible with it. The symptom that results retains but distorts the memory of its cause; it allows a provisional resolution of the conflict. Over the next few years, this notion of compromise (*Kompromiss*)—a stabilization that is always at risk of breaking down—would come to be central to Freud's view of psychical mechanisms. Conflict and compromise would come to seem the norm rather than the exception of mental life, now thought of as an inevitable and perpetual struggle between what unknown instinctual forces may seek, and what consciousness or circumstances may refuse.

The question of women is another area in which the *Studies* appears retrospectively to anticipate later theories. Although all its case studies, including the small or partial ones that are dotted about, are of women, the *Studies on Hysteria* are not presented as studies of femininity. After the 1890s, not only did hysteria fade from psychoanalytic focus, but the default psychoanalytic subject underwent a change of sex from (aberrant, hysterical) female to (ordinary, Oedipal) male. And then much later when the question of women's difference was raised as a separate issue in the 1920s, the old theory of hysteria was itself like an unexcavated 'buried city', underlying the emergent theory of women's early development, now in contrast to men's.

[42] The beginnings of this generalization can already be seen in the *Studies*. After he has quoted Miss Lucy's knowing–not-knowing sentence, Freud adds a footnote that almost takes this is an ordinary or universal phenomenon—'I have never managed to give a better description than this of the strange state of mind in which one knows and does not know a thing at the same time.' He then describes an experience of his own in which a visual perception that did not fit his expectations, and must somehow have seemed repellent for him not to see it as it was, is a 'blindness of the seeing eye' (in German, 'eyes': '*Blindheit von sehenden Augen*'), *SE* ii. 117; *GW* i. 175. Here can also be glimpsed the germ of Freud's later theorization of male fetishism in the short essay of 1927 ('Fetishism', *SE* xxi. 152–7; 'Fetischismus', *GW* xiv. 311–17), and more generally of the process by which a boy gradually, but only gradually, comes to realize that girls have no penis. At first, he fends off—does not see—the disagreeable sight, just as the fetishist's substitute serves the function of continuing to keep it out of view. See further Ch. 5, pp. 140–2, below.

In these later writings on femininity, Freud considers the centrality of the early relationship of mother and daughter, again using an archaeological metaphor. The newly discovered significance of the first importance of the mother–daughter relationship is compared to the recent retrieval of the remains of the Minoan-Mycenaean civilization beneath and before that of the golden age of Greek culture in the fifth century BCE. In thus rectifying what is now exposed as an omission, Freud makes visible the sparse attention to mothers and to relationships between women more generally in the *Studies on Hysteria* (and the 'Dora' case of 1905). Anna O.'s mother, for instance, has only a fleeting role in the case history, as the author of the diary that testifies to the accuracy of Anna's relivings of the same days of a year before when her husband, Anna's father, was dying. Because he is interested in the mother's words only as evidence for what actually happened, Freud does not look at how mother and daughter have each in one sense been engaged in the same process, with their own times and ways of marking and remembering those days. There is no discussion of the mother–daughter relationship itself. Similarly, Frau Emmy von N.'s relationships with her two daughters, her only immediate family at the time of her analysis, are explored much less than the connection of her present illness to her husband's untimely death, and the possibility of a practical cure if she were to remarry.

But from the point of view of the larger issues surrounding women's development in Freudian theory, the discovery of mothers is not necessarily a happy addition to the family. Mothers are identified with a moment of prehistoric exoticism, with a little-known and unsophisticated culture that came before the democracy and the intellectual achievements of fifth-century Greece, regarded in Freud's time not just as the beginning of European culture but as a high point of civilization that would never be equalled. This pattern perfectly fits the Freudian theory of femininity as it came to be settled in the 1920s and 1930s: women never have the chance to move out of the restrictive world of the family into the wider republic of equal citizens who have gone beyond the pre-modern world of their infancy at home. Hysteria here makes a kind of return, incognito, in the inter-war decades, when some of its features reappear in the form of a protesting, inherently unsatisfied and misfit femininity. This femininity is like a mythicized version of the situations of most of Breuer and Freud's nineteenth-century women patients. It puts women into a necessarily subordinate, secondary role: not men, not full subjects, and never quite reconciled to their situation. At the same time, unlike the *Studies*, it considers women's troubles not just individually but in structural terms. Women suffer not only from reminiscences, but from the difficulties of becoming and being women in a world that marks their difference in such a negative way, as being all-but-men.

In Freud's later femininity papers, the significance and complexity of sexuality in male and female development is axiomatic. By contrast, we might imagine from much of the literature that relates to the *Studies on Hysteria*, and in particular to the Anna O. case, that sexuality was yet to emerge as an explicit issue in Freud's, and especially in Breuer's, account. It seems to be there and not there, appearing for a moment only to be quickly tidied away again. Speaking of Anna O., Breuer famously declared that 'the element of sexuality was astonishingly undeveloped'.[43] Starting with Ernest Jones in his biography of Freud, generations of subsequent commentators have gone back to this fateful remark. It would be interesting enough for Breuer to have said that Anna O. happened to lack one admittedly major feature of normal human character, when that very 'element' later came to be seen as so central to the psychoanalytic conception of human development. But it was another thing entirely that he subsequently seemed to have made his claim defensively. Breuer's account does not report the alleged final episode of Anna's consultations, when she is said to have announced the imminent arrival of 'Dr Breuer's baby'.[44] Breuer's failure to acknowledge this putative event in his write-up then stands in sharp contrast to Freud's remarks at the end of the book, where he begins to explore the curious way in which patients 'transfer' to the doctor feelings they have experienced in relation to someone else. In his own denouement we can see Freud on the way to what would become the fully fledged theory of transference as a vital component in analytic work. Rather than the new symptom adding to analytic work, as a further 'obstacle', it could instead provide an alternative means of understanding what was essentially the same problem: 'The patients, too, gradually learnt to realize that in these transferences on to the figure of the physician it was a question of a compulsion and an illusion which melted away [*zerfließe*] with the conclusion of the analysis.'[45] Again, there is a magical element, with an involuntary 'compulsion' and 'illusion' apparently dissolving into

[43] Breuer, *Studies*, *SE* ii. 21; *GW* 221: 'Das sexuale Element war erstaunlich unentwickelt'.

[44] See Ernest Jones, *Sigmund Freud: Life and Work*, i (London: Hogarth Press, 1954), 246–7.

[45] Freud, *Studies*, *SE* ii. 304; *Studien*, *GW* i. 310.

thin air. But from this perspective, the difference between Breuer and Freud would be that Breuer himself repudiated, chose to ignore, what he regarded as the embarrassment of Anna O.'s feelings for him: Bertha Pappenheim falling for Josef Breuer, not a patient predictably making a transference onto her doctor. So the narrative sequence of the *Studies* themselves seems to foreshadow the breaks that were about to occur.[46] Breuer, it appears, withdraws from the awkwardness of a personal involvement, whereas Freud comes to claim that 'the whole process followed a law' which has nothing to do with individual qualities.[47]

There is thus, for Freud, a move away from the question of what happened or what the patient thought (in past reality) to that of how events and feelings that occur to the patient are processed—'dealt with'—or not. The point of an analysis would then be not so much to seek out some ultimate precipitating cause—the 'foreign body' or 'buried city' of Breuer and Freud's metaphors—as to enable a changed understanding, through the 'transferred' relationship to the analyst and the artificial situation of the sessions themselves. Here, for instance, the terms point to much later formulations:

> Even when everything is finished and the patients have been overborne [*überwältigt*] by the force of logic and have been convinced by the therapeutic effect accompanying the emergence of precisely these ideas ... they often add: 'But I can't *remember* having thought it.' ... Are we to disregard this withholding of recognition on the part of patients, when, now that the work is finished, there is no longer any motive for their doing so? Or are we to suppose that we are really dealing with thoughts which never came about, which merely had a *possibility* of existing, so that the treatment would lie in the accomplishment of a psychical act which did not take place at the time?[48]

The emphasis is on 'the accomplishment of a psychical act', here and now. What matters is the sense of completion, a process allowed to come to an end and an event that can now be seen to have been unfinished, unhappened, in its own time.

In that notion of a 'psychical' act lies one germ or seed of the end point of Freud's rapidly changing hypotheses at this time about the significance of sexuality. For a while in the years immediately

[46] On the break between Breuer and Freud see John Forrester, 'The True Story of Anna O.', in *The Seductions of Psychoanalysis: Freud, Lacan and Derrida* (Cambridge: Cambridge University Press, 1990), 17–29.

[47] Freud, *Studies, SE* ii. 304; *Studien, GW* i. 310.

[48] Freud, *Studies, SE* ii. 300; *Studien, GW* i. 306.

following the publication of the *Studies* in 1895, he took seriously the hypothesis that such children's 'seduction', pathological on the part of the perpetrators and harmful to the victims, was in reality extremely widespread. Then, in what is quaintly referred to as his 'abandonment' of the seduction theory, he changed his mind. Sexuality was indeed at the centre; but usually as something imagined, rather than actually undergone, by the child. This move ushered in the concept of psychical reality that we can already see adumbrated in the preliminary idea of transference and the primacy of a 'psychical' act.[49]

In this connection, we might consider how sexuality appears in the earlier world of the *Studies on Hysteria*. There is Breuer's revealing remark, raising and dropping the question in a single sentence. Yet elsewhere, and by both authors, the importance of sexuality is affirmed as clearly as it ever would be in subsequent Freudian writings, and almost as a matter of course. In speaking about Frau Emmy von N., Freud sounds like Breuer in relation to Anna O.: 'amongst all the intimate information given me by the patient there was a complete absence of the sexual element, which is, after all, more liable than any other to provide occasion for traumas.'[50] 'After all'—'*doch*'—makes it seem uncontroversial and obvious.

Freud goes on to say that rather than take Frau Emmy at her word, or her silence, he assumes that there must have been a process of censorship involved, an exclusion of what was undoubtedly there. Censorship was to be a persistent analogy of Freud's for thinking about how one part of the mind bans the thoughts of another. Here it is taken to be motivated by embarrassment; but beneath this, it is assumed that Frau Emmy von N. has 'sexual needs [*sexuellen Bedürfnisse*]', 'and that at times her attempts at suppressing this most powerful of all instincts had exposed her to severe mental exhaustion.'[51] As in later Freudian theory, sexuality is acknowledged to be of pre-eminent importance, and in women as much as in men. But unlike the later view, sexual satisfaction is not in itself a complicated matter: get Frau Emmy a new husband, Freud implies, and her troubles might be over.

[49] The argument about the reality, prevalence, and effects of child sexual abuse has since returned—for instance in the 1980s when investigations in parts of England were pursued on the assumption that great numbers of small children were regularly abused, and in the 1990s, in a therapeutic context, as a controversy about the truth or falsehood of patients' claims to have recovered memories of childhood sexual abuse in the course of therapy.

[50] Freud, *Studies*, *SE* ii. 103; *Studien*, *GW* i. 160.

[51] Ibid.

This view of the sexual instinct as naturally needing a fulfilment thwarted only by lack of opportunity, or by forms of shame, is neatly articulated by Breuer:

> Sexuality at puberty appears ... as a vague, indeterminate, purposeless heightening of excitation. As development proceeds, this endogenous heightening of excitation, determined by the functioning of the sex-glands, becomes firmly linked (in the normal course of things) with the perception or idea of the other sex—and, indeed, with the idea of a particular individual, where the remarkable phenomenon of falling in love occurs.[52]

Breuer describes the romantic destiny of physical changes in lyrical terms, so that perfect union with someone of the other sex perfectly fits and fulfils the growing urge. By the time of the *Three Essays on the Theory of Sexuality* (1905), Freud had elaborated a view of sexuality diametrically opposed to this one, which survives only as the starting point to be debunked and dismantled. Human sexuality does not naturally seek or find the outlet or partner that, from a biological point of view, should secure the reproduction of the species; instead, what needs to be explained is how it comes about that most humans ultimately do behave according to the norm.

To illustrate the difference, we may consider an essay of 1908. 'Hysterical Phantasies and their Relation to Bisexuality' begins with a classic daydreaming scene—straight out of the *Studies on Hysteria*, it might seem, except that here the dreamy girl is not sitting up at night by a sick-bed, but walking down the street. It is tempting to read this as emblematic of a move from the nineteenth to the twentieth century. The woman has left the house and is now moving in the urban, public spaces that had previously been largely out of bounds for ladies. And yet, for the time being, the tale the woman is telling herself is a classic love story of feminine abandonment by a more powerful man. As though watching a silent movie, the dreamer works herself up to climactic tears as she walks along, sympathizing with herself as a pitiful, devoted victim. The driving force of the dream is the fantasy, if not the reality, of a romantic completion like Breuer's version.

In its last section, though, the essay moves beyond the habitual, or conscious fantasy. Freud postulates that bisexual fantasies, where the subject alternates between one identity and the other, are 'common enough'; he gives as examples a person who while masturbating 'tries

52 Breuer, *Studies, SE* ii. 200; *GW Nachtragsband*, 258–9.

in his [or her] conscious phantasies to have the feelings both of the man and of the woman in the situation which he [or she] is picturing', and the woman who, during a hysterical attack (and so unconsciously) 'simultaneously plays both parts in the underlying sexual phantasy.'[53] Both parts, not all four: implicitly the man and woman with whom both subjects identify themselves are each involved in sexual encounters with the other sex, not with another man or another woman. In other writings, Freud would also explore these further permutations of the normal pairing, which follow from his own undoing of its naturalistic premises. And the breakdown can go further than the three possible couples (man–woman, man–man, woman–woman), beyond the assumption of two participants and beyond the specification of one sex or another. In '"A Child is Being Beaten"' (1919), for instance, which analyses a number of conscious and unconscious fantasies, the sex of the participants is often unclear, and so is their number.[54]

In moving from the sentimental daydream to the performance of double sexual roles, 'Hysterical Phantasies' appears as a striking anticipation of a postmodern culture in which it is regarded as possible to choose forms of sexual identity and sexual practice which would scarcely have been thinkable, let alone liveable, for Freud's contemporaries. The present language of options and preferences, in every field from sex to computers, naturalizes the presentation of a world imagined in terms of mobility and multiple choices. Unlike in Freud, there is no sense here that choices may not be consciously controlled, or that they may involve conflicts with other choices not made—including ones that do not appear as part of the available selection at all.

In the later text there also seems to have been a change of emphasis from 'Hysterics suffer mainly from reminiscences', to something like 'Hysterics suffer mainly from fantasies.' In the interval between the *Studies* and this essay, Freud had published *The Interpretation of Dreams*; hysterical symptoms are now said to represent the fulfilment of a wish or 'the realization of an unconscious phantasy'. The last section of the essay gives a list of some characteristics of the 'hysterical symptom [*hysterische Symptom*]'; it is full of bizarre overlapping categories, as Freud points out himself. Only the first two numbered points bear a

[53] Freud, 'Hysterical Phantasies and their Relation to Bisexuality' (1908), *SE* ix. 165, 166; 'Hysterische Phantasien und ihre Beziehung zur Bisexualität', *GW* vii. 198, 198.

[54] See Freud, '"A Child is Being Beaten"' (1919), *SE* xvii. 179–204; '"Ein Kind wird geschlagen"', *GW* xii. 197–226.

trace of the hysteria of the mid-1890s, mentioning mnemic symbols, traumatic experiences, and conversion. And of these the first and last are placed in quotation marks—now as if doubtfully, whereas in the *Studies* the same punctuation had been used to highlight a new term in need of explanation: 'If, for the sake of brevity, we adopt the term "conversion" to signify the transformation of psychical excitation into chronic somatic symptoms ... '[55] The seven further points then draw on the general psychoanalytic theory that has been elaborated in the interim period. From the new perspective, hysterical symptoms are substitute formations, compromises between a sexual wish and its suppression. Sexuality has become, as it would remain for Freud, both the cornerstone and the stumbling block of mental life; no one is fixed from the start in a given sexual identity—as man or woman, or as desiring one or the other sex.

Another change apparent from the nine points is that hysteria has ceased to be treated distinctly as an illness. In one way this is indicated by the fact that the noun does not appear, only the adjective. 'Hysterical' symptoms or fantasies are now like the everyday madness of dreams; they sound far removed from the debilitating and exceptional condition named by 'hysteria'. By this point, hysterical phenomena, like other neurotic symptoms, are primarily of interest not in themselves or in their differences from what is normal, but rather for their capacity to show up, in an exaggerated form, what is true of all: here, that 'the postulated existence of an innate bisexual disposition in man is especially clearly visible in the analysis of psychoneurotics.'[56] This changed perspective is occasionally to be glimpsed in the *Studies on Hysteria*, as with Breuer's suggestion that behaviours like blushing or crying are ordinary examples of the bodily manifestation of feelings that occurs in hysterical conversion.[57] But the weight of this argument has shifted. The point now is not primarily to understand an illness whose mechanisms may have small-scale analogues in ordinary oddities, but to see how the sexual peculiarities of neurotic people are only a particularly marked manifestation of a universal potential. It is as though the radical new theory of hysteria had rapidly faded away, remembered only as the confused beginning of psychoanalysis.

In the years since the *Studies on Hysteria*, Freud had written extensively on such topics as dreams and fantasy, jokes, and the madness of everyday

[55] Freud, *Studies*, *SE* ii. 86; *Studien*, *GW* i. 142.
[56] Freud, 'Hysterical Phantasies', *SE* ix. 165–6; *GW* vii. 198.
[57] Breuer *Studies*, *SE* ii. 220; *GW Nachtragsband*, 279.

life, each the subject of books that were read and rumoured far beyond the medical community. So his own interests, and the broader theory of psychoanalysis, were moving beyond hysteria, beyond mental illness, and beyond particular cases, to the psychology of ordinary life. In one way, madness was being brought down to earth; in another, real life was being rendered sensational. In the postulated division between the unconscious and conscious mind, Anna O.'s 'double consciousness' was universal. In the *Studies*, before psychoanalysis had itself become the talk of the town, Freud had expressed anxiety about the generic category into which his writing might fall and the kind of reading experience it might attract. He worried about whether what he was writing was more entertaining than scientific: 'it still strikes me myself as strange that the case histories I write should read like short stories and that, as one might say, they lack the serious stamp [*Gepräges*] of science.'[58] But he also represented the course of a psychotherapy on the analogy of a popular modern form of literary suspense:

> [I]nterruptions which are imperatively prescribed by incidental circumstances in the treatment, such as the lateness of the hour, often occur at the most inconvenient points, just as one may be approaching a decision or just as a new topic emerges. Every newspaper reader suffers from the same drawback in reading the daily instalment [*täglichen Fragments*] of his serial story, when, immediately after the heroine's decisive speech or after the shot has rung out, or some such, he comes upon the words: 'To be continued.'[59]

Here, far from appearing apart, the everyday and the dramatic are inseparably joined. Fictional drama is deliberately produced and paced for the newspaper serial, while the drama of an analytic unravelling seems automatically to plot itself in relation to the time of the daily session. In both cases, the sensational story is both within and marked off from daily life.

As this passage also suggests, with most of the patients described in the volume there are no formal boundaries to therapeutic sessions. Their hours are not fixed, sometimes seeming infinitely elastic, and meetings with the doctor happen not in a professional consulting room but in the patient's own home, where he is known to the family. Miss Lucy R. is the patient who happens to initiate the beginnings of future therapeutic formalities. As a governess, neither her time nor her home is her own.

58 Freud, *Studies*, *SE* ii. 160; *Studien*, *GW* i. 227.

59 Freud, *Studies*, *SE* ii. 297, tr. mod.; *Studien*, *GW* i. 303.

It is therefore she who visits Freud rather than the other way round, for sessions that are at set times and of more or less fixed duration. The different kind of thinking and experience of the analytic session is thus partitioned off and, ideally, the patient acquires the ability to use this differentiation so as not to be 'obsessed ... in the interval between two treatments' by something that has come up, and instead to 'learn in the end to wait for the doctor'.[60] But theatricalization does not disappear with the development of more formal separations between the time of therapy and the ordinary life that continues to be lived on either side of it. The theory of transference, which Freud is beginning to develop at the end of the *Studies*, consolidates these kinds of change. The real-life doctor exits from the analytic stage, to be replaced by whatever cast of characters, seen as such, the patient may put in his place. The impersonal suspension of normal social exchange then provides the space for the patient to come to understand the roles into which she is casting both herself and the analyst in the conversation. And at the same time, the newspaper serial comparison involves a form that, like the soap opera today, is at once modern, dramatic, quotidian, and potentially never-ending.

At the very end of his concluding essay in the *Studies*, Freud announces: 'it is only with the last words of the analysis that the whole clinical picture vanishes'.[61] This conjures up exactly the same theatrical and magical scenario as with the hypothetical disappearance of the symptom gone 'for ever'. We have seen how the ghost of hysteria, vanished if not banished from the horizons of twentieth-century psychoanalysis, has never stopped coming back, in many kinds of guise. In one way, perhaps the only element that really did go for ever was the belief in the possibility of a total cure, once and for all. More than forty years after the *Studies*, in 'Analysis Terminable and Interminable' (1937), Freud stated clearly the limits of psychoanalytic treatment, which can never produce, nor should it, a patient immune to the unforeseeable experiences that may come her way in life after therapy. Where they are known, the subsequent histories of patients suggest that the end of the treatment with Breuer or Freud did not render them proof against further mental troubles.[62] And already at the end of this text, Freud

60 Freud, *Studies*, *SE* ii. 298; *Studien*, *GW* i. 303.
61 Freud, *Studies*, *SE* ii. 299; *Studien*, *GW* i. 304.
62 See Appignanesi and Forrester, *Freud's Women*, ch. 3.

delicately shifts the focus away from the idea of an invading element that needs to be got rid of to that of a more or less enabling mental environment. He deploys a direct analogy with surgery:

I have often in my own mind compared cathartic psychotherapy with surgical intervention. I have described my treatments as psychotherapeutic operations; and I have brought out their analogy with the opening up of a cavity filled with pus, scraping out a carious region, etc. An analogy of this kind finds its justification not so much in the removal of what is pathological as in the establishment of conditions that are more likely to lead the course of the process in the direction of recovery.[63]

Here Freud is moving the sense of 'cathartic'. The aim now is not so much to cut out a noxious element that can be isolated and permanently removed as to alter the environment within which the patient will deal with what she encounters in her present and future life. (It is confusing that Freud chooses a strictly medical analogy for talking about the hysteric for whom, in particular, the body is troublingly implicated with the mind.) The job of the surgeon/therapist sounds much more like a routine operation of clearing out, clearing a passage. It is not very exciting; and in due course it will need doing again.

At a later stage in his concluding discussion of therapeutic practice, Freud speaks of the need for a 'regular clearing up [*die jedesmalige Beseitigung*]', as more symptoms are generated during the course of an illness.[64] The ordinariness and regularity of the treatment is suggested in relation to Frau Cäcilie M.: 'For a few hours after a purgation [*Reinigung*] of this kind during hypnosis she used to be quite well and on the spot.'[65] It is, he says, 'a Danaids' task',[66] characteristically turning to Greek mythology for something that Anna O. herself presented in rather more modern and mundane terms when she called it her 'chimney-sweeping'. This latter expression is recorded in the same breath—of Breuer's, if not hers—as the talking cure, and it too is in English in her utterance and in the German text: 'the apt and serious "*talking cure*" and the humorous "*chimney-sweeping*".'[67] Breuer thus brushes off the chimney-sweeping

63 Freud, *Studies*, *SE* ii. 305; *Studien*, *GW* i. 311.

64 Freud, *Studies*, *SE* ii. 264; *Studien*, *GW* i. 262.

65 Freud, *Studies*, *SE* ii. 70; *Studien*, *GW* i. 123.

66 Freud, *Studies*, *SE* ii. 263; tr. mod.; *Studien*, *GW* i. 262. Strachey's translation in fact substitutes Sisyphus the boulder-roller for Freud's (female) Danaids, whose endless task it was to fill leaky containers with water. That alteration is the starting point of Ch. 3.

67 Breuer, *Studies*, *SE* ii. 30; *GW Nachtragsband*, 229.

as just Anna's little joke, and pursues it no further. But in fact it is suggestive in a number of ways.

Chimney-sweeping might, at a push, have something in common with the dramatic model. As dark conduits between the interior and the outside world, chimneys do evoke something of the ghostly ambiguity of the hysterical symptom as intrusive foreign body, a nebulous and unwelcome visitor to the patient no longer master or mistress in their own house. But chimney-sweeping is not normally to do with getting rid of intruders. What is removed is only the unmourned ashes and dust of daily life. And the blackness of the chimney is not in itself threatening or ominous; it is the remains of a warm hearth. So chimney-sweeping might point towards the move away from the rigid separation implied by the metaphor of the foreign body. No house (or body, or subject) is at any time complete and whole, without openings through which outsiders, welcome and unwelcome, come and go. Otherwise, there would be no circulation, no life, and no history. Thus it is not the foreign body as such which is the source of trouble, but the way in which it can be received. Freud's analogy with the surgical operation points to exactly this modification: the task of analysis now is to enable the patient (like the bodily environment) to be able to take in and respond to what comes her way. And indeed Freud does himself take up Anna O.'s suggestion in his final contribution to the volume: 'A very great deal can be done for such patients by means of prolonged supervision and occasional "chimney-sweeping".'[68]

The *Studies* conclude with the almost painfully modest promise that psychotherapy can do no more than to try to transform 'hysterical misery into common unhappiness [*gemeines Unglück*]', enabling patients to 'arm' themselves better against that unhappiness.[69] There is also something ordinary about chimney-sweeping. It is a messy job that has to be done regularly in order for life to continue as normal but that, unlike a theatre, public or private, goes on *behind* the scenes. It is a necessary and dirty task—domestic, but semi-external, and usually undertaken by paid outsiders. It is best not seen but unnoticed, showing up only negatively, when it hasn't been done. Dramatic denouements seem to be in another world from the regular household work that is never over because there will always be new experiences to be cleared up and dealt with.

[68] Freud, *Studies*, *SE* ii. 264–5; *Studien*, *GW* i. 263.
[69] Freud, *Studies*, *SE* ii. 305; *Studien*, *GW* i. 312.

Breuer in particular stresses the way that patients' troubles are often derived from aspects of their domestic role. Of his two typical situations giving rise to hysterical daydreaming, sick-nursing involves, as well as continual anxiety, hard work and repetitiveness. Like chimney-sweeping, it also involves working and waking in the dark, having to live according to another rhythm from the natural alternations of day and night. In these connections, Breuer and Freud's use of metaphors of wiping away, sweeping up, and brushing away to describe their removal of symptoms begins to make the process of therapy sound like a matter of housework. At the other extreme from the dramatic model, this analogy associates the talking cure with routine, daily life—necessary household maintenance. Like all domestic tasks, chimney-sweeping is never finally done. It doesn't vanish, never to return.

And no more did the hysteria of the 1890s disappear without a trace, forgotten in the subsequent emergence of new kinds of twentieth-century symptom, and buried like a lost city under the modern developments of later psychoanalytic and psychiatric doctrines, disputes, and institutions. Instead, we have found the subject of hysteria returning again and again—to haunt with the shadow of its strangeness, with the sense of something remaining from the nineteenth century which will never quite go away.

Catharsis, too, recurs. Aristotle does not suggest that a tragedy's catharsis is somehow final; it only operates in relation to the particular play being watched, which will be followed in any case by another play, just as the competitions at which tragedies were performed would be followed by others. Dramatic, but not final. To be continued.

3

Fifty–Fifty: Female Subjectivity and the Danaids

Who the hell are the Danaids? Unless you have specialized knowledge, it is unlikely that you would have much idea beyond, perhaps, a vague sense of the Danaids as mythological and female. If you were really well informed, you might have them down as residents of Hades, and if you had got that far you would probably be able to name some of the others they work out with in that infernal gym: Ixion and Tantalus and Sisyphus, for instance. You might even know that, unlike others doing time down there, the Danaids are not one but fifty: the fifty daughters of Danaus. (Or rather, as it will become clear, the fifty daughters of Danaus minus one.) They massively outnumber all the other celebrities from hell, and yet they fade into the background by comparison. Perhaps this is because they are not individuals. Or perhaps it is because they are women. Whatever the explanation, it would seem that the Danaids have not, at least of late, had a significant role as poetic figures or as subjects of common allusion; they have remained in or returned to obscurity—unrepresented, with barely the ghost of a mention in handbooks of classical mythology.

But if this may be more or less true for the recent English-speaking tradition (there are counter-examples, as we will shortly see), it is probably not so for some European countries.[1] My tale of the Danaids is prompted, in fact, by a striking instance of this hypothetical Anglo-Continental division, when the Danaids, in the process of being moved from German to English, were simply lost in translation. Towards the end of the *Studies on Hysteria* there is a passage in which, thinking about the problems of the newly discovered talking treatment for hysterical illness, Freud turns to consider a practical problem that has emerged:

[1] In 2003 my unrandom survey of a handful of (mainly) academics revealed an alarming 100% Danaid-recognition rate among the French.

the sheer time it takes. In James Strachey's 1955 translation for the *Standard Edition*, Freud says: 'The physician will not be spared the depressing feeling of being faced by a Sisyphean task.'[2]

The Sisyphean task evokes a more familiar image from Greek mythology. Sisyphus, most people do remember, was the one who had to keep on rolling the boulder up the hill until, just when it was getting to the top, down it rolled again. It seems an evocative analogy for the effort and the frustrations of the therapist, always about to reach the end of the job but always thwarted at the last minute by the patient's force of resistance to moving on and her readiness to fall back into her previous situation. In terms of the history of psychoanalytic theory and practice, it is a prescient declaration, depressingly prescient: more than forty years after the *Studies on Hysteria*, Freud would write the long essay called 'Analysis Terminable and Interminable', in which the same problem of the endless analysis is addressed, itself apparently a problem that had never been resolved. More than a century on, the ball is still rolling as analysts seek to respond to patients' needs or demands for less frequent sessions and a shorter overall period of therapy than in what is provocatively referred to as the 'classic' Freudian analysis, five times a week for an indefinite length of time.[3]

But actually, it turns out that Freud makes no mention of Sisyphus. Instead, where the English has 'Sisyphean task', the German has *Danaidenarbeit*, 'Danaidean task'—and, in addition, '*Mohrenwäsche*', or whitewashing.[4] The '*Mohrenwäsche*' or 'Moors' wash' (the inverted commas are Freud's) conveys the mildly racialized suggestion of an attempted cover-up, light on dark, its impossibility indicated by its having to be done over and over again, and never successfully. But in English you would never know, for it has disappeared without trace; no blank space or substitute appears to mark its absence or alteration. The 'Danaidean task', on the other hand, seems to have been supplanted in Strachey's translation by the Sisyphean task. Presumably Strachey did not imagine his educated English readers would know the meaning of the allusion, and so put in its place something comparable that they might be expected to understand.[5] Like Sisyphus, the Danaids were

[2] Freud, *Studies on Hysteria*, *SE* ii. 263.

[3] See e.g. Elisabeth Roudinesco, *Why Psychoanalysis?* (1999), trans. Rachel Bowlby (New York: Columbia University Press, 2001), 141–2.

[4] Freud, *Studien über Hysterie*, *GW* i. 262.

[5] The first translation of the *Studien* into (American) English did away with the mythology and metaphors altogether: neither Sisyphus nor Danaids nor 'Moor's wash'

condemned in hell to a perpetual punishment performing a single, repetitive task that could never be completed, and therein lies the similarity which justifies Strachey's substitution. The Danaids' job is doubly dispiriting. Over and over again they fill containers with water, and the containers have holes in them. It looks in one way like an image of the futility and the endlessness of domestic labour, constantly interrupted, never done, always to be begun again.[6] The equipment is damaged and further effort only leads to further waste.

Now Sisyphus, as an alternative to the Danaids, is in fact not an obviously appealing figure. In some accounts he is something like an ex-con man, who arranged for his funeral rites to be incorrectly performed so that after his death he could get back out of the underworld again on a technicality. Then Sisyphus can also readily be linked to the common image of the shrink as charlatan, in a way that the Danaids can't: in other words, he generates new associations. What is more, the English mistranslation acquired a certain *ex post facto* authenticity. Sisyphus did not remain as just part of a passing phrase in the text, but even found his way into the index of the *Standard Edition* in his own right, through no virtue or crime of his own–that is, despite the fact that he is not even mentioned by Freud! Yet still, the solitary figure of the man struggling with the resistant stone has a touch of the noble hero about him, and in the wake of Albert Camus's absurdist version of the Sisyphus myth, this was the dominant image at the time of Strachey's translation in the mid-1950s; the English translation of *The Myth of Sisyphus* came out in the very same year.[7] Compared with this, the crowd of women sloshing away is hardly a picture of existential endeavour and muscular machismo.

can be discerned in A. A. Brill's version: 'The physician will not be spared the depressing impression of fruitless labor' (*Studies in Hysteria* (Boston: Beacon Press, n.d.), 197).

Not surprisingly in view of readers' likely familiarity with them, French translations of the *Studien* have not abolished the Danaids, having no practical reason to. Just like the English 'Sisyphean task', the expression 'un tonneau des Danaïdes', 'a Danaids' barrel', is commonly used in French to mean useless effort. Anne Berman's translation, like Strachey's from the mid-1950s, renders Freud's sentence: 'Le médecin aura alors l'impression pénible d'accomplir une tâche analogue à celle des Danaïdes ou un "blanchiment de nègre"' (*Études sur l'hystérie* (1956; Paris: PUF, 1992), 212). The transformation of the '*Mohrenwäsche*' into a 'negro-whitening' maintains the racial element suppressed in the English, although 'blanchiment de nègre' is not an established phrase but an invention for the purpose of the translation, which makes the change from Moors to 'nègre' intriguing.

6 On the likening of the analytic task to domestic work in the *Studies on Hysteria*, see Ch. 2, pp. 72–3, above.

7 See Albert Camus, 'Le mythe de Sisyphe', in *Le mythe de Sisyphe* (1942; Paris: Gallimard, 1961), 159–66; 'The Myth of Sisyphus', in *The Myth of Sisyphus*, trans.

On the other hand, much is lost by dropping the Danaids. By only a small shift of focus, it is possible to see in those leaky vessels and involuntary flows a picture of femininity as a dismal subjection to both dysfunctional biology and uselessly repetitive, unskilled work. In the early 1960s a French feminist, Evelyne Sullerot, made the contrast between women's and men's daily lives in terms of the Danaids and Sisyphus—another sign of the Danaids' greater familiarity in continental Europe, especially since Sullerot was writing for a popular readership: 'Every day they [women] fill the Danaids' container. Sisyphus pushes up his rock, which rolls back down, and everything has to be started over again each day. He is seized by a feeling of absurdity, but he puts all the force of his arms into the effort and sees clearly that the important thing is not the rock but the struggle to which he is condemned. But we Danaids fill containers with holes in them: the substance escapes from us through our fingers.'[8]

Sullerot was not the first feminist to throw in the Danaids *contra* Sisyphus. In an English poem of the early eighteenth century called *The Thresher's Labour*, the Wiltshire farm labourer and poet Stephen Duck had taken Sisyphus as an emblem of the endlessness of men's agricultural work: 'Like *Sysiphys*, our Work is never done; | Continually rolls back the restless Stone'. To which, in *The Woman's Labour*, her witty response to Duck of 1739, Mary Collier, a Hampshire washerwoman, directly riposted:

> While you to *Sysiphys* yourselves compare,
> With *Danaus*' daughters we may claim a share;

Justin O'Brien (London: Hamish Hamilton, 1955), 96–9. Camus summarizes several very different versions of the story of how Sisyphus came by his punishment. One of these, to which much the most space is allotted, involves a twisted version of marital brutality, possibly on both sides. Sisyphus had decided to test his wife's love by ordering her, after his death, to throw his unburied body into the middle of the public square. He woke up in Hades, was 'annoyed [*irrité*] by an obedience so contrary to human love', and got permission from Pluto to go back to the world to punish his wife. His own violation of the terms and conditions for this—he didn't come back to the underworld of his own accord—then led to the rock punishment. The wife's fate, above or below, is not recorded. Did she willingly or unwillingly obey the (husband's own) demand to transgress the laws of love and religion, thereby making herself into a kind of anti-Antigone?

[8] Evelyne Sullerot, *La vie des femmes* (Paris: Gonthier, 1965), 94. Sullerot continues: 'We use things. The important thing for us is not the effort, but this substance that gets used up under our fingers, beneath our eyes, and ends up haunting us. What we think about is no longer the effort begun over again each day, but this trickling away of things we lack, constantly, inescapably, in the shorter or longer term.' Sullerot goes on to give examples of the things whose wearing out prompts this kind of relentless and futile female repair work, often because of poverty: shoes, socks, or sheets.

For while *he* labours hard against the Hill,
Bottomless Tubs of Water *they* must fill.[9]

It now begins to seem that in suppressing the Danaids in favour of Sisyphus, Strachey, consciously or not, might have been doing more than covering over an obscure mythological reference that he assumed would be lost on his readers; he was also removing associations that would have been other than desirable. For the analogy, after all, is with the analyst: it is the analyst's labour that is Danaidean. At a time when there were as yet no women analysts in reality, and when almost all the patients, and all of those in the *Studies on Hysteria*, were women, Freud makes the suggestion that the doctor is like the Danaids, doing a menial feminine job without satisfaction or prospects. No wonder he calls this a 'depressing' thought; though the German '*verstimmende*', with no conveniently available adjectival equivalent in English, has more the sense of being put into a bad mood—pissed off. An irritating idea, these Danaids, and perhaps Strachey did well to delete them from psychoanalytic history. Or perhaps not. What *is* the task of the translator?[10] This is one question raised by the Danaids' disappearance. Strachey's choice also raises more general questions about the nature of work. What is a task or a job, whether chosen or assigned (a difference that cannot always be maintained)? What is a man's job? What is women's work? Feminism has typically manifested itself as refusing the assignment of women to 'reproductive' tasks, bearing and raising children and maintaining the household. In this context the Danaids appear as a spectacular illustration of female labour reduced to utter uselessness: they have neither husbands nor children to tend, and their one, unvarying task is not just eternally repeated, but never accomplished at all.

But if, like the rest of Hades' prison population, the Danaids have no future, they certainly have a history, and this shows them up in a stronger shade of darkness. Behind their eternal drudgery lies another kind of act altogether. What they are being punished for is murder: all but one (in some versions two) of the fifty of them killed their husbands, the fifty

[9] Stephen Duck, *The Thresher's Labour*, in *Two Eighteenth Century Poems*, ed. E. P. Thompson and Marian Sugden (London: Merlin Press, 1989), 12; Mary Collier, *The Woman's Labour*, ibid. 23.

[10] Alluding to Walter Benjamin's essay, 'The Task of the Translator', which discusses translations in relation to the 'afterlife [*Überleben*]' and 'continuing life [*Fortleben*]' of literary works (in *Illuminations*, trans. Harry Zohn (New York: Schocken, 1969), 69–82, 71; 'Die Aufgabe des Übersetzers', in *Illuminationen* (1955; Frankfurt am Main: Suhrkamp, 1977), 50–62, 51).

sons of Aegyptus, on their joint wedding night. For the movie, there is obviously a choice of several titles: 'Fifty Ways to Lose your Lover'; 'Fifty Brides for Fifty Brothers'; or—the clear winner—'Fifty Weddings and Forty-Nine Funerals'. The Danaids move from murderous protest to deadly resignation. In its entirety, their story resembles the bizarre generic mélange of the TV soap opera. It consists of an implausible combination of murders, marriage break-ups, and faulty household appliances, and it goes on and on and on. It is a strangely naturalized combination of the dramatic and the domestic, of the utterly aberrant with the numbingly normal; of the one-off horrific catastrophe with the serial continuity of an unchanging existence that simply continues as it is.[11]

Literary and philosophical representations of the Danaids have picked out different aspects of their remarkably multifaceted story. They appear in various surviving Greek and Latin works, sometimes fleetingly (as well-known mythological characters) and sometimes in leading roles. To begin with, and most substantially, they are the subjects of Aeschylus' play the *Suppliants*, which is concerned with the first part of their story. This play was the first in a full trilogy about the Danaids; the other two plays are lost. In the *Suppliants*, the fifty daughters of Danaus arrive from Egypt in Greek Argos with their father to demand asylum. Danaus' daughters are running away from their fifty cousins, their uncle's sons the Aegyptii, whom they refuse to marry. As is usual in tragedy, they make their request for asylum as a supplication, in the name of the gods—but their arguments are various, including the claim to be Argive themselves in origin, the claim that women are vulnerable to some men and so need protection from other men, and the claim that women have the right to refuse suitors not to their taste. Eventually they are granted protection by the Argive polity, just before the ship bearing their hot pursuers docks in the harbour. After various negotiations, however, matters are settled for the time being and the Aegyptii back off.

It is thought that the two subsequent tragedies in the trilogy, one of which was called *The Danaids*, must have dealt with the next stage of the story in which the Danaids do marry their cousins, after a fashion. The ending of the *Suppliants* suggests some counter-arguments to the

[11] As long ago as 1838, the German scholar P. F. Stuhr argued 'that the water-carrying was to be considered as a symbol of house-work, and that the Danaids' punishment was the pointless, hopeless life of one who had not fulfilled herself as a housewife' (A. F. Garvie, *Aeschylus' 'Supplices': Play and Trilogy* (Cambridge: Cambridge University Press, 1969), 235).

Danaids' resistance to marriage, which perhaps open the way to a genuine capitulation that might have happened before the wedding and its tragic aftermath. The Athenian audience for the *Suppliants* would have been familiar with the myth of the Danaids and so would have known that the end of this play was 'to be continued' and roughly what was to happen; they would then have watched the two further plays the same day, as well as a fourth, more lightweight and bawdy, satyr play, in this case probably about Amymone, another one of the fifty daughters. The absence of the follow-up plays makes it impossible to know how Aeschylus imagined the ethics and the erotics of the Danaids' murders—issues which Horace and Ovid, many centuries later, would sharply moralize by singling out the non-murdering Danaid as a romantic heroine and damning her sisters as wicked. But the *Suppliants* is nonetheless a rich and peculiar source, not least because of its unusual mode of characterization.

The play is distinctive because its chorus, the Danaids themselves, is not, as is most common in tragedy, a background source of moral commentary and lyrical interludes, perhaps with occasional interventions in the action. Instead, it is a collective protagonist. This used to lead critics to suppose that the play must be Aeschylus' earliest; because of its active chorus and group heroine it was regarded as 'primitive' or 'archaic'. But the discovery in the early 1950s of a papyrus proving that the *Suppliants* was in fact produced much later than had been supposed, probably in 463 BCE, began to change this argument.[12] More recently, critics and translators have seen other qualities in the play and have challenged as anachronistic the criteria which demoted it because of its relative lack of complex characterization in a recognizable modern sense.[13] But in so far

[12] For those who clung to the theory of an early *Suppliants*, one hypothesis was that Aeschylus had somehow had the thing stored away for later use. Richard Lattimore nicely debunked this many years ago: 'to postulate that Aeschylus put this one on ice for years and then brought it out seems to me to be a desperate means of defense for a position which may not be worth defending' (*The Poetry of Greek Tragedy* (Baltimore: Johns Hopkins Press, 1958), 12). Another counter-argument claimed that the performance could have been a revival; D. W. Lucas, again already in the 1950s, characterized this in the same way as 'a desperate hypothesis' in *The Greek Tragic Poets* (1950; 2nd edn. London: Cohen & West, 1959), 64.

[13] See Janet Lembke, Introduction to her translation of Aeschylus, *Suppliants* (New York: Oxford University Press, 1975), 3–20; Froma I. Zeitlin, 'The Politics of Eros in the Danaid Trilogy of Aeschylus', in *Playing the Other: Gender and Society in Classical Greek Literature* (Chicago: University of Chicago Press, 1996), 123–71. Most enthusiastic of all in his claims for the interest and complexity of the play is Michael Ewans: 'For me ... *Suppliants* is Aischylos's greatest surviving drama outside the *Oresteia*', 'Introduction', Aischylos, *Suppliants and Other Dramas*, ed. and trans. Michael Ewans (London: J. M. Dent, Everyman), p. xxxix).

as our interest in the Danaids has to do with the kinds of subjecthood that they exemplify, this collective agency may be the most interesting feature of the play. Here is a body of women—fifty women—demanding asylum in a state that they take to be hospitable to their concerns, and fleeing from what they identify as a threat of subjugation to masculine power against their will.[14] In this sense, the Danaids are a band of proto-feminists, using the state to help them *as women*, with their womanhood represented as a vulnerability in the face of unwarranted male demands; the Greek word most used in this connection is *hybris* and here seems to mean principally a violent lust.[15] Pointing up the issue of sexual symmetry, the same word *stolos*—a band or group, with connotations of a military expedition—is used of both collectivities.

It could be objected that the Danaids are only following their father, refusing the men on his behalf, as it were. But this does not detract from their adherence to a kind of daughterly feminism in which, although they shuttle from one form of paternal protection to another, from Danaus to the Argive king, they still know and claim a right to resist the violence of a different version of masculinity that they refuse. Like so many individual tragic heroines, from Antigone to Electra to Medea, these women are by no means shy of asserting themselves; they both declare and justify their refusals. In making their claims on both civic and sexual grounds, they deliver rhetorical arguments as good as they get. And even though they are obeying their father, the refusal and revulsion are clearly as much their own. They seem to see themselves as having equal rights—an equal right to men, but also the right to make claims *as women* in relation to the impositions of male sexuality and marriage.

Against this assertive and anti-sexual femininity,[16] masculinity has more than one manifestation in the play. The Aegyptii are repeatedly

[14] In *Mutterrecht* (1861), J. J. Bachofen said that in all versions of the legend, 'right' is on the side of the Danaids—the right to murder as well as the right to reject the men—and '*freche gottverhaßte Gewalt*', 'insolent odious power', on the side of the Aegyptii. '[W]hich is patently untrue', comments Garvie in parentheses after citing this (*Aeschylus' 'Suppliants'*, 213); but Bachofen's radical view of the play (and myth) in the categorical terms of sexual conflict and justice is interesting in its own right.

[15] The word occurs as a noun or adjective nine times in the play (at ll. 31, 80, 103, 426, 487, 528, 817, 845, 880); in all but one of these cases it is used by the Chorus in reference to the Aegyptii. The exception is line 487, when King Pelasgus tells Danaus that the people of Argos will hate the *hybris* of the 'male band [*arsenos stolou*]' when they see the signs of the women's supplication.

[16] At one point (ll. 854–7), there may be a hint of a refusal of maternity, too. Arguing with the Egyptian herald who has now arrived, the chorus say (in one conjecture) that they wish never again to see the fertilizing, life-engendering waters of the Nile; see Eschyle, *Les Suppliantes*, ed. and trans. Paul Mazon, with an Introduction and Notes

spoken of in images of brute force, as opposed to the considerate humanity of Pelasgus, the king of Argos. Above and beyond both him and the Aegyptii is Zeus, curiously combining the masculinity of both. He is at once the predatory male who went after Io, the Danaids' Greek ancestor, and also the arbiter and conciliator. He is represented (twice) as holding the scales of justice, *balancing* powers and rights in an image of the equitable political negotiation between conflicting claims. Here is Janet Lembke's translation of one of these passages; the chorus of Danaids is pleading with Pelasgus to do what they ask:

> We share
> one blood and
> spring from one vigilant God Whose hands
> weighing human differences fairly dispense
> vengeance to the profane
> blessings to the reverent.[17]

In a literal translation, the lines might read:

> On both sides [*amphoterois*] Zeus our common ancestor inspects these matters, making now one side and now the other preponderate [this whole clause translates a single word: *heterorrepês*], appropriately distributing penalties to the bad on the one hand, holy things to the lawful on the other. (*Suppliants*, ll. 402–6)

The to-and-fro oscillation of paired opposites is apparent: two sides to the scales, two sides to the sentence, this way and that way in an alternation marked by the characteristic prefixes *amph-* (both) and *hetero-* (the other of two).

But it is not clear that the scales are balancing like with like or that the grounds for the arbitration are shared between the different parties; arguably, if they were, there would be no dispute. There are too many different claimants and hypothetical terms of engagement. These include: the Danaids (fleeing the Aegyptii) versus the Aegyptii (pursuing the Danaids); the Danaids seeking asylum versus the Argives defending themselves from possible attack; the claims of kinship versus the claims of what we might call international justice; marriages of convenience

by Jean Alaux (Paris: Les Belles Lettres, 2003), 63–4. (Other texts make the Aegyptii the subject: the negative wish is that *they* ('you') may never again see the Nile.) On the *Suppliants*' use of the regular Greek association of the Nile with male fertility, see Phiroze Vasunia, *The Gift of the Nile: Hellenizing Egypt from Aeschylus to Alexander* (Berkeley: University of California Press, 2001), 43–7.

[17] Aeschylus, *Suppliants*, trans. Lembke, 39–40.

versus forced marriages; incestuous marriage versus exogamous marriage; religious versus civic duty. The Danaids ask for protection on a number of disparate counts: in the name of the gods; as foreigners with a right to asylum; as originally natives of Argos; as vulnerable women in need of male protection against male assaults; as women who resist marriage as subjugation: 'May I never become the slave of men's power' (l. 392). Pelasgus is put in the double bind characteristic of the supplication scenario. If he and his people agree to the Danaids' request, then they will be liable to invasion by the pursuing army. But if they refuse, they will be liable to the wrath of the gods: as is customary, the Danaids are making their plea on holy ground. To drive home the point, they even threaten to hang themselves if they are refused, an action that would magnify the pollution or *miasma* incurred by the Argives. The Danaids' collective suicide threat would perhaps have been recognized by the audience as ironically linked to the mass murders they do ultimately commit. Whether it is a challenge or a cry of despair, or both, this move, in which the women graphically point to the damage they plan to do with their brooches, is something other than a reasoned argument about the justice of their case. Yet it comes just before Pelasgus departs on his mission to consult with the Argive people, who take a vote on the matter in a proto-democratic way, '*dêmou kratousa cheir hopêi plêthynetai*' (l. 604), 'the people's hands ruling according to the majority'. This line is historically the first surviving occurrence of the combination of *dêmos* and *kratein*, the elements of 'democracy': thus the word originates as a response to a collective female demand.

As an upholder of the law of the land, Pelasgus also believes in the local variability of justice, at least in some matters. It seems to be a moot point whether the Danaids' marriage to their cousins is illegal or, on the contrary, positively prescribed by law (to keep property in the family). That both possibilities seem to be conceivable, with nothing between them, is a perfect illustration of the arbitrariness of kinship rules as described by Claude Lévi-Strauss, the only cultural universal being that there *are* such rules, not that their content is fixed in any way.[18] With a sense of cultural relativity, Pelasgus asks them about the practice where they come from, with the implication that that should be the paramount criterion. His questioning of the Danaids about legal matters is itself expressed in the form of a hypothetical court case: 'If

[18] See Claude Lévi-Strauss, *Structures élémentaires de la parenté* (1949); trans. James Harle Bell and John Richardson Sturmer, ed. Rodney Needham, *The Elementary Structures of Kinship* (Boston: Beacon Press, 1969).

the sons of Aegyptus are your rulers by the laws of your country [*nomôi poleôs*], claiming to be your nearest relations, who would want to speak in opposition to them?' (ll. 387–9). The notion of personal preference in the matter of marriage partners might seem to be very far off the agenda, especially when there are fifty women and fifty men involved. Yet Pelasgus does specifically put the question of the women's feelings: '*potera kat' echthran ê to mê themis legeis?*' (l. 336): 'Do you mean you can't stand them or that it's not the custom?'

One strand of the Danaids' case is their claim that Argos is their rightful homeland. They make much of their direct descent from the Argive Io, the daughter of the river Inachus. Her misfortune had been to attract the attention of Zeus, seen in this connection not as absolute judge but rather as habitual seducer. In the version that the Danaids recapitulate here, Zeus' eye fell on the lovely Io; Hera, Zeus' wife, turned Io into a cow; Zeus consequently turned himself into a bull, so Hera put Io under 24-hour, 100-eye surveillance from the watchman Argos. Zeus' response to this was to have Argos killed by his messenger Hermes. Then Hera set a gadfly, an *oistros*, onto Io, which stung her into perpetual flight. The original mad cow, Io then ran about in a frenzy all over the world, touring the whole of Asia before finally fetching up in Egypt. There she was caressed by Zeus, as a result of which she gave birth to a son called Epaphus ('touch'). Epaphus was the great-grandfather of Danaus and Aegyptus. In coming to Argos, the land of their great-great-great-grandmother, the Danaids then claim to be returning home.

Yet the presence of their ancestor Io in the Danaids' thoughts—they recount her story at length—shows up a rather curious elision in their immediate history. They think back through their foremother, apparently; but who, exactly, is their mother? Or rather, who are their mothers? For that matter, who are the mothers of Aegyptus' boys? A father can have any number of offspring, be it fifty or five hundred, but naturalistic limits are placed on women's reproductive capacity. The excessive numbers of Danaids (and Aegyptii) and the absence of any mothers seems like a caricature of a fundamental biological dissymmetry of the sexes. No woman could single-wombedly bear a whole army of children in her lifetime, but a man could conceivably engender fifty offspring in a week or two. Or even, today, in a few seconds, since new reproductive technologies have made it possible to separate out sperm so as to fertilize any required number of eggs. Indeed the fifty daughters on one side, fifty sons on the other might now suggest a fantasy of high-tech multiple births, pre-selected for their sex.

The Danaids seem, from this perspective, almost inhuman in the very singleness of their multi-mindedness. If they have no mother or mothers, they never mention the fact, instead sustaining themselves on their dream of Io. They do not miss their mothers, and nor do they seek to find someone else to love one-to-one. Instead, they are driven, all together, by their one aim of avoiding the fifty ties, or the fifty-fold tie, to their cousins. It is this, and this alone, that unites them. The play gives no evidence of sisterly affection or particular relationships between sisters. They think *as one*, with the conventional first-person singular speeches of a chorus; there are no factions or internal differences and no primary motivator. Unlike the relationship between Antigone and Ismene (in Sophocles' *Oedipus at Colonus* and *Antigone*), or between Electra and Chrysothemis (in Sophocles' *Electra*), there are no inter-sisterly politics here. The myth as commonly reported makes their father the instigator of their predicament, since he is in dispute with his brother, refusing his daughters in marriage either as the main issue or as a corollary to a general quarrel about their division of authority and land. But Aeschylus' play makes no mention of this background. The Danaids' own collective refusal of and revulsion against the Aegyptii is the starting point; there is only this motive and it seems to originate with them, just as the lustful aggression they attribute to their cousins is another kind of datum, according to the Danaids the sole defining motivation on the men's side.

Richard Seaford discusses the Danaids as part of his compelling demonstration of a pervasive ambivalence in Greek tragedy about the moment of marriage, often subverted by elements of protest and lamentation.[19] Other commentators go so far as to suggest that the *Suppliants* is not only a play about these particular characters, or about ancient Greek culture or myth; it is about adolescent femininity in general. The Danaids are simply going through a phase, acting out a moment in female development when male sexuality is both feared and rejected as daughters remain, for the time being, daddy's girls.[20] The girl or *parthenos* is also, from this perspective, seen as untamed, like a wild filly that will later be willingly or unwillingly brought under control; critics point to other places in Greek literature where young women are represented as similarly frisky figures. The word that hovers around here is *domestication*, a term that can encompass both the anthropological

[19] See Richard Seaford, 'The Tragic Wedding', *Journal of Hellenic Studies*, 107 (1987), 106–30, esp. 110–19.

[20] Froma I. Zeitlin gives a comprehensive account of interpretations of the Danaids' sexual predicament in *Playing the Other*, 153–60.

and the animal.[21] Just as cows or foals are brought under the yoke, so nomad races settle down in one place, and so lively young girls will eventually settle down as women: civilized, homely, subject to routine. The consensus is that the Danaids have no *particular* cause for complaint; though their complaint, if the critic is a feminist, may be justified in general.[22] Their objection to arranged marriages, their flight from Egypt and seeking of asylum, are a dramatization of the girlish condition, seen as complex and fraught with ambivalence.

If for the moment we follow the hypothesis of a normal female tendency to domestication preceded by youthful refusal, it is interesting to ask what it is that the Danaids do want. What they *don't* want seems easier to answer. It is what they are running away from and what is pursuing them: the Aegyptii. But they also seem to be attached to an idea of home, praising both the places they claim as their countries, Argos and Egypt, in lyrical descriptions. There is a moment when Pelasgus, after the Egyptian herald has retreated, offers a guide to the local housing options: 'There are many kinds of home in the city. My own accommodation is by no means on a small scale. You can choose to live in large dwellings with lots of other people. But if you would rather, it's also possible to live in single-style units' (ll. 959–63). They are to have rooms of their own, privately or publicly, singly or together. '*Monorrythmos*', the word I have tendentiously translated as 'single-style' is a one-off word, this being its only occurrence in extant Greek literature; it is a compound of *mono-*, single, and *rythmos*, rhythm or shape. The passage does seem to suggest a kind of lifestyle choice; a decision about where to live is a decision about how to live, and it is significant that the women are given a choice at all.

The Danaids' status more generally points to a double entitlement. Their claim for consideration is '*xenikon astikon th' hama*' (l. 618): they are both 'townspeople' and foreigners or guests, to be cared for according to the laws of hospitality. The oddity of this is that these are normally mutually exclusive possibilities: either you claim rights as a citizen, or

[21] On the associations of the word 'domestication' in relation to critical theory and feminism, see Rachel Bowlby, 'Domestication', in Diane Elam and Robyn Wiegman (eds.), *Feminism Beside Itself* (New York: Routledge, 1995), 71–91.

[22] In strikingly contemporary language, Michael Ewans refers to a history of 'pre-feminist male indifference to a woman's right to dispose of her own body' in relation to this play; he notes that 'A remarkable number of male interpreters have diagnosed the Danaides as suffering from a pathological aversion to marriage, because they assert their right not to marry men they do not want' (Introduction, Aischylos, *Suppliants and Other Dramas*, p. xlii).

you claim the different rights of a non-citizen. The Aegyptii, it might also be said, could make the same double claim: they are after all the Danaids' cousins, and they too are descendants of Io. But it is never suggested that they might do this. Instead, their name itself seems to determine that the Aegyptii belong where they came from, in Egypt.[23]

The Danaids, as we have seen, identify themselves as Egyptian-Argive, or Argive-Egyptian, while the Aegyptii remain unequivocally Egyptian. Mothers' lines of descent (Io, a great-great-great-grandmother, is on the paternal side for both Danaids and Aegyptii) are never mentioned either; if the however many mothers come from different countries, as other sources suggest, we are not told so.[24] All these relational sleights of hand are overlaid by the play's use of a rhetoric of civilized versus barbarian.[25] The Aegyptii verge on the bestial; they are uncontrollable. The Danaids are returning to the justice and calmness of Argos, and fleeing the violence of the *barbaroi*. But ethnic differences also feature in the exchanges between the chorus and the king. Pelasgus' first reaction to the Danaids is that they can't possibly be Greek because of the way they look. When Danaus is about to go round the town to gather support for his daughters' case, he takes an escort to avoid harassment. Yet despite this visual prejudice—clearly they cannot 'pass'—the Argive identity awarded to or recognized for the Danaids is apparently not related to the colour of their skin.[26]

[23] Phiroze Vasunia pursues this question in *The Gift of the Nile*, 40–3.

[24] Robert Graves, drawing on several sources, says that both the Danaids and Aegyptus' sons were 'born of various mothers': 'Libyans, Arabians, Phoenicians, and the like' in the case of the Aegyptii, 'Naiads, Hamadryads, Egyptian princesses of Elephantis and Memphis, Ethiopians, and the like in the case of the Danaids' (*The Greek Myths*, 2 vols. (1955; 2nd edn. Harmondsworth: Penguin, 1960), i. 200). Campbell Bonner, on the other hand, in his compendious study of the Danaid myth, does not actually bring up the issue of mothers but says: 'There are also varying statements about the wives of the two brothers. Each had only one wife, according to Hippostratus' ('A Study of the Danaid Myth', *Harvard Studies in Classical Philology*, 3 (1902), 130).

[25] Edith Hall points out Aeschylus' linguistic indication of the Egyptians' barbarity by the use of 'cries, repetition, and alliteration' (*Inventing the Barbarian: Greek Self-Definition through Tragedy* (Oxford: Clarendon Press, 1989), 118). Like *stolos* (band), *barbaros* is used in relation to both the foreign men *and* the foreign women. The word occurs a number of times, e.g. at l. 235, when King Pelasgus, arriving on the scene for the first time, asks: 'Where has this crowd come from, with such un-Greek-looking clothes, luxuriously clad in barbarian robes and headgear, to whom I'm speaking?' (ll. 234–7). As well as neatly identifying the barbarian and the non-Greek, the king's opening question is an elaborately ornate version of the customary identity check on foreign arrivals, '*tis kai pothen?*', 'Who are you and where do you come from?'

[26] On the ethnicity of the Danaids in relation to that of the Aegyptii see further Vasunia, *The Gift of the Nile*, 41, 47–53.

The *Suppliants* leaves the Danaids' story in suspense. The Aegyptii have been driven back from Argos, and the women are installed as residents of their new home city, in a kind of sheltered accommodation where they will be safe from the invading horde of Aegyptii. It is not the classic kind of end to a tragedy. No one has been murdered or committed suicide; instead there have been pleas and threats and negotiations, and a provisional settlement, in both senses of the word. The Danaids' extraordinary acts of violence are unrepresented. If the other two plays in the trilogy survived, the murders would not of course have been shown on stage, but reported by a messenger. That the plays themselves have disappeared, and are thus only a matter of conjecture, reinforces the sense of the Danaids' doom. The murders are unwitnessed, a missing but reconstructed link in the dramatic history that seems to take the Danaids straight from Argos to Hades.[27]

Pindar's version of the myth, in contrast, seems to forget Hades along with the need for punishment. The Danaids make a brief appearance in the ninth *Pythian Ode*, in relation neither to the murder nor to the punishment but to an interim moment of their father finding second husbands for them all. Or all but two: Pindar actually specifies the number of forty-eight, *tessarakonta kai oktô* (l. 113) without mentioning the original fifty. Elsewhere we learn about Hypermestra, the one who stayed married the first time around, by refraining from murder, while a second sister, Amymone, seems to have been turned into a fountain after a brief encounter with the god Poseidon. The Danaid story is told in Pindar as a hint to a royal father as to how to get your daughters married off quickly: Danaus was known to have organized a foot-race for suitors to come and compete, with the individual girls as prizes in some sort of pre-arranged pecking order. The speedy marriage, '*ôkutaton gamon*' (l. 114), matches the race itself. Significantly, the women are called *parthenoi* (l. 113), implying a status as both daughters and virgins; no mention is made in the poem of either their first weddings or their crime.[28]

[27] One fragment that does survive from the later tragedies is part of a speech by Aphrodite in praise of love. It is thought that this could have been spoken at the trial undergone by the one defecting sister, Hypermestra, who refused to murder her man. While the other sisters do eventually receive the water-pouring punishment in hell, it may be that initially the situation evoked here was such that Hypermestra could be prosecuted for her non-murder, because it involved breaking a vow, perhaps to her father, perhaps now the king.

[28] Pindar, *Olympian Odes, Pythian Odes*, ed. and trans. William H. Race (Cambridge, MA: Harvard University Press, Loeb Classical Library, 1997), 352–3.

In his 1902 study of the myth, Campbell Bonner pointed to the anomalies in this strand of the legend, 'the more flattering form', inconsistent with the trajectory that takes the women from crime to punishment.[29] He argued that the foot-race and second marriages must be a later addition, in fact a 'white-washing' to cover the story of the 'blood-guilty brides'.[30] A number of theories were being brought to bear at this time to explain the myth and to attempt to date-sort its diverse elements and explain their inclusion or rejection for different ideological ends. J. J. Bachofen's *Mutterrecht* (1861), the work that made the case for an ancient world of 'mother right' having preceded the patriarchal culture that superseded it, had taken the Danaid myth as one illustration of the transitional phase between the two. The women's refusal is consistent with the female choice of the first period; their punishment reflects the new regime of female subjection to men.[31] Jane Harrison considered the development of the myth in terms of a gradual 'moralization' linked to this hypothetical sexual-cultural revolution: 'Of old the Danaides carried water because they were well-nymphs; the new order has made them criminals, and it makes of their fruitful water-carrying a fruitless punishment—an atonement for murder'; moreover their crime, from the punishing patriarchal perspective, 'is clearly not only that of murder, but of rejection of marriage'.[32] In both Bonner's and Harrison's studies, the water-carrying aspect of the punishment becomes a focal point of the argument. Did the Danaids begin mythical life as water nymphs, or were they retrospectively given that early identity as an explanation for their particular water-related punishment? For Harrison, the marriages-and-murders story is yoked onto the innocence of the primitive, mother-era version, in which the Danaids are 'well-nymphs'.

[29] Bonner, 'A Study of the Danaid Myth', 134. [30] Ibid. 134, 144.

[31] On Bachofen's interpretation of the Danaid myth see above, n. 14, and see Bonner, 'A Study of the Danaid Myth', 145. It is interesting too that the Danaids' water-carrying punishment (as opposed to their crime or any other of the stories attributed to them) inspired a number of English paintings at this time—several, in particular, by J. W. Waterhouse, and a 'Labour of the Danaids' of around 1878 by John R. Weguelin.

[32] Jane Ellen Harrison, *Prolegomena to the Study of Greek Religion* (1908; 3rd edn. Cambridge: Cambridge University Press, 1922), 620. More recent commentators have followed Harrison in discussing the ambiguity of myth in relation to a female body either intact or else 'uninitiated' in relation to marriage, identifying the Danaids' situation as 'between' virginity and womanhood; their punishment perpetually repeats the filling and the leaking of the resisted event. See Giulia Sissa, *Le Corps virginal* (Paris: Vrin, 1987), 147–94; Jean Alaux, Introduction, Eschyle, *Les Suppliantes*, ed. and trans. Paul Mazon (Paris: Les Belles Lettres, 2003), pp. xxv–xxvi.

For Bonner, the 'blood-guilty brides' is the *sine qua non* of the Danaid myth, both the oldest and the distinctive part.

From Campbell Bonner's perspective, three elements of the myth—the second marriage, the sister who did not kill (Hypermestra), and the water-nymph beginnings, linked to Amymone—are all to be seen as second in time and secondary in importance to the core marriage-murders. In Latin poetry, the versions of Horace and Ovid both concentrate on the exceptional Danaid in the murder story: Hypermestra. In Horace's *Odes* III xi, Hypermestra is '*splendide mendax*' (l. 35), 'nobly cheating' on her father, and she is offered to the poem's addressee as an exemplum of proper femininity.[33] Lyde, in the poem's present, is refusing to yield to the appeals of her lover (she is like a gambolling filly who fears touching); one alone among the Danaid sisters had the maturity to accept marriage. But the poem moves from Lyde to Hypermestra (who is not named) via a wayward sequence of connections. The argument goes like this: Lyde, you are not succumbing to my lyre. But even the criminals performing their punishments in Hades stopped work to listen when they heard the music: Ixion, Tityus, and the Danaids. Hey, let me tell you about the Danaids! They all murdered their men, a wicked sisterhood, '*scelestas ... sorores*' (ll. 39–40), except for that one in a million, '*una de multis*' (l. 33), who superbly defied her father and saved her husband. She is an exemplary girl for all time, '*in omne virgo | nobilis aevum*' (ll. 35–6). Hypermestra herself then appears, telling her new husband Lynceus to rise up and run away while there is time; she says she doesn't care if her father puts her in prison and banishes her to live among the savages for her act of clemency, and finally, as she urges him to hurry, she asks him to have an elegy in her memory engraved on her tombstone. She swaps her life for his, but also requests to be allowed to survive in story, as she is now doing in another way through this poem.

Hypermestra is presented as standing out from the crowd, and also as a model of behaviour for all time. After her death, she will live on, her good memory preserved on the tombstone; her afterlife is counterposed to that of her sisters, who are not just averagely unexceptional women,

[33] The *splendide mendax* Hypermestra is exemplary in a quite different way as well. In his edition of book III of Horace's *Odes* (London: Macmillan, 1952), T. E. Page's note on the phrase ignores the woman and the ethics but describes it as 'Probably the best known instance in Latin of oxymoron' (p. 84).

but wicked ones. The framing of the poem does hint at a romantic involvement on Hypermestra's part: Lyde is being asked to succumb to the poetic music of her lover. Here, though, the speaker's logic becomes very shaky. By the end, the identification offered to Lyde is with the nobility of Hypermestra and her consciously chosen act in sparing Lynceus. But the bridge that takes the poem to Hypermestra is the suggestion that the lyre, and by extension the lover, are irresistible, not a matter of choice or virtue at all. This is an inevitable capitulation, not a conscious commitment. And to make the point even more peculiar, the proof of this seductive power is that even the inhabitants of Hades, among them the Danaids, stopped what they were doing when Amphion came down to charm them with his music.

Ovid's poem about Hypermestra (*Heroides*, XIV) follows on from Horace's. It takes the form of a dramatic monologue, a letter written from prison by Hypermestra to Lynceus, explaining with a messenger speech's sense of dramatic tension and sensational titillation just what went on during the wedding night turned bloodbath. The sisters wait as 'armed brides', '*armatas nurus*' (l. 24), until the brothers-cousins-bridegrooms turn up 'merry' ('*laeti*', l. 31) with drinking and overeating; they can do nothing but lie down and sleep, pressing into the couch ('*premunt*', l. 32) with their dead weight. Hypermestra all but does the deed, having heard the sounds of her sisters' acts in the middle of the night. There follows a lengthy passage in which Hypermestra reports her own lucid but contradictory nocturnal meditation on the ethics of the question. It is the fear of her father, described as '*violentus*' ('violent', l. 43) and '*saevus*' ('savage', l. 53) that moves her, 'three times', in the epic mode of ghostly hesitation, to raise the sword to kill him. But in her ultimate refusal to do the deed there is also an element of rebellion against this cruel father, with whom she and her sisters have to roam the world because of his dispute with their uncle: '*cum sene nos inopi turba vagamur inops*' (l. 62): 'with a helpless old man we wander about as a helpless crowd'. At this point Hypermestra could make a move to identify herself and her sisters with their cousins, equally subject to the demands of the old men's quarrel. But in fact she does the opposite. The brothers are treated as extensions of their father; they 'have deserved this death [*hanc meruere necem*]' (l. 61).

What holds Hypermestra back is not love for Lynceus or even, primarily, duty either to him personally, him as her husband, or him as a human being. '*[T]imor et pietas*' (l. 49), 'fear and piety', are the abstracted considerations that determine her non-doing. *Timor* is not really, as one early twentieth-century translator wishfully has it, 'tenderness'.[34] The word involves apprehensiveness, anxiety, respect; nothing personal or amorous or feminine is involved. Hypermestra does not see why she should have to accept the guilt of murder: '*quo mihi commisso non licet esse piae?*' (l. 64): what have I done, what act have I committed, that I should not be allowed to be 'pious'?—in other words, to be within the ethical law, free from the taint of a wrongdoing.

Up to this point Hypermestra is arguing in terms of human morality in general. But she also makes a contrast between men's and women's spheres of action:

> quid mihi cum ferro? quo bellica tela puellae?
> aptior est digitis lana colusque meis. (ll. 65–6)

What have I to do with the sword? What is the point of warlike weapons for a girl? Wool and the distaff are better suited to my hands.

Men are killers and women are weavers; murder is not my job. This might seem, obliquely, to add force to the implied claim that the bridegrooms do deserve to die, being identified with their father's alleged crime in a way that the daughters are not identified with their own father's actions. It also has the effect of further depersonalizing Hypermestra's act, or her failure to act. Piety and respectful fear, those neutral civic virtues, are no longer the issue; *as a woman* she cannot do it, it's not an appropriate act.

Hypermestra in effect breaks up the sisterhood; her defiance of their kind of defiance makes the murders now appear as individually chosen acts, since there is one who has gone her own way. With the opposite emphasis, this same assertion of personal choice occurs in Euripides' *Phoenician Women*, in which Antigone threatens Creon with Danaid-esque behaviour. She will murder her fiancé, his son, if he refuses to relent and allow her to bury her beloved brother: 'That night [of the marriage] will see me one of the Danaids' (l. 1675). Antigone singles herself out (she uses the word 'one', '*mian*') as a potential bad Danaid, not as the good one. Her situation has in common with that of the Danaids that she is engaged to her cousin, but her euphemistic or dysphemistic indication of her murderous thoughts is a remarkable instance of a mythical shift of emphasis: 'I'll do a Danaid on you', Antigone says in effect, using the story to get what she wants in the present time of her own story.

[34] Ovid, *Heroides and Amores*, trans. Grant Showerman (Loeb Classical Library, 1914; Cambridge, MA: Harvard University Press, 1963), 175.

The Roman focus on Hypermestra suggests a poetic interest in the psychology of romantic love. But in fact, as we have seen, it is not really so. Ovid's poem is a prisoner's defence and request for assistance from the one she has rescued; there is only one allusion to amorous attraction, which is the telling of Io's story. Horace's ode, on the other hand, *is* a love poem, but the bizarre sequence of steps in the argument that leads to Hypermestra does not present her as a lover, only as the one virtuous Danaid.

Ovid's Hypermestra tells the story of Io, just as the Danaids collectively do in Aeschylus' *Suppliants*. In Ovid, the importance of the connection and the excuse for the narrative is not Io's Greekness but her troubled life of wandering far from home; indeed, Hypermestra seems to reverse the Aeschylean attributions by making her Greece a distant place of exile and Egypt, implicitly, home: '*regnoque domoque | pellimur; eiectos ultimus orbis habet*' (ll. 111–12): 'We are driven from our kingdom and our home; we are cast away to the farthest ends of the world'. Ovid narrates Io's story at much greater length in the *Metamorphoses* (it also appears in Aeschylus' *Prometheus Bound*); and Hypermestra's abbreviated version leaves out features related in detail in the other text: Io's surveillance by Argos, set to watch her by Hera/Juno, and Argos' murder by Hermes/Mercury, Zeus/Jupiter's appointed hit man. The shorter version also omits the specific source of Io's frenzied rushing about the world: Hera's maddening gadfly who pursues her relentlessly until finally she collapses by the Nile. One element, however, that does appear in both Ovid's Io stories brings back the question of Freudian substitutions together with Freudian versions of femininity. It is what we might call Io's anti-Narcissus moment.

After she has been changed into a heifer, Io looks in the water and what she sees is a cow. She cannot believe, but has to believe, it's her; and in the *Heroides* version it is the shock of this sighting, not the goading gadfly, that sends her wild and wandering. She can't stand to look at what she recognizes as now herself:

> per mare, per terras cognataque flumina curris;
> dat mare, dant amnes, dat tibi terra viam.
> quae tibi causa fugae? quid tu freta longa pererras?
> non poteris vultus effugere ipsa tuos. (ll. 101–4)

Over the sea, over lands and related rivers you run; the sea, the rivers and the land all give you passage. What's your reason for running away? Why do you wander over the broad seas? You won't be able to run away from your own face.

Narcissus' story, like Io's, is told in the *Metamorphoses.* Narcissus falls in love with the image he doesn't initially realize to be his own; Io runs away from the image she can't bear to see, but does see, as her own. Narcissus dies after being captivated by his own beauty, and Io's life is ruined by her seeing and recognizing the unbeautiful cow that she is. 'Ioistic' behaviour might make a counterpart or alternative to Freud's 'narcissistic' model, particularly in the light of the resonances of sexual difference here. Io is no self-admiring Dorian Gray, his outward appearance immaculate even as his image secretly grows old and repulsive.[35] Instead, she sees very well the change in her, the loss of her youthful beauty, and she cannot live with it; her life henceforth is a flight from the unattractive image of herself.

Io's feminine reaction also resembles Freud's account of the way that women encounter sexual difference: with an immediate acknowledgement but also a protest, in the face of an irrefutable visual perception.[36] Freud's own discussions of femininity as such occurred after his general theory of human development, based on the story of Oedipus, was well established. He had drawn on Greek tragedy for his paradigm of the common story for men, and when he turned to consider the distinctiveness of women's development, the Oedipus model remained the pattern; women's failure to fit it became the explanation for all their difficulties of adjustment in adult life. Women's problem was that they started off thinking they were like boys, but then had to face the fact that they weren't: this was the shocking realization of 'castration'. After that, their lives could only be a matter of more or less manageable negotiation with a fundamentally thwarted existence, in which any solution, even the normal one of settling down as a wife and mother, was still to be regarded as following on from this determining disappointment.

[35] See Oscar Wilde, *The Picture of Dorian Gray* (1891). In developing his theory of narcissism, Freud does not refer to Ovid, the principal source for the Narcissus myth; instead he takes up and characteristically universalizes a category that had been proposed in the late nineteenth century to describe specific perversions involving sexual attraction to one's own body. The French psychologist Alfred Binet and the British sexologist Havelock Ellis had used the term before it was introduced into German in 1899 by the criminologist Paul Näcke. (See Elisabeth Roudinesco and Michel Plon, *Dictionnaire de la psychanalyse* (Paris: Fayard, 1997), 707.) In regard to their origins, then, Narcissus and Oedipus are not classical brothers in the psychical pantheon. Freud himself engendered Oedipal Oedipus on the basis of his knowledge and experience of Sophocles' tragedy; the Narcissus of narcissism was already grown up—Binet's first use of the term was in 1887—at the time when Freud adopted him around 1910.

[36] On women's 'recognition' of sexual difference in the Freudian account, see Chs. 5 and 6, below.

In the 1970s and 1980s, the usefulness of Freud's model of female development provoked heated argument among feminists.[37] His theory gives women no identity of their own; whether they protest or succumb, whether they are feminists or paid workers or mothers, or any combination of these, everything they do, once they have realized that they are women, meaning not-men, is related to what now must be seen as their lost masculinity. They never get over it; to be a woman is to be a disappointed boy. This perspective seems to leave no possibility for escape from what is pessimistically presented as an inevitable doom. Modern women can do better, so the argument ran; they need not be caught in this pre-modern dungeon. But for those on the other side of the argument, the sense of entrapment did not appear as a negative quality, since it provided an account of why women, even when apparently emancipated, set free from their prison, still found themselves afflicted by personal unhappiness and sisterly strife in ways that seemed to defy rational explanation.

In thinking back through the Danaids it is not my intention to propose their story as a new paradigm of female development, but to suggest that its very contradictions and complexities could have added something to Freud's consideration of the difficulties of female subjectivity. The Danaids are formidably effective campaigners, attuned to the pragmatic need for 'spin' or *peithô*; they are also, like Oedipus (and like numerous tragic heroes and heroines) murderers; and, in a third incarnation, they are downtrodden domestics. Their story is not a single one, generically or morally; the perspective is always moving around, as if it were impossible to gain a distinct view of their position or condition. At different points they exemplify both the resentment and the resignation that Freud attributed to women as typical reactions to the discovery of their difference from men. Yet the Danaids never see themselves as having been deprived of masculinity: it is as women that they articulate a resistance to the *hybris* of men, a refusal of female subordination to male power.

Beyond this, the teasing fifty–fifty symmetry of the Danaids and their cousins, the girls and the boys, points to other issues in modern political and feminist argument.[38] How should we differentiate a group

[37] Juliet Mitchell's *Psychoanalysis and Feminism* (1973) was the first book to make the case not just for the helpfulness, but for the indispensability of psychoanalysis to feminist understanding.

[38] Fifty-strong single-sex groups are not unusual in classical mythology. Speaking of female monsters in folktales, in which 'the qualities of bloodthirstiness and lasciviousness are frequently conjoined', Campbell Bonner darkly suggests that 'Similar ideas may underlie the account of Heracles' relation to the fifty daughters of Thespius' ('A Study of

identity from an individual one, or a two-person one, and what is the validity or force of a group identity *according to sex* (as opposed to class, or ethnicity, or nationality, or any number of other categories)? Is sexual difference still, as Freud assumed, the primordial distinction in the acquisition of human identities? To speak of two sexes, of 'the' two sexes, with their 'equal' rights, fifty–fifty, necessarily rules out the differences that may render their respective claims or qualities radically incompatible and not susceptible to such balancing of like with like according to a common criterion. The Danaids versus the Aegyptii represent two groups identically matched, apparently equal (because equal in number), and yet two groups so different that they are ever and eternally two—ever and eternally either in love or at war.

In keeping with this suggestive multiplicity of the Danaids myth, three nineteenth-century versions bring out very different aspects of it. Schopenhauer used the endlessness of the Danaids' labours as an image for the insatiability of desire, as in this passage from *The World as Will and Representation*:

> For we untiringly strive from desire to desire, and although every attained satisfaction, however much it promised, does not really satisfy us, but often stands before us as a mortifying error, we still do not see that we are drawing water with the vessel of the Danaides, and we hasten to ever fresh desires.[39]

Here the Danaids are neutral both morally and sexually. That their continued labours are a punishment is not said, and they are not marked out as women; they are given as a general figure for the ceaseless renewal of

the Danaid Myth', 153). The fifty Nereids (the daughters of Nereus) appear for instance in Euripides' *Ion* (l. 1081) and Sophocles' *Oedipus at Colonus* (l. 718), where they are 'hundred-footed [*hekatompodôn*]'. As with the Danaids plus the Aegyptii, fifty always seems to suggest its double—and in fact the Nereids themselves sometimes number a hundred (see R. C. Jebb (ed.), *Sophocles: Plays: Oedipus Coloneus* (1900; London: Bristol Classical Press, 2004), 123). Nor are the Danaids and the Aegyptii the only example of a fifty–fifty match of young men and women. The *Iliad* mentions the fifty sons and fifty daughters of Priam and Hecuba, and Virgil refers (*Aeneid* II. 501) to the ensuing *centumque nurus* or 'hundred brides'—the fifty daughters plus fifty daughters-in-law. Maternal capacity is an unspoken problem, since Hecuba is the acknowledged mother of all the hundred sons and daughters in this story. The scholiast Servius 'has a worried note, and speculates upon polygamy', R. G. Austin tells us in his own note to the line (Virgil, *Aeneid II*, ed. Austin (Oxford: Clarendon Press, 1964), 194).

39 Arthur Schopenhauer, *The World as Will and Representation* (1819), trans. E. F. J. Payne, 2 vols. (New York: Dover, 1969), i. 318. Other references to the Danaids in this connection occur at i. 196 and i. 362; in the first of these, Ixion and Tantalus join them as symbols of the ever unsatisfied subject.

wishing.[40] This is a pre-Freudian idea. In *The Interpretation of Dreams*, wishing is what gets the mental apparatus going and keeps it going, as well as setting up the elementary structures of an imagined sequential time; there is also, in the passage quoted, the suggestion of a subjective blindness like the Freudian unconscious. But Freud gives no mythical identity to his universal desiring and dreaming subject: no compulsive classical wishers—no Danaids, for instance—take their place alongside Oedipus and Narcissus.

My second example is Baudelaire's poem 'Le tonneau de la haine' (The Barrel of Hatred). Here the Danaids in their Hades phase are linked to a hatred whose primary and appalling quality is its inexhaustibility, that of the barrel that can never be filled: 'La haine est le tonneau des pâles Danaides'—'Hatred is the barrel of the pale Danaids'.[41] Punishment and crime are tied relentlessly together; the endlessness of the Danaidean task is matched by endless murders, as corpses are resurrected by Vengeance only to be once again put down. But then in mid-poem the personifications and the mythology give way to a pub drunk, 'un ivrogne au fond d'une taverne' (l. 9), whose thirst keeps popping up again like the hundred-headed Hydra that won't be killed; the difference is that drinkers, in this sense 'happy', eventually fall asleep, whereas hate never ever lets up:

—Mais les buveurs heureux connaissent leur vainqueur,
Et la Haine est vouée à ce sort lamentable
De ne pouvoir jamais s'endormir sous la table. (ll. 12–14)

[But happy drinkers know their conqueror, | And Hate is condemned to this wretched fate | Of never being able to go to sleep under the table.]

40 Schopenhauer is close to two classical philosophical personifications of endlessly unsatisfied desire which all but name the Danaids. In the 'mythologizing' passage of Plato's *Gorgias* (493a–b) referred to above (Introduction, p. 8, n. 18), a leaky jar appears as an image for the desiring part of the mind in stupid (*anoêtoi*) or 'uninitiated' people; in Hades this doubles into an image of fruitless labour as they carry water in a perforated sieve to pour into a leaky jar. Lucretius (*De rerum natura*, book III) has a catalogue of the characters from hell, wittily demythologizing—and remythologizing—them one at a time by declaring that Tantalus or Sisyphus or Ixion do not exist; rather these people are to be found as particular types in the real world. Sisyphus is a stressed-out workaholic, who never achieves what he is aiming for. Right after him come those who are always feeding up their ungrateful natures with good things but are never satisfied ('*satiareque numquam*', l. 1004); these suggest the story of 'those girls in the flower of their youth' ('*aevo florente puellas*', l. 1008) forever pouring liquid into a perforated vessel. They are not named.

41 Charles Baudelaire, 'Le tonneau de la haine' (1851), in *Œuvres complètes*, ed. Claude Pichois (Paris: Gallimard, Pléiade, 1975), i. 71, l. 1.

Ultimately Baudelaire's poem ends in bathos—with the slumbering drunk displacing the pale Danaids, the man the women, the unviolent layabout the murderers, the happy the hating, and the everyday the mythological. The drunk's sleep is the rest and respite that never come for the hatred that is here identified with the Danaids—punishment and crime, out of time, without end.

Finally, the Danaids really were taken up as mythological analogues for the troubled lives of modern feminists, and in English too. Mona Caird's New Woman novel *The Daughters of Danaus* was published in 1894, exactly contemporary with Freud and Breuer's *Studien über Hysterie.* Caird explains her allusions to the myth of the Danaids throughout; she does not assume that her readers will know the story. But she uses it, nonetheless, to elaborate her feminist critique. Youthful Danaid rebelliousness is initially seen in the form of wild Celtic dancing and animated debating of modern ideas, Emerson especially. Then, like the migration from Egypt to Greece, the scene moves from Scotland to the 'home' counties of southern England. The protest against marriage, first resisted and then reluctantly accepted, does not go as far as murder, but the heroine does run off, post-maritally, to Paris, there to cultivate her musical genius and (almost) have an affair. She leaves behind two small sons as well as a husband but takes with her, in proto-twenty-first-century mode, an adopted daughter (and a nanny). And then, faithful to the final phase of the myth, the Danaid returns and submits herself once more to a life of eternal domestic tedium, varied only by her relationships with various mentor figures, mostly men (with one of whom she all but has an affair). Lumberingly, the prose spells out the collective conventional dullness and stress:

> And the same savage story was written, once more, on the faces of the better dressed women: worry, weariness, apathy, strain; these were marked unmistakeably, after the first freshness of youth had been driven away, and the features began to take the mould of the habitual thoughts and the habitual impressions.[42]

Caird's description of the visible effects of the well-off women's weary existences reads like an anticipation of Freud's sad picture, in one of his

[42] Mona Caird, *The Daughters of Danaus* (1894; New York: Feminist Press, 1989), 465. Ann Heilmann sees the novel primarily as a version of the Medea story rather than that of the Danaids; Caird is shifting the emphasis 'from Medea's violent transgression [in killing her children] to her artistic aspirations' (*New Woman Strategies: Sarah Grand, Olive Schreiner, Mona Caird* (Manchester: Manchester University Press, 2004), 223). The novel mentions Euripides' *Medea* just once (p. 95). Heilmann's downplaying of the title Danaids reflects and reinforces their obscurity, both a century ago and now.

later writings, of the typical woman of about 30. Her 'psychical rigidity' makes it seem that 'there are no paths open to further development', as though 'the difficult development to femininity had exhausted [*erschöpft*] the possibilities of the person concerned.'[43] This is the miserable anti-parable of the Danaids, a 'before and after' myth of feminist rage followed by stressed and depressed middle age.

[43] Freud, Lecture XXIII, 'Femininity' (1933), *New Introductory Lectures on Psycho-Analysis, SE* xxii. 135; 'Die Weiblichkeit', *Neue Folge der Vorlesungen zur Einführung in die Psychoanalyse, GW* xviii. 144–5. On this passage see further Ch. 6, pp. 165–7, below.

4

The Other Day: The Interpretation of Daydreams

It almost seems to go without saying that dreams in *The Interpretation of Dreams* are creatures of the night. Shady, enigmatic, mysterious, they draw unto them all the accumulated metaphorics of a symbolic division between darkness and light. They belong to a nether world which has no place on the surfaces of daytime life—as in this passage including a famous Freudian citation:

In waking life the suppressed material in the mind is prevented from finding expression ... but during the night ... this suppressed material finds methods and means of forcing its way into consciousness.

Flectere si nequeo superos, Acheronta movebo.

The interpretation of dreams is the royal road to a knowledge of the unconscious activities of the mind.[1]

Freud quotes Virgil in the original Latin (and in the German text the 'royal road' is the '*Via regia*'). Thus he sets up a grand classical and epic connection—this will be his *magnum opus*—just at the moment when he is evoking the strangeness of the movement into the night and the underworld: 'If I cannot turn the higher powers around, I will move Hell.'[2] But the separation itself seems to be a sure one. Sleep and 'night' go together as surely as 'waking life' and the day. Dream,

[1] Freud, *The Interpretation of Dreams* (1900), *SE* v. 608; *Die Traumdeutung*, *GW* ii–iii. 613.

[2] The speaker of the line from the *Aeneid* (VII. 312) is in fact Juno, the goddess hostile to the Trojans' resettlement in Italy and their future foundation of Rome in the wake of their defeat by the Greeks; at this point building works have just begun. In his edition of the poem, R. D. Williams calls it 'A line of chilling simplicity and finality' (*The Aeneid of Virgil: Books VII–XII* (London: Macmillan, 1973), 190). Juno determines, if she cannot persuade her divine colleagues, to seek help from hell (and she immediately summons the monstrous, fury-inducing Allecto). 'Acheronta' marks this hell as Greek, in both name and form (a Greek accusative is kept within the Latin sentence). In

sleep, night-time, darkness all come to shade into one another to the point that they appear to be inseparable. As though to acknowledge that there is something about this obscurity that is more than the evidence allows—since it is obvious that sleep, and dreams, can occur in daylight as well as at night—Freud sometimes uses the expanded term 'night-dreams', *Nachtträume*. Without darkness, without the night, dreams would carry no mystery; there would be nothing to interpret.

Yet the day is far from being absent from these nocturnal phenomena. It enters into Freudian night-dreams in two regular manifestations, each of which is considered at some length in the *Interpretation*. First, the use of the term 'night-dreams' is partly, of course, a way of marking the existence of daydreams. And second, there are the ubiquitous features known as 'day's residues', *Tagesresten*: something from the previous day, Freud claims, goes into the making of each and every dream.

At first sight, daydreams and day's residues appear rather different: daydreams are comparable to night-dreams, while the day's residues contribute to their making. But this initial division is complicated by the fact that daydreams themselves can also appear as part of the content of dreams. In this instance, daydreams function as ready-prepared, unobjectionable material that can be used by the dream without more ado, in this respect like the day's residues. The other case, that of the comparison of dreams to daydreams, is itself used for two opposite purposes: daydreams show something about dreams either because they are like them, or because they are not. This is partly because different features of dreams and daydreams are being utilized in each instance, but also because there are important variations in how Freud conceives of the relative importance of each.

The day's residues are subject to other ambiguities of deployment. Freud states unequivocally that every dream includes something that derives from the previous day. That something is there, however, not because of its significance, but because it has none: being recent and new, the day's residues qualify under the purely negative condition of being insignificant, free of associations. It is this that gives them the capacity to act as a 'cover' for the real thoughts of the dream, which cannot obtain free expression by themselves. The day is of merely passing significance,

Freud's text it is 'the suppressed [mental] material [*Das seelisch Unterdrückte*]', which is pushing for a hearing—from below. But the reference to the 'royal road' in the following gnomic utterance suggests a contrary identification of the avenging Juno with Freud the interpreter-explorer intrepidly entering and stirring up Greek hell.

in two senses: the obvious one, whereby it matters only while it lasts, until it is past; and a second, whereby it enables the night-dream's thoughts to 'pass', to appear to be as trivial and innocuous as the day's are supposed to be.

These enigmatic and elusive appearances of the day, in a context for the most part resolutely nocturnal, can themselves easily pass unnoticed. This chapter pursues some of the peculiarities that attach to the day in the dream, and the dream in the day, in relation to the kinds of story or fantasy that dreams and daydreams are said to develop. What is the significance of the day's actual ubiquitousness, but alleged insignificance in the Freudian dream? With this question in mind, Freud's reference to a story by the late nineteenth-century French novelist Alphonse Daudet in one of his discussions of daydreams offers a minor road which ends with a different view.

DAY'S RESIDUES, NIGHT'S SURVIVALS

Freud insists that all dreams find some material out of 'day's residues', from the thoughts and activities of the very day before. All dreams, it is claimed, make use of impressions from the day that immediately precedes the sleep of the dream; their usefulness is premised on the need for a cover or surface of indifference to hide dreams' real motives and meanings. This, day's residues are uniquely suitable to provide:

> Both groups of impressions satisfy the demand of the repressed for material that is still clear of associations—the indifferent ones because they have given no occasion for the formation of many ties, and the recent ones because they have not yet had time to form them.
>
> It will be seen, then, that the day's residues, among which we may now class the indifferent impressions, not only *borrow* something from the *Ucs.*, when they succeed in taking a share in the formation of a dream—namely the instinctual force which is at the disposal of the repressed wish—but that they also *offer* the unconscious something indispensable—namely the necessary point of attachment for a transference.[3]

As the language of borrowings and offers suggests, a kind of deal is struck. The deal depends on a negotiation between the ephemeral in quest of continuation and the permanent in search of short-lived daylight. The day's residues gain some temporary extension of their role when they

[3] Freud, *Interpretation*, *SE* v. 564; *Die Traumdeutung*, *GW* ii–iii. 569.

get to participate in a dream, and the dream acquires a means of gliding its instinctual disturbances into an acceptable form. In what we shall see is a persistent attribution in many contexts, that which belongs to the day is taken to be transitory and thereby also trivial, while that which belongs to the night is durable to the point of timelessness, loaded with a pressure of meaning that must out into the temporal.

It is significant that, in contrast to the usual emphasis in his outlining of this kind of structure—in relation, for instance, to the formation of neurotic symptoms—Freud here suggests not so much the negative aspect of a compromise, where a bargain is struck by each contributor making concessions, as the positive gains associated with a move that is beneficial to both parties. In the neurotic structure, the repressed wish gets itself out in the form of a symptom, but not as a fulfilment; while the ego keeps the wish from coming out openly, but only by allowing the symptom. The day's residues, on the other hand, have nothing to lose, being otherwise destined only to get lost. They are dismissed again and again: 'unimportant details of waking life ... worthless fragments of waking life'; 'remnants of trivial experiences'; 'the "dregs" of daytime recollections'; 'indifferent refuse left over from the previous day'.[4]

The rhetoric of rubbish apparent here is linked sometimes to an idea that such detritus has to be disposed of—as it were, by a daily refuse collection. Freud rejects this theory in relation to dream-content only because it implies an impossible task of working over for dreams to accomplish, not because he thinks that there is no disposal to be done: 'The night would not be long enough to cope with such a mass [*Summe*]. It is far more likely that the process of forgetting indifferent impressions goes forward without the active intervention of our psychical forces.'[5] What is revealing about the form of this refuse-refusal is its premise of rational order: the night, with the dreams that take its time, is conceptualized as a given period for the achievement of necessary work, rather than—for instance, and as elsewhere—as a phase in which the normal orders of time and reason are suspended altogether.

The treatment of the remains of the day as superfluous waste for throwing out puts them at the opposite extreme from the dream-thoughts that instigate dreams. These stay put come what may; they are

[4] Freud, *Interpretation*, *SE* iv. 174, 177, 178; v. 589; *Die Traumdeutung*, *GW* ii–iii. 180 ('Nebensächliches aus dem Leben ... den wertlosen Brocken des Tageslebens'), 183 ('Reste von nebensächlichen Erlebnissen'), 184 ('den "Schlacken" der Tageserinnerung'), 594 ('die gleichgültigen Abfälle des Tages').

[5] Freud, *Interpretation*, *SE* iv. 178; *Die Traumdeutung*, *GW* ii–iii. 184.

full of significance whereas the day's impressions have none whatever; and they are virtually indestructible whereas the day's remains are (literally) ephemera, lasting only for a day, with no enduring value. A further radical distinction is suggested by the 'mass' of indifferent impressions in the passage quoted above. 'Crowds [*Scharen*] of such impressions enter our minds and are then forgotten',[6] Freud says a little earlier: on one side, teeming in from the day, is a number so large, it is implied, that it could not possibly be incorporated or assimilated; on the other is the small, select, and well-defined group of the repressed wishes. Such polarization is typical of the way in which Freud establishes his two-tier systems—in this instance, as often, contrasting a surface (of transient dailiness) with the underlying depths of timeless significance and potency.

The day's residues serve primarily as only the veil or excuse for the dream-thoughts, the wishes to which they offer a means of muffled expression. For although Freud does discuss the possibility of a contribution to dreams of thoughts and worries and wishes from daily life in their own right, as independent instigators, he nonetheless affirms that they are not sufficient in themselves to get a dream going: 'In my view, therefore, wishful impulses left over from conscious waking life must be relegated to a secondary position in respect to the formation of dreams.'[7] In this connection, daily life seems to be at once crucial and trivial: necessary to give the unconscious wish a hearing or a sighting, but of no importance in comparison to the psychical interests that are older, more deeply established. This accords, as we shall see, with one of the ways in which daydreams are differentiated from dreams.

DAYDREAMS, NIGHT-DREAMS

Daydreams flit in and out of the *Interpretation*, in various guises and various kinds of connection and disconnection with the night-dreams that form the main focus of the book's inquiry, its 'royal road' to the unconscious. They are protean and contradictory in their appearances—sometimes just a bit of a dream, sometimes similar to night-dreams, and sometimes their antithesis. In the later, theoretical parts of the book, Freud deliberately draws on daydreams as both counter-example and analogy to elucidate his claims for the significance

[6] Freud, *Interpretation*, *SE* iv. 176; *Die Traumdeutung*, *GW* ii–iii. 182.
[7] Freud, *Interpretation*, *SE* v. 554; *Die Traumdeutung*, *GW* ii–iii. 559.

of night-dreams in their relations to unconscious wishes. As we shall see, these passages resonate with others in essays of the following years, in the course of which daydreams gradually come to serve as adumbrations or exemplary modes of what he is by now exploring under the term 'fantasy'.

To begin with, then, daydreams can appear as extensions or analogues of dreams. In this connection, Freud makes a minor argument out of their shared name. A footnote in the German glosses the term *Tagtraum*—specified as a literal translation of the English 'day-dream'—with both French and English: '*rêve, petit roman—day-dream, story*'.[8] The connection here has to do with narrative form: the unity which characterizes the stories of daydreams resembles the surface appearance of night-dreams produced in the process of secondary revision (we shall come back to this aspect of the comparison). In a passage from the eighth of the *Introductory Lectures* (1916–17), Freud again makes the point about linguistic continuity. In this instance, he even goes so far as to refer to dreams as 'a "nocturnal day-dreaming" [*ein "nächtliches Tagträumen"*]', thereby making the daydream into the default mode of which the night-dream would be just a special case. Here the point of similarity is not the story as a whole but the happy ending attributed to daydreams: 'Linguistic usage, therefore, has a suspicion of the fact that wish-fulfilment is a chief characteristic of dreams.'[9]

The clearest and largest claim for the importance of daydreams in the *Interpretation* makes them an alternative 'royal road', a kind of *Autobahn* to the unconscious constructed after the first arrival at the destination: 'They share a large number of their properties with night-dreams, and their investigation might, in fact, have served as *the shortest and best approach* [*den nächsten und besten Zugang*] to an understanding of night-dreams.'[10] And in a footnote later in the same section, added in 1909 and italicized in the German but not in the English translation, this considerable overlap of features becomes, unequivocally, 'the complete analogy between night-dreams and day-dreams', '*die volle Analogie des nächtlichen Traumes mit dem Tagtraume*'.[11]

The usefulness of daydreams to the study of dreams on the grounds of shared components is emphasized in later writings. In 'Hysterical Phantasies and their Relation to Bisexuality', we read: 'They are justly called

[8] Freud, *Die Traumdeutung, GW* ii–iii. 495. All four examples are italicized.

[9] Freud, Lecture VIII, *Introductory Lectures on Psycho-Analysis, SE* xv. 130; *Vorlesungen zur Einführung in die Psychoanalyse, GW* xi. 129.

[10] Freud, *Interpretation, SE* v. 492, italics added; *Die Traumdeutung, GW* ii–iii. 496.

[11] Freud, *Interpretation, SE* v. 494; *Die Traumdeutung, GW* ii–iii. 298.

"day-dreams", for they give us the *key* [*Schlüssel*] to an understanding of night-dreams—in which the *nucleus* [*Kern*] of the dream-formation consists of nothing else than complicated day-time phantasies of this kind that have been distorted and are misunderstood by the conscious psychical agency.'[12] And in the twenty-third of the *Introductory Lectures*, in a long section on daydreams, Freud summarizes: 'We know that such day-dreams are the nucleus and prototype [*Kern und Vorbild*] of night-dreams. A night-dream is at bottom nothing other than a day-dream that has been made utilizable owing to the liberation [*Freiheit*] of the instinctual impulses at night, and that has been distorted by the form assumed by mental activity at night.'[13]

Running through these passages are the two models, of part and paradigm. On the one hand, daydreams contribute to dreams: they form a core or nucleus and provide materials that go into the composition of the night-dream. On the other hand, daydreams resemble night-dreams. They could equally well have been used as a key to understanding that which night-dreams enable us to understand, since they are similar in psychical function—'the complete analogy', no less. Let us look first at the second of these aspects.

Daydreams, like night-dreams, are narratives which lead to satisfaction by representing the fulfilment of wishes. In the lecture on 'Children's Dreams', Freud says:

> Incidentally, if our experience in dreams is only a modified kind of imagining made possible by the conditions of the state of sleep—that is, a 'nocturnal day-dreaming'—we can already understand how the process of constructing a dream can dispose of the nocturnal stimulus and bring satisfaction, since day-dreaming too is an activity bound up with satisfaction and is only practised, indeed, on that account.[14]

Such wishes, for both kinds of dream, are long-lasting—dating back, apparently, to the earliest period of life. From the *Interpretation*: 'Like dreams, they are wish-fulfilments; like dreams they are based to a great extent on impressions of infantile experiences; like dreams, they benefit by a certain degree of relaxation of censorship.'[15] Daydreams can also

[12] Freud, 'Hysterical Phantasies and their Relation to Bisexuality' (1908), *SE* ix. 159–60, emphasis added; 'Hysterische Phantasien und ihre Beziehung zur Bisexualität', *GW* vii. 192.

[13] Freud, Lecture XXII, *Introductory Lectures, SE* xvi. 372–3, emphasis added; *Vorlesungen, GW* xi. 387–8.

[14] Freud, Lecture VIII, *Introductory Lectures, SE* xv. 130; *Vorlesungen, GW* xi. 129.

[15] Freud, *Interpretation, SE* v. 492; *Die Traumdeutung, GW* ii–iii. 496.

be unconscious, Freud goes on to say—as far from waking awareness as dreams themselves. They too may point towards something that is constantly undermining the apparent unity and simplicity of daytime consciousness and aims. Like dreams, they are a piece of normality which verges on being, and is structured like, a neurotic symptom. They may be the immediate forerunners of a hysterical episode, or they may precede a dream that is itself interchangeable with a hysterical attack.[16]

But daydreams are also said to resemble not so much dreams in general as one particular aspect of their form and function: what Freud calls 'secondary revision [*die sekundäre Bearbeitung*]'. The longest section on daydreams in the *Interpretation* occurs in the part dedicated to that fourth feature of the dream-work; in it, the unifying, reconstructive effect is said to be epitomized by daydreams:

> The function of 'secondary revision', which we have attributed to the fourth of the factors concerned in shaping the content of dreams, shows us in operation once more the activity which is able to find free vent in the creation of day-dreams without being inhibited by any other influences. We might put it simply by saying that this fourth factor of ours seeks to mould [*gestalten*] the material offered to it into something like a day-dream.[17]

Here too, Freud both makes an analogy of daydreams and, at the same time, offers them as component parts of dreams. He continues:

> If, however, a day-dream of this kind has already been formed within the nexus of the dream-thoughts, this fourth factor in the dream-work will prefer to take possession of the ready-made [*bereits ... gebildet*] day-dream and seek to introduce it into the content of the dream. There are some dreams which consist merely in the repetition of a day-time phantasy [*Tagesphantasie*] which may perhaps have remained unconscious.[18]

The alleged likeness of daydreams to dreams thus subtends very different—and conflicting—emphases. Daydreams are considered either as touching on the unconscious, repressed thoughts that are the origin of night-dreams, or as resembling only the not-dream part of the dream—its presentable, outside, external face as formed in the process of secondary revision.

[16] The first suggestion is made in 'Hysterical Phantasies' (*SE* ix. 160; *GW* vii. 192), as well as in the *Interpretation* (*SE* v. 491; *GW* ii–iii. 495), the second in a 1909 footnote to the *Interpretation* (*SE* v. 494; *GW* ii–iii. 494).

[17] Freud, *Interpretation*, *SE* v. 492; *Die Traumdeutung*, *GW* ii–iii. 496.

[18] Freud, *Interpretation*, *SE* v. 492; *Die Traumdeutung*, *GW* ii–iii. 496–7.

In later writings, this point slides into the suggestion of an obviousness that attaches to daydreams; it is this which might have made them a more accessible, less twisting road to the understanding of wish-fulfilment as the primary feature of dreams. The word that that tends to be used here is 'transparent' or 'see-through': '*durchsichtig*'. In the fifth *Introductory Lecture*, for instance, Freud states: 'The content of these phantasies is dominated by a very transparent motive.'[19] And in the eighth: 'at one point we hoped to approach an understanding of the problems of dreams from the fact that certain imaginative structures which are very transparent to us are known as "day-dreams".'[20]

These references to transparency may be compared to a pair of architectural similes that occur in the course of the discussion of daydreams in the *Interpretation*. Here is the continuation of Freud's enumeration of the points of similarity between daydreams and night-dreams:

> If we examine their [daydreams'] structure, we shall perceive the way in which the wishful purpose that is at work in their production has mixed up the material of which they are built, has rearranged it and has formed it into a new whole. They stand in much the same relation to the childhood memories from which they are derived as do some of the Baroque palaces of Rome to the ancient ruins whose pavements and columns have provided the material for the more recent structures.[21]

In addition to its derivative, re-make status, the Baroque comparison functions to suggest the ornateness, the complexity, and above all the finished appearance of a daydream, as of a dream which has been through the process of revision. But here, when the 'complete analogy' is still being considered, the structure is opaque rather than transparent: this is a front which obscures what lies behind it, rather than serving as a window on the wish.

In the other instance, we move once again from the analogy to the component part, as daydreams are considered in their capacity to furnish one of the elements—the outward front—for the total building which will make up the dream: 'there is one case in which [secondary

[19] Freud, Lecture V, *Introductory Lectures*, *SE* xv. 98; *Vorlesungen*, *GW* xi. 95.

[20] Freud, Lecture VIII, *Introductory Lectures*, *SE* xv. 130; *Vorlesungen*, *GW* xi. 129.

[21] Freud, *Interpretation*, *SE* v. 492; *Die Traumdeutung*, *GW* ii–iii. 496. In this comparison, ancient Rome in its ruins represents the wildness of unreconstructed wishes. In Freud's quotation from the *Aeneid* in the passage at the start of this chapter, ancient Rome, about to be built, was in the opposite position, representing the civilized destiny and destination of Aeneas and contrasted to the instincts thwarting its achievement in the person of Juno.

revision] is to a great extent spared the labour of, as it were, building up a façade for the dream—the case, namely, in which a formation of that kind already exists, available for use [*seiner Verwendung harrend*] in the material of the dream thoughts.' This formation is then described as a '"phantasy"', which is in turn elucidated as being like a '"day-dream"' (Freud's inverted commas signifying a new concept in the first instance and a new linguistic coinage, as we have seen, in the second).[22] The daydream becomes not just ready-made but made for a purpose, labour-saving and (literally) 'awaiting its use'.

It is at points like this that the use of daydreams as counter-comparison, rather than as analogy, begins to appear more sharply. Unlike the dreams of sleep, daydreams in this instance are said to show their meaning on the surface: there is no subterranean layer to be plumbed. As such, they can provide the varnish on a dream, appearing as a gloss for the unpresentable materials underneath. In themselves, they are what they seem: straightforward—unified, and unidirectional—stories of wish-fulfilment. This leads to further differences, some of them mentioned more than once, some only implied, and some where there is no consistency—what Freud instances as a difference in one place, he may assume as a common feature in another.

Minimally, the dream occurs during sleep, the daydream when the subject is awake. The distinction is barely more than physiological; what is interesting is the way that it comes, surreptitiously, to be mapped onto others, in particular the opposition of night and day. Freud assumes, without question, that daydreams are unlike night-dreams because 'their relation to sleep is already contradicted by their name'.[23] As natural, in appearance, as the difference between sleeping and being awake, this opposition takes on the greatest symbolic importance and makes way for others, some explicit and some not.

A contrast regularly stressed by Freud concerns the dreamer's belief in the dream. Where dreams carry conviction, daydreams do not: they 'are *thought*, even though vividly imagined, and never experienced as

[22] Freud, *Interpretation*, *SE* v. 491; *Die Traumdeutung*, *GW* ii–iii. 495. *Phantasie* is intended as a semi-technical term in German, and the invention of a new word 'phantasy' to translate it into English reinforces that separation but also creates a new difference from the existing 'fantasy'. French (*phantasme/fantasme*) as well as English psychoanalytic theory has sometimes sought to maintain the distinction as between unconscious and conscious fantasy. In general, I have not used 'phantasy' as a separate term; the case of daydreams renders the distinction between the two particularly fragile.

[23] Freud, Lecture V, *Introductory Lectures*, *SE* xv. 98; *Vorlesungen*, *GW* xi. 95.

hallucinations'.[24] You are always aware of daydreaming, so that in some sense you are knowingly in two places, two times, at once, with the difference between the orders of reality clearly maintained: 'we do not experience or hallucinate anything in them but imagine something, we know that we are having a phantasy, we do not see but think [*sieht nicht, sondern denkt*].'[25]

Another marked difference is that the dreamer has no control over the dream, but some control over the daydream.[26] There are also alleged differences of form and medium. Drawing together a number of these distinctions, Freud states that 'dreams differ from day-dreams ... in the fact of their ideational content being transformed from thoughts into sensory images, to which belief [*Glauben*] is attached and which appear to be experienced.'[27] He goes on to qualify this by a caveat based upon personal experience: not all dreams make ideas into images, witness one of his own discussed earlier in the book. The criterion of conviction is not, however, affected, he says; it is just that the normal pattern puts seeing with believing.

Freud's own difference from the norm of experiencing hallucinatory images in dreams is also mentioned in a footnote added in 1909 to the principal discussion of daydreams in the *Interpretation*. Immediately before the declaration of 'the complete analogy between night-dreams and day-dreams', Freud states: 'Incidentally, I underestimated the importance of the part played by these phantasies in the formation of dreams so long as I was principally working on my own dreams, which are usually based on discussions and conflicts of thought and comparatively rarely on day-dreams [*seltener Tagträume, meist Diskussionen und Gedankenkonflikte*].'[28] Here, the assumption about the predominance of sensory images in dreams, as opposed to daydreams, seems to be reversed. For most people, not for Freud, daydreams, as bearers of

[24] Freud, Lecture VIII, *Introductory Lectures*, *SE* xv. 130; *Vorlesungen*, *GW* xi. 129. The English translation, but not the German, italicizes *gedachte* ('thought').

[25] Freud, Lecture V, *Introductory Lectures*, *SE* xv. 98; *Vorlesungen*, *GW* xi. 95.

[26] However, in a passage added to the *Interpretation* in 1909—the year after 'Creative Writers and Day-dreaming'—Freud provided an interesting qualification to this by granting some initiative to some dreamers. There are those 'who thus seem to possess the faculty of consciously directing their dreams. If, for instance, a dreamer of this kind is dissatisfied with the turn taken by a dream, he can break it off without waking up and start it again in another direction—just as a popular dramatist may under pressure give his play a happier [*glücklicheren*] ending' (*SE* v. 571–2; *Die Traumdeutung*, *GW* ii–iii. 577).

[27] Freud, *Interpretation*, *SE* v. 535; *Die Traumdeutung*, *GW* ii–iii. 540.

[28] Freud, *Interpretation*, *SE* v. 494; *Die Traumdeutung*, *GW* ii–iii. 498.

what is not discursive or ideational, would be more dream than the dream—the key to dreams because they are hyperdreams, not milder versions.

A further apparent difference between dreams and daydreams concerns the temporal direction of the wishes represented in them. For although Freud says in the *Interpretation* that daydreams, like dreams, are derived from and resuscitate childhood wishes, nonetheless when he comes to talk about them in essays of the subsequent years, the two wishful modes that he names as being those that are typically expressed in daydreams are both of them turned towards the future, rather than returning to an image of ancient satisfactions. These two wishful modes, of which there will be more to say, are ambition and love.

Sometimes the difference of temporal orientation disappears, when the fulfilment of the future-directed wish is interpreted as being, in effect, a return to the securities or supremacies of the idealized early years. So a man seeking work who dreams, as he walks to a job interview, of marrying the boss's daughter and inheriting the business himself, elicits, in 'Creative Writers and Day-dreaming' (1908), the following interpretation:

> In this phantasy, the dreamer has regained what he possessed in his happy childhood—the protecting house, the loving parents and the first objects of his affectionate feelings. You will see from this example the way in which the wish makes use of an occasion in the present to construct, on the pattern of the past, a picture of the future.[29]

But even if a Freudian future can always be found to hark back, at some level, to a memory or an ancient desire, still in the case of the daydream the wishes are resolutely forward-looking in their mode of return, seeking to find a replacement, a new story, even if it does take the older one as its model.

And indeed at other moments the forward orientation of the daydream appears unequivocal. For Freud also claims that daydreams are modified throughout the subject's life: they do not remain fixed once and for all at the time of their origin, or by reference to an earlier period. From 'Creative Writers':

[29] Freud, 'Creative Writers and Day-dreaming', *SE* ix. 148; *GW* vii. 218. The title of the essay is in fact 'Der Dichter und das Phantasieren'—'fantasizing' (or 'phantasying', as Strachey would put it: he uses this form for instance on p. 146) rather than 'daydreaming'. '*Tagtraum*', Freud's usual word for 'daydream', appears in the essay too, twice highlighted, as elsewhere, with inverted commas because it is adopted as a Germanization of the English word.

We must not suppose that the products of this imaginative [*phantasierenden*] activity—the various phantasies, castles in the air and day-dreams—are stereotyped [*starr*] or unalterable [*unveränderlich*]. On the contrary, they fit themselves in to the subject's shifting impressions of life, change with every change in his situation [*Lebenslage*], and receive from every fresh active impression what might be called a 'date-mark'.[30]

Freud repeated this stress on the changing rather than the fixed quality of daydreams in the *Introductory Lectures*:

In other respects these day-dreams are of many different kinds and pass through changing vicissitudes [*Schicksale*]. They are either, each one of them, dropped after a short time and replaced by a fresh one, or they are retained, spun out into long stories and adapted to the changes in the circumstances [*Lebensverhältnisse*] of the subject's life. They go along with the times, so to speak [*Sie gehen sozusagen mit der Zeit*], and receive a 'date stamp' which bears witness to the influence of the new situation.[31]

'Date stamp' and 'date-mark' translate the same word *Zeitmarke*: a 'time-branding', or dated trademark. Freud puts it in inverted commas as though to patent a new expression, one which itself offers a suitably modern image for fantasy's way of keeping up with what's new, of never passing its 'sell-by' date. Although the earlier passage does go on to refer to the present occasion's capacity to make a connection with an older experience of wish-fulfilment, there is no mention in either of a kernel or core fantasy that would remain the same from the beginning. Daydreams are modified in relation to a changing life 'situation' or 'circumstances'. They seem to have no necessary continuity, but merely 'fit themselves in' ('*schmiegen sich*', with a sense of cosiness); they 'go along with the times', malleable to the mark of each new impression encountered.

Something comparable to this outward impressionability is going on in the categorization of the changing wishes as either ambitious or amorous, despite the inner continuities that such specification might suggest. The two modes are differentiated by the sex of the daydreamer: women's dreams are of love, men's are ambitious. But at the same time, Freud regularly subsumes each of the two into the other: an ostensibly ambitious outcome in a man's daydream should be understood as secondary to a primary aim, which is that of pleasing a woman, while a woman's love-dreams are in reality the only expression allowed to her ambition.

30 Freud, 'Creative Writers', *SE* ix. 147; 'Der Dichter', *GW* vii. 217.

31 Freud, Lecture V, *Introductory Lectures, SE* xv. 98–9; *Vorlesungen, GW* xi. 95–6.

This extract from the fifth of the *Introductory Lectures* gives a typical summary of these attributions and their mobility, beginning with the factor of obviousness or transparency that is consistently associated with the meanings of daydreams:

> The content of these phantasies is dominated by a very transparent motive. They are scenes and events in which the subject's egoistic needs of ambition [*Ehrgeiz*] and power or his erotic wishes find satisfaction. In young men the ambitious phantasies are the most prominent, in women, whose ambition is directed to success in love, the erotic ones. But in men, too, erotic needs are often enough present in the background: all their heroic deeds and successes seem only to aim at courting the admiration and favour of women.[32]

It is common enough, not to say standard, for Freud to find that binary distinctions—as here, between male and female wishes, and correlatively between the erotic and the ambitious—turn out to be not so distinct after all. In this instance the explanation, or further complication, of the initial situation—ambition and love, one assigned to each sex—not only merges the terms, but also takes it for granted that women are ambitious too. Men's ambitions may well be love-driven—'often enough [*oft genug*]'—and in women, categorically, no exceptions, 'their ambition' is redirected: literally, 'they have thrown their ambition into success in love'. Novelistically, both sexes start off with a supply of ambition; the daydreaming difference relates pragmatically to women's love-centred lives.[33] This claim for the social contingency of daydreams accords with the inversion of the habitual Freudian structure in the 'date-stamp' passages cited above: for once, what matters is the date or the 'moment', historical or daily.

DAYDREAMING IN FICTION

There is a further occasion in the *Interpretation* when Freud is led to adopt his analogy of dreams to daydreams. He is arguing that in dreams, 'the thought is represented as an immediate situation with the "perhaps" omitted', and that dreams thus adopt the present tense in representing their wish as fulfilled, replacing the hesitation of the optative grammatical mood—'would that ... '—with a straightforward

32 Freud, Lecture V, *Introductory Lectures*, *SE* xv. 98; *Vorlesungen*, *GW* xi. 95.

33 For another covert reference to women's ambition in Freud, see further Ch. 6, pp. 165–8, below.

declaration: 'We need not linger long over this first peculiarity of dreams. We can deal with it by drawing attention to conscious phantasies—to day-dreams—which treat their ideational content in just the same manner.'[34] Here, as with other points of correspondence, the likeness to the daydream is assumed, not argued; the daydream is brought in not for itself, but because it serves just as well as a dream for illustration.

This elision is followed by a second one, since the daydream offered as an example is not Freud's or anyone else's, but taken from a work of fiction. The passage continues:

> While Daudet's Monsieur Joyeuse was wandering, out of work, through the streets of Paris (though his daughters believed that he had a job and was sitting in an office), he was dreaming of developments that might bring him influential help and lead to his finding employment—and he was dreaming in the present tense. Thus dreams make use of the present tense in the same manner and by the same right as day-dreams.[35]

We shall return to the themes of this paraphrase, after considering a peculiarity of Freud's use of it. For the example turns out to have an intriguing connection to a real daydream—one of Freud's own.

In *The Psychopathology of Everyday Life* (1901), Freud describes a near error in his redaction of the section of the *Interpretation* in which the literary daydream appears. When he drafted it, he was away on holiday, without his books. He describes how he misremembered the name of Daudet's daydreamer, substituting Jocelyn for Joyeuse, and also changed the plot of the daydream in Daudet:

> I imagined I had a distinct memory of one of the phantasies which this man—I called him Monsieur Jocelyn—hatched out [*ausbrütet*] on his walks through the streets of Paris; and I began to reproduce it from memory. It was a phantasy of how Monsieur Jocelyn boldly threw himself at the head of a runaway horse in the street, and brought it to a stop; how the carriage door opened and a great personage [*eine hohe Persönlichkeit*] stepped out, pressed Monsieur Jocelyn's hand and said: 'You are my saviour [*Retter*]. I owe my life to you. What can I do for you?'[36]

There are in fact other mistakes that Freud retains in his revised remembering of the literary episode, and there will be more to say about them. But the mistake in the name turns out to be a significant one:

[34] Freud, *Interpretation*, *SE* v. 534; *Die Traumdeutung*, *GW* ii–iii. 539–40.

[35] Freud, *Interpretation*, *SE* v. 535; *Die Traumdeutung*, *GW* ii–iii. 540.

[36] Freud, *The Psychopathology of Everyday Life* (1901), *SE* vi. 149; *Zur Psychopathologie des Alltagslebens*, *GW* iv. 165.

'"Joyeux", of which "Joyeuse" is the feminine form, is the only possible way in which I could translate my own name, Freud, into French.'[37]

The suppressed identification and the substitution of a different story then suggest to Freud that the daydream was in fact his own, which leads to a quite fabulous evocation of himself as youthful *flâneur*: 'Perhaps I invented it myself in Paris where I frequently walked about the streets, lonely and full of longings [*einsam und voll Sehnsucht*], greatly in need of a helper and protector, until the great Charcot took me into his circle.'[38] Here we have the classical scene of masculine daydreaming: the modern city street. In this setting, solitude and anonymity facilitate the departure into another mental world, as well as reinforcing the typical plot: the daydreamer's present situation as anyone or no one is replaced by another, in which he acquires a name for himself. In this daydream of Freud's, that element is compounded by the actual naming of great names that become, in effect, the dreamer's new family. First there is 'the great Charcot', '*Meister Charcot*'; finally, the daydreams' wish-fulfilling interfusion of fiction and reality, inside and outside novels, seems to be complete when Daudet himself makes a (literally) guest appearance. With touching irrelevance to his argument, Freud adds a concluding sentence to his happy ending: 'Later I more than once met the author of *Le Nabab* [the novel in which M. Joyeuse appears] in Charcot's house.'[39]

[37] Freud, *Psychopathology*, *SE* vi. 149; *Zur Psychopathologie*, *GW* iv. 166.

[38] Ibid.

[39] Ibid. At the time when Freud was in Paris studying under Charcot in 1885–6, Daudet was at the height of his fame, both in France and abroad; he was as well known and as well regarded as contemporary novelists still famous today such as Flaubert and Zola. A letter to his fiancée Martha Bernays conveys Freud's excitement at meeting such a celebrity: 'The party grew larger and larger; the later guests included Cornu, the famous optician, with a truly inspired expression; M. Peyron, director of the Assistance Publique, against whom the students recently instigated a huge scandal, no one knows why; and (prepare yourself for a surprise) Daudet himself. A magnificent face!' Freud's admiration extends to a full physical description: 'Small figure, narrow head with a mass of black curly hair, a longish but not typically French beard, fine features, a resonant voice, and very lively in his movements.' It is heightened by the sharp contrast that follows: 'Mme D. was also there, and never left her husband's side; she is so unbeautiful that one cannot imagine she has ever been any better-looking; a worn face, prominent cheek bones. She was dressed like a very young woman, although her eighteen-year-old son [Léon], friend of Charcot's son, was present. Daudet doesn't look a day over forty; he must have married very young' (*The Letters of Sigmund Freud*, ed. Ernst L. Freud, trans. Tania and James Stern (1960; New York: Basic Books, 1975), Letter 96, Wednesday, 10 February, 1886, 207–8).

On Daudet's novels see further Murray Sachs, *The Career of Alphonse Daudet: A Critical Study* (Cambridge, MA: Harvard University Press 1965); no monograph has been published on Daudet since this one, in which the decline of interest in him is

And this is not all. Until the 1924 edition of the *Psychopathology*, Freud went on to make further confessions:

But the irritating part of it is that there is scarcely any group of ideas to which I feel so antagonistic as that of being someone's protégé. What can be seen in our country of this relation is enough to rob one of all desire for it, and the role of the favourite child is one which is very little suited indeed to my character. I have always felt an unusually strong urge 'to be the strong man myself'.[40]

A first point about this is its curiously unpsychoanalytic mode of argument: you don't wish to be a protégé for the common-sense reason that any objective observer can see that it's a bad position to be in. Secondly, the passage takes up the ambitious aim which was to acquire such a prominent place in subsequent accounts of daydreams; yet it assumes, equally curiously and perhaps unpsychoanalytically too, that the fantasy as given—of saving a great man who then offers a favour in return—is passive rather than active, the inversion of an ambitious desire, rather than the example of one. Only the later elucidation, that a great man of this type would be like the 'helper and protector' that Charcot represented, makes this explicitly a protégé structure at all, in effect by completing the story to suggest what kind of favour would be involved. In the account of the misremembered daydream, the strengths would seem to be all on the side of the rescuer, not the rescued man.

The structure of this Freudian daydream thus in one way turns the emphasis from physical to social capacities. The act of saving a life is both reciprocated and replaced by symbolically offering a better one. Insofar as this is a daydream of ambition, it seems to involve an unstable rotation between two men's positions of dependence and superiority

already a given. Of all Daudet's novels, Sachs is most critical of *Le Nabab*, and within it most critical of Daudet's portrayal of the Joyeuse family: 'The cloying and tasteless tone, the facile emotion, are unfortunately quite typical of the manner in which Daudet deals with every scene involving the Joyeuse family in *Le Nabab*' (p. 110). He continues: 'No other novel of Daudet's is so heavily larded with this kind of sentimentality—he was thereafter to exercise heroic restraint over these personal outbursts' (p. 111). Sachs's own outburst also doubts whether 'the modern reader' (of the 1960s) will be able to stand the sentimentality, and makes the point that 'M. Joyeuse, who somehow bravely conceals his jobless state from his family for so long, is simply incredible even at the most practical level of realism' (pp. 109–10). Which makes it interesting that the same situation was used a century after Daudet by John Lanchester in his very successful and very funny novel *Mr Phillips* (London: Faber and Faber, 2000); it is true, though, that Mr Phillips is only described on the first day of his redundancy.

[40] Freud, *Psychopathology*, *SE* vi. 149–50; the footnote is not included in the *Gesammelte Werke* or in the separate Fischer paperback of *Zur Psychopathologie*.

in relation to one another, as the initiative and the power move from one to the other. Freud's readiness to make this into an issue of activity versus passivity, with negative connotations attached to the latter and activity appearing to be straightaway threatened by the possibility of slipping into its opposite, may be connected to his initial repudiation of the name 'Joyeuse' that he identifies as the feminine version of his own.

'Hysterical Phantasies' features a feminine version of the 'great man' urban daydream. A woman finds herself in tears in the street from imagining a story in which she has an affair with a locally celebrated musician who abandons her to poverty when she has his child. In this negative version, the culmination leaves the woman with neither love nor money, a fall made the more pronounced by her temporary acquisition of both during her relationship with the pianist.[41] This story in turn suggests links to another of the basic daydreams or fantasies outlined by Freud: the rescue of the fallen woman, a version of which is discussed in some detail in the essay of 1910 entitled 'A Special Type of Choice of Object Made by Men'. Here, the initial focus is on the male *Rettungsphantasie*, a 'fantasy of rescuing' women who are sexually involved with another man. This represents, Freud argues, a repetition of the situation of the boy with his parents, since the mother whom he desires is already attached to his father. The force of the image of the fallen woman is also related, both by contrast and by assimilation, to what he calls the mother-complex (*Mutterkomplex*). As the boy learns about adult sexuality, he is first unable to connect it with his own parents, who seem so remote from such things; but 'when after this he can no longer maintain the doubt which makes his parents an exception to the universal and odious norms of sexual activity, he tells himself with cynical logic [*zynischer Korrektheit*] that the difference between his mother and a whore is not after all so very great, since basically they do the same thing.'[42]

In addition to the fantasy of rescuing a fallen woman, there is also a parallel fantasy in relation to a father-surrogate:

> When a child hears that he *owes his life* to his parents, or that his mother *gave him life*, his feelings of tenderness unite with impulses which strive at power and independence, and they generate the wish to return this gift to the parents

[41] See Freud, 'Hysterical Phantasies', *SE* ix. 160; 'Hysterische Phantasien', *GW* vii. 192–3.

[42] Freud, 'A Special Type of Choice of Object Made by Men' (1910), *SE* xi. 171; 'Über einen besonderen Typus der Objectwahl beim Manne', *GW* viii. 75. Freud's interest in the sexually learning child as a cynic is discussed in Ch. 5, below.

and to repay them with one of equal value. It is as though the boy's defiance were to make him say: 'I want nothing from my father; I will give him back all I have cost him.' He then forms the phantasy of *rescuing* [*retten*] *his father from danger and saving his life*; in this way he puts his account square with him.[43]

Such a calculated equalization—a fair deal and a life for a life—applies in this hostile mode only in relation to the father; it can be modified into other, milder forms:

This phantasy is commonly enough displaced on to the emperor, king or some other great man [*auf den Kaiser, König oder sonst einen großen Herrn*]; after being thus distorted it becomes admissible to consciousness, and may even be made use of by creative writers. In its application to a boy's father it is the defiant meaning in the idea of rescuing which is by far the most important.[44]

Here, then, is the meaning that Freud subsequently gave to the fantasy of rescuing a great man that he describes as his own distortion of the passage from the Daudet novel.

Rescuing a man seems to have to do with power, rescuing a woman with her sexuality: respectively, ambition and love in their more naked forms. The great man rescued in Freud's fantasy is momentarily fallen—from his horse, literally, and thereby also from the power he normally wields. The woman in a rescue fantasy is sexually 'fallen', to be redeemed by the unconditional love offered her by the man who takes her up in spite and because of her situation. It is now he who falls for her, in both senses: falls in love and falls on her behalf.

Yet the differences are not nearly as firm as this summary would suggest. In Freud's study of a case of female homosexuality, in 1920, the falling is made literal in the would-be suicidal act of a young woman who throws herself down the side of a railway cutting. She has 'fallen for' an older woman, who is promiscuous and whom she adores and wants to rescue. As Freud points out, this is the 'Special Type of Choice of Object' situation. He interprets the woman's love as masculine, because its object is the feminine 'special type'; yet in this case, and presumably only because the man in the affair is a woman, he interprets the fall in sexual, not social terms.[45]

[43] Freud, 'Special Type'. *SE* xi. 172; 'Über einen besonderen Typus', *GW* viii. 75.

[44] Freud, 'Special Type', *SE* xi. 172–3; 'Über einen besonderen Typus', *GW* viii. 75.

[45] See Freud, 'The Psychogenesis of a Case of Homosexuality in a Woman' (1920), *SE* xviii. 147–72; 'Über die Psychogenese eines Falles von weiblicher Homosexualität', *GW* xii. 271–302.

The inseparability of sexual and social reversals is also the subject of another passage about Daudet in *The Interpretation of Dreams*. This time, the association is to the opening part of Daudet's novel *Sapho*. In Freud's precis:

a young man carries his mistress upstairs in his arms; at first she is as light as a feather, but the higher he climbs the heavier grows her weight. The whole scene foreshadows the course of their love-affair, which was intended by Daudet as a warning to young men not to allow their affections to be seriously engaged by girls of humble origin and a dubious past [*zweifelhafter Vergangenheit*].[46]

The dream, in Freud's interpretation, involves a woman's sexual and thereby also social rise and fall, and a man's social rising and falling, in relation to the dreamer's brother—all of which features he sees as being intimated by the Daudet parallel. Peculiarly enough, the idea of this particular source-text for the dream is Freud's own—he told the patient that the dream reminded him of the 'well-known', 'masterly introduction' ('*bekannte meisterhafte Introduktion*');[47] but the dreamer accepts its relevance by making a connection to a further work (a play he had seen the evening before) that involves similar themes of the upward and downward mobility of a young girl's sexual and social career.

Some other misrememberings in Freud's deployment of the Joyeuse story from *Le Nabab* are pertinent here, in addition to the one about the name that he identifies himself. For one thing, the story simply does not prove the main point claimed for its illustrative value at this stage in the *Interpretation*. Freud wants it to demonstrate that daydreams, like dreams, are immediate and therefore appear in literature in the present tense; but in the Daudet story they are as often in the imperfect, while the narrative of what is really happening, in the story as opposed to the daydream, is frequently in the present tense.

A second point is related to Freud's interest in daydreams of masculine rescue. In the *Psychopathology*, as we have seen, he claims that his first draft of the passage included a fantasy for M. Joyeuse which turned out, when he later checked it, to have been a complete invention: his stopping a runaway horse and thereby rescuing 'a great personage [*eine hohe Persönlichkeit*]'. Yet in fact such a rescue scene does occur in the daydreams of Daudet's character, who sees himself saving a child from a similar street accident involving a horse and carriage. Only the sequel

46 Freud, *Interpretation*, *SE* iv. 285–6; *Die Traumdeutung*, *GW* ii–iii. 292.

47 Freud, *Interpretation*, *SE* iv. 285; *Die Traumdeutung*, *GW* ii–iii. 292.

is different, in that M. Joyeuse has his imaginary heroism followed up not with grateful promises from an important man, but with a scene in which, having been injured himself, he is surrounded by his anxious and adoring family waiting to see if he will be all right.

So Freud in this instance forgot that he had not forgotten. The street accident rescue fantasy does occur, after all, in the source-text. But it is used to very different ends: in Freud's case, in relation to a question of ambition, with a rejection of the position of beneficiary; in M. Joyeuse's, as a means to return to the unquestioned love of the family fold. Daudet's hero rather desires the situation of childish dependence and centrality, which he seems to have taken as a reward from the child he has just saved, whereas Freud analyses himself as rejecting anything that smacks of the dependent and feminine passivity of the protégé.

In Daudet's story, daydream and reality are hard to differentiate. This is first because, contrary to one of Freud's criteria for daydreams as distinct from dreams, M. Joyeuse's reveries are convincing, like dreams, to the point of complete immersion. He forgets his surrounding reality until it brings him back abruptly. He is walking about, and he lets out a cry at a crucial point in his fantasy, which then 'awakens' him from it.[48] The overlap is also because what he dreams of is never more than what he has or what, during the course of the story, he loses. He has, and continues to have, a doting family of daughters; he has, loses, and then recovers a job with which to support them. While he is out of work, he has to 'play-act' at home, making up stories about the day at work when in reality he has been wandering the streets in search of employment. At the end, he is really rescued by the intervention of a friend of a friend who offers him a job at the same salary as the one he lost.

So while M. Joyeuse's daydreams do indeed conform to the themes of ambition and love, inseparable as they are in Freud, they could hardly be more modest: apart from averting the accident with the horse, or taking vengeance on the imaginary attackers of one of his daughters, his daydream wishes extend to no more than a Christmas bonus from his boss. The figures of the rescuer or the protégé—those that Freud refuses for himself—are, in their small way, common to the plots of the daydreams and the real life. Daudet's is a story of the daydreamer as ordinary man, employee in the modern city, and of the daydream itself as an outlet for underused mental capacities: he describes the surprisingly large number

[48] Alphonse Daudet, *Le Nabab* (1877), in *Œuvres*, ed. Roger Ripoll (Paris: Gallimard, Pléiade, 1990), ii. 544.

of 'those waking sleepers [*dormeurs éveillés*] in whom too restricted a fate pushes down unemployed forces and heroic faculties.'[49] At the same time, the story of M. Joyeuse is itself an idealized representation of the lovable, decent chap for whom all comes right in the end.

Freudian daydreams, whether grandiose or humble, are recognizably social stories—the upwardly or just horizontally mobile wish-fulfilments of modern life, as it is lived and as it is promoted. It is thus appropriate that when Freud writes about the relationship between daydreams and creative writers, he makes a point of dealing with mass-market authors who flatter their reader into identification with '*Seine Majestät das Ich, den Helden aller Tagträume wie aller Romane*', 'His Majesty the Ego, the hero alike of every day-dream and of every story.'[50] Daydreams fit the comparison with novels of modern life, of recognizable aspirations. For ambition and love sound, in fact, less like the dangerous instincts of an anti-social, repressed but irrepressible unconscious, than like the acceptable driving forces that openly move the plots of the standard nineteenth-century novel or personal biography. Freud's confident attribution of a morally educative purpose when he discusses the introduction to *Sapho*—'intended by Daudet as a warning to young men not to allow their affections to be seriously engaged by girls of humble origin and a dubious past'—would seem to accord with this view of a simple and ideologically laden communication from writer to reader.

One swiftly dealt-with night-dream of the *Interpretation* actually features Daudet in person, along with two other contemporary French novelists:

> A young woman had been cut off from society for weeks on end while she nursed her child through an infectious illness. After the child's recovery, she had a dream of being at a party at which, among others, she met Alphonse Daudet, Paul Bourget, and Marcel Prévost; they were all most affable to her and highly amusing. All of the authors resembled their portraits, except Marcel Prévost, of whom she had never seen a picture; and he looked like ... the disinfection officer who had fumigated the sick-room the day before and who had been her first visitor for so long. Thus it seems possible to give a complete translation of the dream: 'It's about time for something more amusing than this perpetual sick-nursing.'[51]

[49] Daudet, *Le Nabab*, 545.

[50] Freud, 'Creative Writers', *SE* ix. 150; 'Der Dichter', *GW* vii. 220.

[51] Freud, *Interpretation*, *SE* iv. 126, ellipsis in text; *Die Traumdeutung*, *GW* ii–iii. 131–2.

From modern writers, complex meanings are not to be sought; to drive the point home, the next sentence goes on: 'These examples will perhaps be enough to show that dreams which can only be understood as fulfilments of wishes and which bear their meaning on their faces [*zur Schau*] without disguise [*unverhüllt*] are to be found under the most frequent and various conditions.'[52]

These considerations seem to be linked to Freud's repeated assertion that daydreams, and the stories that are like them, are transparent in their meaning. All the better, once again, to separate the supposed obviousness of everyday modern life—its moments, its residues, its routines—from the darker depths of the night and the unconscious. It is to Greek tragedy that Freud turns, not to a contemporary novel, when he is seeking a literary analogue for those other, less manifest wish-fulfilments that are also revealed by the analysis of night-dreams: Sophocles, not Daudet. It is there, below and not on the surfaces of daily life, of public spaces and of commonplace dreams of ambition, that he sees the turbulent forces of mental life to lie. In the process, the other day can be casually forgotten.

[52] Freud, *Interpretation*, *SE* iv. 126; *Die Traumdeutung*, *GW* ii–iii. 132.

5
A Freudian Curiosity

There can be no doubt about
Little Hans's sexual curiosity.[1]

In his theories of childhood development, Freud gives curiosity a very grand narrative, linking it in complex ways to what the title of his article of 1907 boldly calls 'The Sexual Enlightenment of Children'. Enlightenment, *Aufklärung*: the term seems to have its full historical and philosophical weight, suggesting the proud achievement of unbiased knowledge in the face of the prejudices and superstitions of a previous age. It is a word Freud uses often in this connection, especially in writings of the early years of psychoanalysis. But whose enlightenment is it and what and how do they learn? In Freud's usage, the sexual enlightenment of children implicitly includes both what they find out (or try to) for themselves, and the question of sex education, what their carers do or should impart to them. Freudian children are passionately curious researchers, fighting for knowledge in the face of the shifty evasions of a prejudiced older generation.[2]

So is Freud. For there is also, at another remove, an analogy, made more or less explicitly, between children's enlightenment and the knowledge claimed for psychoanalysis itself, which enlightens the world in relation to children's sexuality and the sexual aspect of neurotic illness in adults. To begin with, Freud thinks, all children attempt the achievement of personal enlightenment in matters of sexuality for themselves; at the same time, psychoanalysis is itself a form of enlightenment in an area that has been shrouded in mystery. Observation—the direct evidence of

[1] Freud, *Analysis of a Phobia in a Five-Year-Old Boy* ('Little Hans') (1909), *SE* x. 9; *Analyse der Phobie eines Fünfjährigen Knaben*, *GW* vii. 246: 'Die sexuelle Neugierde unseres Hans leidet wohl keinen Zweifel.'

[2] See Adam Phillips, *The Beast in the Nursery* (London: Faber and Faber, 1998), for other reflections on children's curiosity in Freud.

eyes and ears, in studying both the child and the adult patient—reveals and validates a knowledge that comes before the distorted forms of established philosophy and religion. Freud will often goad or cajole readers taken to be unconvinced, if not hostile to psychoanalysis, by insisting that its findings in this field are clear as day, if only they could divest themselves of the prejudices that prevent them from recognizing the truth.

Post-Enlightenment views of children's development tend to look upon them as natural researchers and explorers who come into the world ready to find out and learn and develop. We are born curious; happy the man, be he poet or *flâneur*, who knows how to retain or how to return to that early wondering—both questioning and pleasure—that is confidently attributed to the child. In Western childcare manuals, the standard view today casts the young child as a gifted scientist who engages in all kinds of experimentation with the world around it, adding all the time to its supply of usable knowledge. Children are not necessarily doomed to dumbing or darkening down; offered a stimulating environment, they may go on wondering and extending their spontaneous reach for the light.

Thus in the commonest post-Romantic version of individual development, curiosity comes naturally; knowledge enters and illuminates an open mind. But stories of collective, cultural enlightenment may work in other ways—if, for instance, the sun of knowledge shines in upon a darkness—superstition or ideology—that it must actively drive away. If the knowledge is being claimed as new, its success will require that it expose prior knowledge as clouded—wrong or preliminary or corrupt. Or if, in another scenario, there is nothing new under the sun, enlightenment presents itself as knowledge never before either seen or acknowledged as such. Freud's version of enlightenment moves between these last two, both in relation to the new knowledge that psychoanalysis claims as its form of cultural enlightenment and in relation to the new world encountered by the child. Children's curiosity and striving for knowledge are not spontaneous but emerge, like cultural enlightenment, as a reaction to and a rejection of the claims of the older generation. And they end not so much in knowledge as in failure or further prejudice. At the end of the day, Freudian enlightenment is a depressing business. Enlightenment in psychoanalytical knowledge involves an impossible conversion, to beliefs which are bound to be resisted; it is a revolution in thought whose refusal is inseparable from its acceptance. It is meant to drive out old knowledge or ignorance, but at the same time it is about truths that have allegedly always been there, as if awaiting their recognition.

In relation to psychoanalytic knowledge, Freud does not only employ enlightenment as a standard metaphor; he also refers directly to the history of sun-knowledge. In the 1910 text on Leonardo da Vinci, to which we shall return, Leonardo is credited with having anticipated Copernicus's hypothesis that it is the earth that orbits the sun, and not the other way around. At the end of 'The Resistances to Psycho-Analysis' (1925), the Copernican discovery is linked both to Darwin's theory of evolution and to psychoanalysis itself. All three met with resistance because they not only transformed the frame of reflection, but brought about what Freud calls 'a severe blow [*Kränkung*] to human self-love [*Eigenliebe*]'.[3] Psychoanalysis is elevated to the role of paradigm theory, since its own frame, here involving collective human 'self-love', can be used in a general way for the interpretation of other challenges to anthropocentrism. At the same time, a significant advance in knowledge goes together with a diminishment of human pretensions. Enlightenment thus begins to look less straightforward in its structure, as an apparently clear line of progressive illumination is muddied or muddled by the inevitable intervention of human *Eigenliebe*. Revolutionary progress in human knowledge directly concerns it; and self-love in the form of resistance necessarily impinges upon the acceptance of such new knowledge.

In one of the lectures he delivered at Clark University in Worcester, Massachussetts, in 1909—enlightening America or else 'bringing them the plague', as he is supposed to have said—Freud's theme, as often, was the reluctance of those encountering it for the first time to believe what psychoanalysis had to say about sexuality. Freud puts his American audience in that position, and offers them a parable of conversion. Others have felt this way—they 'began by completely disbelieving' the claim about the significance of sexuality—until 'their own analytic experiences [*Bemühungen*] compelled [*genötigt*] them to accept it'. The initial situation is not just indifference or neutrality or ignorance; it is disbelief, even *complete* disbelief. The change from one belief to another

[3] Freud, 'The Resistances to Psycho-Analysis' (1925), *SE* xix. 221; 'Die Widerstände gegen die Psychanalyse', *GW* xiv. 109. Strachey's translation also speaks of a 'blow to men's narcissism', repeating the phrase in order to break up a long sentence into two, but the word *Narzißmus* does not appear in the German.

is brought about not by persuasion (by another) but by new knowledge based on the evidence of 'their own ... experiences'. And this evidence is irresistible: belief is *compelled.* They have heard the truth with their own ears. And it turns out that there are cases of such hypothetical converts available in the present entourage, 'a few of my closest friends and followers' who have accompanied Freud on the journey to Worcester. They are now themselves the evidence: 'Enquire from them, and you will hear that they all began by completely disbelieving ... '.[4]

There is a hesitation here between the language of science and truth, and the language of religion and belief. Scientifically, an experiment is validated by the subject's own senses, the neutral truth observed. Religiously, one belief is exchanged for another, or disbelief becomes belief. Both aspects are included in the reference immediately afterwards to 'a conviction of the correctness [*Richtigkeit*] of the thesis'. There is a personal assurance about the correctness, and there is the question of the correctness itself, which is not the same. Freud then goes on to elaborate a fascinating analogy in relation to the process of conversion, or learning, here drawing on the difficulties rather than the opportunities of the analytic situation. Patients, it seems, are as reluctant to reveal what is sexual as sceptics are to believe in its importance:

> A conviction [*Überzeugung*] of the correctness of this thesis was not precisely made easier by the behaviour of patients. Instead of willingly presenting us with information about their sexual life, they try to conceal it by every means in their power. People are in general not candid [*aufrichtig*] over sexual matters [*sexuellen Dingen*]. They do not show their sexuality freely, but to conceal it they wear a heavy overcoat [*eine dicke Oberkleidung*] woven of a tissue of lies, as though the weather were bad in the world of sexuality. It is a fact that sun and wind are not favourable to sexual activity in this civilized world of ours; none of us can reveal his [or her] erotism freely to others. But when your patients discover that they can feel quite easy about it while they are under your treatment, they discard this veil of lies [*Lügenhülle*], and only then are you in a position to form a judgement on this debatable question.[5]

Here we have—at least at first sight—a classic scenario of surface falsehood and underlying truth. Freud is surely hamming it up with that heavy masculine overcoat obscuring the sexuality beneath it, equivalent to the teasingly feminine 'veil' of lies. Yet in one way there is nothing

[4] Freud, 'Fourth Lecture', *Five Lectures on Psycho-Analysis*, *SE* xi. 40; *Über Psychanalyse: Fünf Vorlesungen*, *GW* viii. 42.

[5] Freud, *Five Lectures*, *SE* xi. 40–1; *Über Psychanalyse*, *GW* viii. 42.

enigmatic about this fabric of lies, which serves to protect sexuality against the bad weather of the civilized world it has to live in. Exposure would be inappropriate, it is implied; in this world the weather is bad, the sun is the wrong sun—'sun and wind are not favourable'. In these adverse circumstances, it would not be right to reveal what is underneath the coat. Only in the specific enabling situation of the treatment, where the weather is good, is it feasible to take the coat off.

The tensions revealed in this passage are indicative, I think, of a problematic which surfaces repeatedly in Freud's discussions of sexuality and enlightenment in relation to the new knowledge of psychoanalysis. Psychoanalysis is enlightenment, in an emancipatory view of the new science as illumination—as a demonstration and observation of unbiased truth against the darkness of other views, those associated with false civilization and religion. But Freud also insists that one object of knowledge for psychoanalysis is, precisely, the resistance to knowing or seeing the truth as it is. 'People ... in general' do not want to know, in particular do not want to know about sexuality; and why, as well as what, they don't want to know is part of what psychaoanalysis endeavours to unravel or lay bare.

THE STORK GIVES BIRTH TO THE CYNIC

Children too in Freud's theory have variable sexual beliefs, and their own resistances to sexual knowledge. They are sexually curious, not innocently non-sexual before puberty as the culture likes to pretend. But their 'enlightenment' in sexuality is not straightforward. It is neither an innate knowledge nor a process of simply seeking or simply acquiring information, but involves instead a tortuous and tangled process of development. Children's preliminary sexual speculations, as described in detail in the 'Little Hans' case study of 1909, and summarized at the same time in 'The Sexual Enlightenment of Children', typically involve different theories of the origin of babies and the difference of the sexes. Linked as they evidently are, these two questions are generally represented as separate issues, so that which of them comes first, in importance and in time, is itself, for Freud, a significant question, as we shall discover. The idea of children's sexual enlightenment makes the 'age' that of an individual rather than a culture: even though it may happen in comparable or even identical ways for all children, they each have to follow the path to sexual knowledge on their own, making mistakes, suffering setbacks, and with luck (but it does not always happen) achieving a solution. As we trace the various versions of this path that Freud maps out, we shall see that to reach the state of enlightenment, if you do, is not, in practice, to find either happiness or the truth; at best you acquire a belief.

Curiosity, *die Neugierde*—the first stage on the way to getting knowledge—is not a natural, primary disposition in Freudian children. It is, however, presented as a universal stage of development, which descends upon children as a compelling response to a change, or potential change, in their situation. In most of Freud's descriptions, the first such change, chronologically and in other respects, is the birth of a sibling, or the observation and inference of the likelihood of such an event from the evidence of other families. A new child decentres the place of the older one; and children then asking the question 'Where do babies come from?' express both the urgency of that particular need to know, and also a wish to master, to explain for themselves, the altered situation.

The question, Freud claims, persists, because it does not meet with an adequate answer. Children are told a story, but it is an absurd one, the fable of the stork that brought the new baby out of the water. And they readily cotton on to its fabrication, to its being no better than a cloak for the truth that is actually being covered up. This, says Freud, has two crucial results. First, there begins a mistrust of grown-ups as fundamentally deceitful, saying one thing but knowing another; and a corresponding segregation of children's own thoughts and discoveries as secret from grown-ups. Knowledge becomes something hidden, valuable, and open to wilful distortion or dissimulation in the mode of its presentation. It is not simply or primarily a nugget of truth, possessed or not possessed, but a token of exchange to be traded and tricked over in a battle between those deprived of it and those who want to keep it to themselves. Second, Freud claims, children set off on a path of solitary research. In the logic of his own story, this does not follow directly since the self-imposed isolation is only from adults. So he assumes, without making it explicit, that the disappointment in relation to adult communications of knowledge will have a knock-on effect on children's relations with their peers. Instead of banding together in a research group in competition with the grown-ups, they all go their own lonely ways.

Initially, the child endowed grown-ups, the parents in particular, with omnipotence and knowledge. Parents, Freud says in 'Family Romances', are 'the source of all belief', and he is fond of making this structure the prototype of religion, in which God takes over the parental role.[6] The premise is that such a strong foundation is both necessary and bound to be challenged. The stability of the child's world gets shaken up in one way by the intrusion, or feared intrusion, of another child, but the security of *belief*, in the parents, is a slightly different matter, even though it is linked to this earth-shatteringly unhappy event. The parents' failure to give a truthful answer to the baby question produces an indeterminacy in relation to knowledge: about who knows it, and what they do with it. It now becomes part of a power game, involving quest and concealment, and the child sets off on its own to pursue it independently of the adults. This is the religious secession, born of scepticism, that becomes for Freud the forerunner and prototype of all intellectual inquiry.

There is, however, a sting in the tail of what partly develops as a classic myth of heroic resistance to superstition and triumph over obstacles. The young researcher never quite makes it. And in fact, it is not clear whether there might have been, or should be, an end to be reached: whether the quest for sexual knowledge or for knowledge in general has a conclusion. The child researcher comes up with various unsatisfactory hypotheses and encounters various impediments to knowledge, but his or her attempts to find out are also thwarted by what Freud presents as an internal difficulty, the immaturity of the sexual apparatus. Inconclusiveness, the inability to get at the answer or solve the enigma, is inherent to children's investigations. And that is not the end of it. In 'On the Sexual Theories of Children' (1908), Freud witheringly

[6] Freud, 'Family Romances' (1909), *SE* ix. 237; 'Der Familienroman der Neurotiker', *GW* vii. 227. Strikingly, the essay begins: 'The liberation [*die Ablösung*] of an individual, as he grows up, from the authority of his parents is one of the most necessary though one of the most painful results brought about by the course of his development'; this inevitable emancipation then comes to pass through the gradual shift in the young subject's understanding of his parents' place in the world: 'For a small child his parents are at first the only authority and the source of all belief.... But as intellectual growth increases, the child cannot help discovering by degrees the category [*die Kategorien*: in fact 'the categories'] to which his parents belong. He gets to know other parents and compares [*vergleicht*] them with his own' (*SE* ix. 237; *GW* vii. 227). It is this early comparative sociology which leads to envy and to the ensuing replacement, in fantasy, of the child's own parents with others of preferable status. Particularly noteworthy in this connection is the persistence of comparison as a mode of childish learning. In the fateful instance of grasping the difference between the sexes, discussed below, the Freudian boy and girl make a traumatic contrast: one sees in the other the dreaded reality of what he now fears might become of him, the other sees the superior reality of what she thereby realizes that she will never have; this sexual comparison, marked by disturbance, predominates as a turning point in his later writings.

declares that 'the first failure has a crippling effect on the child's whole future'.[7]

Adult research, it then comes as no surprise, is equally problematic, equally sad. Is it worth interminably seeking to know when what you thereby don't do is to live the rest of your life? This is the point that Freud makes, in striking language, in relation to Leonardo, the boy researcher who never gave it up: 'The postponement of loving until full knowledge is acquired ends in a substitution of the latter for the former. A man who has won his way to a state of knowledge [*zur Erkenntnis*] cannot properly be said to love and hate; he remains beyond love and hatred. He has investigated [*geforscht*] instead of loving.'[8] What is perhaps most remarkable about this is the endorsement of the childhood order of things. Loving (and hating) comes first; the urge to know is secondary, and should not, now, overlay and replace the primary importance of loving well. The position of knowledge is represented as a kind of aloofness, away from the world and from the reality of life; it is not a noble goal. Nor is it being attributed to a follower of philosophy, that branch of knowledge-seeking which regularly incurs Freud's snide devaluation. Leonardo's researches were practical as much as theoretical, like those of psychoanalysis itself. Freud's identification with Leonardo the artist-scientist, the great man who was ahead of his time in his thinking, is clear. This leads him even to wonder why it was that this all-round Renaissance man who was involved in so many forms of investigation was interested only in external things, not also in 'the investigation of [human] mental life', '*der Erforschung des Seelenlebens der Menschen*'; in his world there was '*für die Psychologie wenig Raum*', 'little room for psychology'.[9]

In Leonardo, Freud constructs the peculiar case of a man whose urge to know is to be understood both as a dangerous instinct that has got

[7] Freud, 'On the Sexual Theories of Children', *SE* ix. 219; 'Über infantile Sexualtheorien', *GW* vii. 181. The German *lahmend*, literally 'laming', suggests Oedipus, whose actual laming had occurred in his infancy and whose solving of the Sphinx's riddle did not provide a finally settling truth for the city of Thebes or for his own life.

[8] Freud, *Leonardo da Vinci and a Memory of his Childhood* (1910), *SE* xi. 75; *Eine Kindheitserinnerung des Leonardo da Vinci*, *GW* viii. 142.

[9] Freud, *Leonardo*, *SE* xi. 76–7; *Eine Kindheitserinnerung*, *GW* viii. 143. The first phrase could more literally be translated as 'the investigation of the spiritual life of men' or 'of the life of the soul in men'. Strachey's capsule 'mental life' is a good example of what Bruno Bettelheim identifies as his tendency to undercut the humanistic connotations of *die Seele* (the soul) in favour of a more scientific language. Freud is not suggesting that Leonardo might have been a modern scientist. See Bettelheim, *Freud and Man's Soul* (1982; New York: Vintage, 1984), esp. 70–8.

out of hand, coming to dominate his existence in a debilitating way, and at the same time as the source of nothing less than an intellectual revolution:

And finally the instinct, which had become overwhelming [*übermachtig*], swept him away until the connection with the demands of his art was severed, so that he discovered the general laws of mechanics and divined the history of the stratification and fossilization of the Arno valley, and until he could enter in large letters in his book the discovery: *Il sole non si move* [The sun does not move].[10]

Leonardo may have shown the relations of sun and earth to be other than they appeared, he may have enlightened the world with a finding that altered the focus of all human knowledge; but the impetus is pathological, a single instinct that has taken over. He discovers new connections in one field, but at the cost of losing the links and the balance in himself.

More than any other text of Freud's, the study of Leonardo treats the instinct for knowledge—curiosity—as though it is on a par with the two primary instincts with which he is concerned at this time, the sexual and the self-preserving: 'When we find that in the picture presented by a person's character a single instinct [*einen einzigen Trieb*] has developed an excessive [*überstark*] strength, as did the craving for knowledge [*die Wißbegierde*] in Leonardo ... '.[11] And this is so even though he also provides one of the most detailed of his descriptions of how this extra instinct arises as a secondary formation, following the thwarting of the child's first sexual question. Because it is presented as a full-blown instinct in its own right, the instinct for knowledge has to suffer a subsequent fate that resembles that of the sexual instinct: at a certain point its childhood freedom has to be curbed because of adverse circumstances and turned in other directions, each of which is more a compromise than a continuation. Let us look at this process in more detail.

THE FIRST FIRST QUESTION

Freud enters into speculation about the peculiarities of Leonardo's situation as a child in order to answer the question of how he became

[10] Freud, *Leonardo*, *SE* xi. 76; *Eine Kindheitserinnerung*, *GW* viii. 143.
[11] Freud, *Leonardo*, *SE* xi. 77; *Eine Kindheitserinnerung*, *GW* viii. 144.

the exceptional man that he was. In doing so, as happens so often in the case studies, he in fact comes to show that the abnormal example is only a strong instance of the normal. The question is where does Leonardo's '*übermachtig*', 'overwhelming' instinct for knowledge come from, and Freud's preliminary answer is to set it alongside the sexual instinct, asserting that the force of both in children is underestimated. He has been describing the way in which what were formerly sexual instinctual forces will end up being directed towards professional activity in adult life:

There seem to be special difficulties in applying these expectations to the case of an over-powerful [*übermachtigen*] instinct for investigation [*Forschertriebes*], since precisely in the case of children there is a reluctance to credit them with either this serious instinct or any noteworthy sexual interests. However, these difficulties are easily overcome. The curiosity [*Wißbegierde*] of small children is manifested in their untiring love of asking questions [*deren unermüdliche Fragenlust*]; this is bewildering to the adult so long as he fails to understand that all these questions are merely circumlocutions and that they cannot come to an end because the child is only trying to make them take the place of a question which he does *not* ask. When he grows bigger and becomes better informed this expression of curiosity [*Wißbegierde*] often comes to a sudden end.[12]

There is something familiar in this combination of endlessness and sudden end in a childhood phenomenon: it is just what happens to the sexual instinct itself. Sexuality and what is here called an 'instinct for investigation'—an enquiring mind—seem destined to meet; they in fact turn out to be inseparable. Freud continues:

Psycho-analytic investigation provides us with a full explanation [*Aufklärung*] by teaching us that many, perhaps most children, or at least the most gifted ones, pass through a period, beginning when they are about three, which may be called the period of *infantile sexual researches* [*Sexualforschung*]. So far as we know, the curiosity [*Wißbegierde*] of children of this age does not awaken spontaneously, but is aroused by the impression made by some important event—by the actual birth of a little brother or sister, or by a fear of it based on external experiences—in which the child perceives a threat to his selfish interests.[13]

Again, the 'threat to his selfish interests', literally 'glimpsed [*erblickt*]' by the child, recalls another, better-known infantile scene, when the boy is confronted by the fact of girls' lack of a penis and infers that

[12] Freud, *Leonardo*, *SE* xi. 78; *Eine Kindheitserinnerung*, *GW* viii. 145.
[13] Freud, *Leonardo*, *SE* xi. 78; *Eine Kindheitserinnerung*, *GW* viii. 145–6.

the castration with which he has been threatened is a real possibility. This scene is elaborated much later in Freud's own researches than the present passage; as we shall see, it forms a crucial element in what I will call the second first question.

It should by now be clear that Freudian curiosity is always, primarily, sexual curiosity—or at least, as with the question of new babies, a curiosity that finds a sexual answer. Freud may hesitate, as we shall see in more detail, about which sexual question comes first—whether it is the origin of babies, or the difference between the sexes, or (a distant third) the obscure problem of '"being married"', '"*Verheiratetsein*"', what exactly it might be that couples do with each other.[14] But ultimately, in a striking reversal of the Genesis story, it is sexuality that precedes and engenders curiosity and knowledge, rather than the other way around. 'Thirst for knowledge [*Wißbegierde*] seems to be inseparable from sexual curiosity [*sexuelle Neugierde*]', Freud says in the 'Little Hans' case.[15] In German the link is verbally more explicit, between the (general) *Wißbegierde*, 'thirst for knowledge' or 'knowledge-longing', and the (specific) '*sexuelle Neugierde*', 'sexual curiosity', sexual longing-for-new. (*Wißbegierde* is also sometimes translated as 'curiosity', as indicated in passages already quoted, in the *Standard Edition*.) Yet it is not just that sexuality spurs the curiosity; ultimately sexuality and curiosity are bound together, emerging as the joint source of the explanatory stories that human beings seek.[16] The urge to know matters more than the knowledge itself, its truth or falsehood.

So far, in the discussion of Leonardo, Freud has described the typical development of curiosity. There is a slight hesitation about its applicability. Although we have moved swiftly from the one great man to 'small children' in general, Freud is not sure whether to go to the opposite extreme and make this a universal. Many? Most? The most gifted? He asks the question but passes on to the sexual connection, which becomes the focus:

> Researches are directed to the question of where babies come from [*woher die Kinder kommen*], exactly as if the child were looking for ways and means to avert so undesired an event [*unerwünschtes Ereignis*]. In this way we have

[14] Freud, 'Sexual Theories', *SE* ix. 222–3; 'Sexualtheorien', *GW* vii. 184.

[15] Freud, *Analysis of a Phobia, SE* x. 9; *Analyse der Phobie, GW* vii. 247.

[16] This is one implication of Jean Laplanche and J.-B. Pontalis's enlightening essay 'Fantasme originaire, fantasmes des origines, origine du fantasme' (1964), trans. as 'Fantasy and the Origins of the Unconscious' in Victor Burgin, James Donald, and Cora Kaplan (eds.), *Formations of Fantasy* (London: Routledge, 1986), 5–34.

been astonished to learn that children refuse to believe the bits of information [*Auskünften*] that are given them—for example that they energetically reject the fable of the stork with its wealth of mythological meaning—, that they date their intellectual independence from this act of disbelief, and that they often feel in serious opposition to adults and in fact never afterwards forgive them for having deceived them here about the true facts of the case.[17]

The starting point is the child's rejection of myth—and interesting mythology at that, 'the fable of the stork with its wealth of mythological meaning [*die mythologisch so sinnreiche Storchfabel*]'. Out with the stories, rich though they may be; the child requires nothing less than 'the truth': 'the true facts of the case' in the passage above translates the straightforward '*die Wahrheit*'. Here we have the same conjunction of tactics and reactions noted in relation to the Clark University lecture, from the year before the Leonardo text. In the initial stage, there are three points of interest. First, research is not spontaneous but triggered by an event. Second, it is not disinterested: the event impinges, or is felt to, upon the child, and that is the reason for starting investigations. Third, the aim of research is not knowledge for its own sake but applied knowledge: to find out how to prevent the occurrence or recurrence of the '*unerwünschtes Ereignis*'. The aim is both negative and self-interested; and at this point the only reason for calling the research sexual has to do with the true answer, of which the child is ignorant.

The second stage comes with children's dissatisfaction at the responses they get. Where first they unquestioningly believed, now they 'refuse to believe [*den Glauben verweigert*]' and 'energetically reject [*energisch abweist*]'. Disbelief is not just a state but a positive 'act [*Akte*]'; it is like a secession from the parents, to whom they are henceforth in 'serious opposition'. This involves both 'intellectual independence [*geistige Selbständigkeit*]' and the more personal motive of revenge for a wrong committed. Knowledge is now understood to be bound up with the possibility of withholding it from another, or dissimulating it by presenting a false version. Belief in the parents is withdrawn not because they are themselves lacking in the truth, but because they have kept it back. These elements are clearly brought together once again in 'On the Sexual Theories of Children':

[F]ar more children than their parents suspect are dissatisfied with this solution and meet it with energetic doubts, which, however, they do not always openly

[17] Freud, *Leonardo*, *SE* xi. 78–9; *Eine Kindheitserinnerung*, *GW* viii. 146.

admit.... It seems to me to follow from a great deal of information I have received that children refuse to believe the stork theory and that from the time of this first deception and rebuff they nourish a distrust of adults and have a suspicion of there being something forbidden which is being withheld from them by the 'grown-ups', and that they consequently hide their further researches under a cloak of secrecy [*mit Geheimnis verhüllen*].[18]

The language of secrecy and disguise is the same as that used in the Clark lecture to describe the cloaking of adult sexuality.

The final part of the passage from *Leonardo* describes the results of children's subsequent researches: 'They investigate along their own lines, divine the baby's presence inside its mother's body, and following the lead of the impulses of their own sexuality [*von den Regungen der eigenen Sexualität geleitet*] form theories of babies originating from eating, of their being born through the bowels, and of the obscure part played by the father.'[19] Here we can see another explanation of children's theories slipping in alongside the primary impetus to find the truth that the parents have not imparted. The young researchers are 'following the lead' of the oral and anal stages of their development, a lead which is both a forward direction and a limitation: it is not yet the whole story. They have rejected the parental mythology and replaced it with their own; neither is *die Wahrheit*.[20]

These two aspects are elaborated further both in 'On the Sexual Theories of Children' and in the 'Little Hans' case, with a slightly different line-up of infantile theories. In the essay Freud makes two supplementary, closely related claims. The first is that each of the mistaken hypotheses does in fact contain 'a fragment of real truth [*ein Stück echter Wahrheit*]';[21] and the second, that there is a specific obstacle to getting at the whole truth, which is children's ignorance, at this stage, of the existence and role of the vagina: of there being a second sex. In the first category, Freud alludes to the fact that 'so many animals' do in fact give birth anally,[22] and describes children's understanding of sexual intercourse, if they chance to witness it, as a violent act. The grain of truth here is the frequent survival in adult sexuality of the sadistic and masochistic trends which dominate during a particular period of

[18] Freud, 'Sexual Theories', *SE* ix. 213–14; 'Sexualtheorien', *GW* vii. 176.

[19] Freud, *Leonardo*, *SE* xi. 79; *Eine Kindheitserinnerung*, *GW* viii. 146.

[20] On the relationship of Freud's theories of children's theory-making to contemporary theories of comparative mythology, see Ch. 1, above.

[21] Freud, 'Sexual Theories', *SE* ix. 215; 'Sexualtheorien', *GW* vii. 177.

[22] Freud, 'Sexual Theories', *SE* ix. 219; 'Sexualtheorien', *GW* vii. 181.

childhood. More locally and realistically, the child may be seeing aspects of a wholly or partly unhappy relationship—'the spectacle [*Schauspiel*] of an unceasing quarrel' carried over into the night, or a mother sexually reluctant because she is afraid of becoming pregnant again.[23] By far the lengthiest account, however, is devoted to the fragment of truth in the assumption attributed to all children that there is only one sex. When small boys—the paradigm here is Little Hans in relation to his baby sister Hanna—see female genitals, they do not see the difference, or see it only as contingent: here is something small that will grow in time. And they are not completely wrong, says Freud, because in evolutionary terms the clitoris really is an undeveloped penis.

Clearly, there is a connection between the one-sex theory and the second of Freud's points, that states: 'his conviction that his mother possessed a penis [*Wiwimacher*] just as he did stood in the way [*stand ... im Wege*] of any solution'.[24] 'On the Sexual Theories of Children' makes the same point with more elaboration: 'at this juncture [the child's] enquiry is broken off in helpless perplexity. For standing in its way [*steht ... im Wege*] is his theory that his mother possesses a penis just as a man does, and the existence of the cavity [*Hohlraumes*] which receives the penis [*Penis*] remains undiscovered by him.'[25] One theory or conviction bars the way to seeing another, but this very theory is naturalized in the image of the all-pervasive penis blocking off other ways of imagining the female sex. For the vagina appears only as complementary, a space which 'receives [*aufnimmt*] the penis'. It is not, for instance, seen as the place from which babies first emerge.

THE SECOND FIRST QUESTION

In the 'Sexual Theories' essay, Freud states very clearly that 'the child now comes to be occupied with the first, grand problem of life [*dem ersten, großartigen Problem des Lebens*] and asks himself the question: "*Where do babies come from?*" '.[26] But even when the issue of the origin

[23] Freud, 'Sexual Theories', *SE* ix. 221–2; 'Sexualtheorien', *GW* vii. 183.

[24] Freud, *Analysis of a Phobia*, *SE* x. 135; *Analyse der Phobie*, *GW* vii. 366. Freud uses *Wiwimacher*, not the technical *Penis*, adopting Little Hans's own vocabulary; though he doesn't here, Strachey usually makes the distinction by translating the colloquial *Wiwimacher*—'weeweemaker'—as 'widdler'.

[25] Freud, 'Sexual Theories', *SE* ix. 218; 'Sexualtheorien', *GW* vii. 180.

[26] Freud, 'Sexual Theories', *SE* ix. 212; 'Sexualtheorien', *GW* vii. 175.

of babies is ostensibly the one to start researches going, it is apparent that more and more it is taken over, in Freud's account, by the related question of the difference between the sexes. Following the trajectory of his own theories, we can see that this parallels or resumes the pattern by which the castration complex comes to occupy the foreground, taking precedence over the Oedipal triangle. The son whose place is challenged by the arrival of a new sibling gives way to the boy whose masculinity is threatened by the existence of femininity.

In Freud's theories of children's theories, the growing dominance of the sexual difference question is signalled expressly in a footnote to an essay of the mid-1920s, 'Some Psychical Consequences of the Anatomical Distinction between the Sexes'.[27] Appearing when and where it does, the changeover evidently has something to do with the conscious turn of attention to girls' sexual understanding, and its possible differences from that of boys. Just as psychoanalytic research is coming to focus on the differences between the sexes, so it finds that children themselves are interested in this very question before any other. In this area, the conditions of research for children turn out to be different from those that surrounded the first first question, that of the origin of babies. These differences can be divided into three categories, all of which are themselves closely connected to the question of sexual difference. There is first the reason for undertaking the research; second, the outcome as it affects the disposition of the researcher; and third, the kind of knowledge that the research produces. Let us take these one by one.

With the question of where babies come from, as we have seen, there is an external reason for undertaking research, namely the arrival or possibility of another child. Where do they come from and, concomitantly, how can they be prevented from turning up in the first place? As we have seen, Freud believes that 'the curiosity of children of this age does not awaken spontaneously [*nicht spontan ... geweckt*]'.[28] With the second question, on the other hand, early research does come naturally, and in boys it is penis-led:

This part of the body, which is easily excitable, prone to changes and so rich in sensations, occupies the boy's interest to a high degree and is constantly setting

[27] Freud, 'Some Psychical Consequences of the Anatomical Distinction between the Sexes' (1925), *SE* xix. 252; 'Einige psychische Folgen des anatomischen Geschlechtsunterschieds', *GW* xiv. 24. The footnote will be discussed below.

[28] Freud, *Leonardo*, *SE* xi. 78; *Eine Kindheitserinnerung*, *GW* viii. 145–6.

new tasks to his instinct for research [*Forschertrieb*]. ... The driving force which this male portion of the body will develop later at puberty expresses itself at this period of life mainly as an urge to investigate [*Forschungsdrang*], as sexual curiosity [*sexuelle Neugierde*].[29]

This time we have an unqualified 'instinct for research' and a curiosity that is unrelated to external events and arises from a biological fact of sexuality.

The essay in which this passage occurs, 'The Infantile Genital Organization' (1923), is generally regarded as a turning point in Freud's own theory because it introduces the concept of the phallic phase, paving the way for the central significance of castration for both sexes. But the passage above, applying to boys, is preceded by an apology for only being able to describe the boy's situation, since 'the corresponding processes in the little girl are not known to us.'[30] Ignorance of girls is now a separate issue.[31] As a barrier for the researcher to full knowledge into children's sexuality it figures just like the child's own ignorance of the vagina in the first account of sexual researches: knowledge of girls is marked in its absence, just like knowledge of the vagina was before. This recognized lacuna then opens up the way for the discussions of differences in girls' development that follow in the next few years, beginning in 1924 and 1925 with 'The Dissolution of the Oedipus Complex' and 'Some Psychical Consequences of the Anatomical Distinction between the Sexes', through to 'Female Sexuality' and the lecture 'Femininity' in the early 1930s, where the girl's difference has become the principal subject of investigation.

In the first account, boys' (and possibly girls') researches into the origin of babies always end in failure from a combination of external and internal factors: lack of evidence (the unknown difference of the sexes) and lack of capacity (the boy's sexual organization is not yet ready for him to imagine the truth). This results, Freud says, in a debilitating

[29] Freud, 'The Infantile Genital Organization' (1923), *SE* xix. 142–3; 'Die infantile Genitalorganisation', *GW* xiii. 295.

[30] Freud, 'The Infantile Genital Organization', *SE* xix. 142; 'Die infantile Genitalorganisation', *GW* xiii. 295.

[31] As early as 1908, however, in 'On the Sexual Theories of Children', the issue was noted: 'In consequence of unfavourable circumstances, both of an external and an internal nature, the following observations apply chiefly to the sexual development of one sex only—that is, of males' (*SE* ix. 211; 'Sexualtheorien', *GW* vii. 173). The terms are frustratingly precise and yet unelaborated. What is the reference of the 'external' and 'internal' conditions, and what is the nature of the inauspiciousness—*Ungunst*—of these circumstances? Nothing more is said on the point.

attitude of mind which never goes away: 'The impression caused by this failure in the first attempt at intellectual independence [*intellektueller Selbständigkeit*] appears to be of a lasting and deeply depressing [*tief deprimierender*] kind'.[32] Or again, in a statement partly quoted already: 'This brooding and doubting [*Grübeln und Zweifeln*] ... becomes the prototype of all later intellectual work directed towards the solution of problems, and the first failure has a crippling effect on the child's whole future.'[33] In this first scenario, the boy winds up depressed and unfit for life. In the second version, though, when the first question, that of sexual difference, is the very one that blocks the solution in the first version, the results, if far from happy, are not quite so dark. Doubt and delay are two elements from the first sequence that maintain their role, but in very different sequences. Doubt or outright disbelief initially represented a loss of trust in parental honesty, the breakaway independent research fostered by the 'energetic rejection' of the stork myth as patently fabricated. The 'brooding and doubting' that remain to haunt the unsuccessful researcher make him sound like a nineteenth-century clergyman, afflicted with nebulous but insoluble 'doubts' about a faith he can neither take on trust any more, nor replace with a compelling confidence of his own.

In the later version, doubt derives from the possibility of there being fellow human creatures who lack a penis. It is once again, but now more directly, related to a threat to the self. The new baby threatened the child's special position vis-à-vis his parents; the threat of castration is directed to what now for the first time emerges as the boy's masculinity, in urgent distinction from the femininity against which it is defended. In every account Freud gives of boys' realization of the difference, the process is a slow one. Like a soundtrack that has to be linked to the appropriate footage, the verbal threat and the visual perception must be brought together before the new conviction clicks into place. Some of Freud's descriptions show doubt and disbelief arising from the first sight of the girl's different genitals, and clarified in the light of an adult's mock threat of castration as a punishment; most often, the threat is itself the first stage, unheeded until connection is made with the same sight. For instance:

[T]o begin with the boy does not believe in the threat or obey it in the least [*keinen Glauben und keinen Gehorsam*]. ... The observation which finally breaks

32 Freud, *Leonardo*, *SE* xi. 79; *Eine Kindheitserinnerung*, *GW* viii. 146.

33 Freud, 'Sexual Theories', *SE* ix. 219; 'Sexualtheorien', *GW* vii. 181.

down his unbelief [*den Unglauben ... endlich bricht*] is the sight of the female genitals. Sooner or later the child, who is so proud of his possession of a penis, has a view of the genital region of a little girl, and cannot help being convinced of the absence of a penis in a creature who is so like himself.[34]

This breaking down of unbelief, leading to inescapable conviction, tells the reverse story from that of the first first question. Here we have the making of a reluctant convert; there it was a reluctant rebel losing his (or her) faith by recognizing a fabricated story for what it is. The combination here of complete scepticism and rebelliousness (literally, 'no belief and no obedience') with forced acceptance ('cannot help being convinced') also repeats the Clark lecture account of the making of psychoanalytic believers: those who 'began by completely disbelieving' Freud's claim about the significance of sexuality were eventually 'compelled ... to accept it' in the light of 'their own analytic experience'.

Less often, the delay is said to occur in the other sequence, between observation (not taken seriously) and threat (which gives it meaning). In 1924, for instance:

It is not until later, when some threat of castration has obtained a hold upon him, that the observation [of a girl's genital region] becomes important [*bedeutungsvoll*] to him: if he then recollects or repeats it, it arouses a terrible storm of emotion [*einen fürchterlichen Affektsturm*] in him and forces him to believe in the reality of the threat which he has hitherto laughed at.[35]

Prior to this essay, as in 'The Infantile Genital Organization' of the previous year, there is a kind of slow-motion skittle effect in the realization. Gradually, more and more women are understood to lack penises after all until finally, when the mother has fallen along with all the rest, it has to be recognized that all women are without one, that to be a woman is to be without a penis, no more and no less.[36] After this, an accommodation is made to the new knowledge which enables the boy to pass definitively from childhood to manhood in a fairly clear-cut way: 'In his case it is the discovery of the possibility of

[34] Freud, 'The Dissolution of the Oedipus Complex', *SE* xix. 175–6; 'Der Untergang des Ödipuskomplexes', *GW* xiii. 397–8.

[35] Freud, 'Some Psychical Consequences', *SE* xix. 252; 'Einige psychischen Folgen', *GW* xiv. 23–4.

[36] Freud, 'The Infantile Genital Organization', *SE* xix. 144–5; 'Die infantile Genitalorganisation', *GW* xiii. 296–7. In this passage the quest for the origin of babies is clearly subsequent to the investigation of the problem of having or not having a penis.

castration, as proved by the sight of the female genitals, which forces on him the transformation of his Oedipus complex, and which leads to the creation of his super-ego and thus initiates all the processes that are designed to make the individual find a place in the cultural community.'[37] The 'proof' compels ('*erzwingt*', 'forces on him') certain changes, but those changes are smooth and sure, neatly resituating the Oedipal prince as one young man among others, out of the family and into the *Kulturgemeinschaft* or 'cultural community'. Failure and depression have gone from the account; instead, this is a modestly happy ending, a new beginning.

The girl's castration story, of course, is rather different. Now it is for her, not for the boy (or the child in general), that there is no settled conclusion, only a set of loose ends and surreal equivalences. Babies remain in her picture (while they have disappeared from the boy's), but strangely transformed. No longer potential rivals whose origins must be sought, they have turned into belated substitutes for unobtainable penises. Leaving aside for the moment the epistemological framework here, it is notable that the girl's pathway to this equivocal knowledge occurs according to a temporal pattern that sharply contrasts with the boy's.[38] The boy takes his time, doubting and delaying, but ultimately comes to terms with it; it provides the means for him to move out into the wider, extra-familial world. The girl sees and understands instantly, without a doubt; but she never really moves on, remaining caught up in the nexus of futile reactions into which castration casts her. Essentially, where the boy (initially) doubts, the girl (subsequently) 'clings' desperately to the impossible hope of one day acquiring what she in fact can never get.[39] She has a moment of illumination, but it is wholly negative:

> A little girl behaves differently. She makes her judgement and her decision in a flash [*im Nu*]. She has seen it and knows that she is without it and wants to have it. [*Sie hat es gesehen, weiß, daß sie es nicht hat, und will es haben.*][40]

[37] Freud, 'Female Sexuality' (1931), *SE* xxi. 229; 'Die weibliche Sexualität', *GW* xiv. 521.

[38] See Toril Moi's trenchant analysis of the different logics ascribed to boys and girls in Freud's account of these developments, 'Representation of Patriarchy: Sexuality and Epistemology in Freud's Dora', in Charles Bernheimer and Claire Kahane (eds.), *In Dora's Case* (London: Virago, 1985), 181–99.

[39] On the girl's hopeless clinging to hope in these essays, see further Ch. 6, below.

[40] Freud, 'Some Psychical Consequences', *SE* xix. 252; 'Einige psychische Folgen', *GW* xiv. 24.

These short declarative clauses stand out in a single paragraph, further exposing the peculiarity of this critical moment of development so unlike others in Freud. This change in the girl's understanding is almost magically immediate, with no doubt or deferral intervening between the perception, the knowledge, and the desire—seen, knows, wants, in Freud's equally hurried shorthand. But it is the whole life afterwards which then slows down almost to the point of immobility. The boy eventually realizes an unwelcome fact whose acceptance can then set him up along new paths in a new world. The girl, even if she does end up in the normal social role of wife and mother, never finally accepts: 'She acknowledges the fact of her castration, and with it, too, the superiority of the male and her own inferiority; but she rebels [*sträubt sich*] against this unwelcome state of affairs. From this divided attitude three lines of development open up.'[41]

It is in fact at the end of the staccato sudden-death paragraph that Freud adds the footnote in which he declares he has changed his mind about children's first research question. Here it is:

This is an opportunity for correcting a statement which I made many years ago. I believed [*ich meinte*] that the sexual interest of children, unlike that of pubescents, was aroused, not by the difference between the sexes [*Geschlechtsunterschied*], but by the problem of where babies come from. We now see that, at all events with girls, this is certainly not the case. With boys it may no doubt happen sometimes one way and sometimes the other; or with both sexes chance experiences may determine the event.[42]

'I believed ... we now see': here is another minor conversion.[43] And how ironic that this should be the one place where the girl's case becomes paradigmatic, while boys are indeterminately one way or the other. (As indeed Freud is here himself, for having said that it 'is certainly not' true that the baby-origin problem is first for girls, he ends by saying that perhaps for both sexes it may be either way round. The only certainty seems to be that the baby question has lost its assumed priority, and probably its actual priority in most instances.) There is also the characteristic masculine situation of deferred understanding,

41 Freud, 'Female Sexuality', *SE* xxi. 229; 'Die Weiblichkeit', *GW* xiv. 522.

42 Freud, 'Some Psychical Consequences', *SE* xix. 252; 'Einige psychische Folgen', *GW* xiv. 24.

43 In the German, Freud simply states a new fact: '*Das trifft also wenigstens für das Mädchen gewiß nicht zu*'; 'we now see that' is an added clarification.

here from 'many years ago', in the early years of psychoanalysis, to the present.[44]

The reversal of babies and sexual difference has further implications, which take us to the third concern in relation to boys' and girls' 'enlightenments': the type of knowledge that is acquired. With the question of where babies come from, the false answer—the stork 'myth'—is simply false: storks don't bring babies. One accurate answer to the question is presumed to be: babies come from inside mothers. Children like Little Hans are said to have worked this out quite well for themselves: 'the change which takes place in the mother during pregnancy does not escape the child's sharp eyes [*die Graviditätsveränderung der Mutter den scharfen Augen des Kindes nicht entgeht*]'.[45] Here a perception of a growing body corresponds to a truth and a kind of solution to the question: babies do come from mothers, and what makes mothers mothers is that they grow bigger with babies inside them. The positive distinction of the larger size is in this instance on the female side.

The sharp-eyed researchers of the first first question are thwarted, as we have heard—first, by the grown-ups' counter-story, and second, by their ignorance of an invisible origin further back along the line, the existence of the vagina, sometimes associated with boys' assumption that all humans have a penis. The sexual difference question is already implied by the hypothesis that the solution for the baby question is not enough: children are supposed to sense that there is something more to be known which they can't yet imagine, and that is where the unknown vagina enters the frame in its significant absence. Whence the second first question and the second set of solutions, this time sexually differentiated just as the question itself is concerned with sexual difference. And now, what both sexes in their diverging ways perceive, eventually or immediately, is not a fact of nature but its meaning: not

[44] And 'many years ago', in 'The Sexual Enlightenment of Children' (1907), he had also on one occasion suggested the hypothesis now being put forward; there 'The second great [*große*] problem which exercises a child's mind—only at a somewhat later age, no doubt—is the question of the origin of babies' (*SE* ix. 135; 'Zur sexuellen Aufklärung der Kinder', *GW* vii. 24). Two sentences later, however, the priority of the question of the origin of babies appears to be strongly affirmed after all, and given an urgency that the sexual difference question lacks at this stage for both Freud and the child: 'Es ist dies die älteste und die brennendste Frage der jungen Menschheit': 'It is the oldest and most burning question that confronts immature humanity.' And the matter described in the previous passage is not the threatening issue that female difference will become in the later theory; it shows 'Little Hans' happily assuming or asking about the 'widdlers' of cows or mothers—and not being contradicted.

[45] Freud, 'Sexual Theories', *SE* ix. 214; 'Sexualtheorien', *GW* vii. 176.

(changing) anatomy but their destiny as men and women in the 'cultural community'. Enlightenment is not, this time, a perception of the truth like Leonardo's precocious hypothesis that 'The sun does not move.' From that point of view sexual difference as castration is no better than the fable of the stork: it is a collective mythology.

Yet this realization is not in itself a cause for either protest or resignation. Freud does not ultimately claim castration is a fact of nature; instead, as Laplanche and Pontalis suggested, children's early questions and solutions can be seen as their initiation into the world of human meanings and myths, where empirical truth has no priority. But we may speculate as to whether, or how much, the earth has moved since Freud's day, now that Little Hans's descendants would be unlikely to hear the stork story other than as a fairy tale and now that the imagined destinies of men and women are far less clearly differentiated than they were then. The Freudian child's researches were ultimately marked by either depression and failure or negative illumination, the reluctant observer finally forced to believe. And so, perhaps, we can be curious about possible different outcomes—other forms of enlightenment—for twenty-first-century children, wherever they may come from.

6

The Cronus Complex: Psychoanalytic Myths of the Future for Boys and Girls

HOPE, PROMISE, THREATEN, AND SWEAR

Students of Greek and Latin used to be taught that special rules applied when composing sentences that involved the verbs 'hope, promise, threaten, and swear'. The quartet is memorably nonsensical, like a stupid jingle you can't get out of your head; at the same time it seems to suggest a kind of incantatory quality: witches brewing a mixed fate. For what the verbs have minimally in common is their reference to the future—or rather, their constructions, different in each instance, of a particular orientation towards the future.[1] 'Swear' has the sense of an oath; it pairs with the 'promise' from which it is separated in the set-piece order of words. 'Hope' and 'threaten' are then left to make a diametrical semantic contrast between two ways of imagining or imposing future possibilities: positive and negative. All four verbs entail the presence of a second verb: 'I promise *to do* that'; 'I hope he *will*'; 'They vowed *to protect* him', and so on.

In Freud the difference of the sexes can be defined through their characteristic orientations towards the future, and 'hope, promise, threaten, and swear' are close to the bone. For it is versions of these verbs that supply the templates for the boys and girls of the future. They open up or rule out certain possibilities, according to their syntactical and semantic nature. In particular, a contrast between hopes and threats is fundamental; it is the structuring distinction that gives each sex its typical character. Femininity *hopes* (to be masculine). Masculinity *is*

[1] See e.g. William W. Goodwin, *A Greek Grammar* (2nd edn. 1894; London: Macmillan, 1974), 275: 'Verbs of *hoping, expecting, promising, swearing*, and a few others, form an intermediate class between verbs which take the infinitive in indirect discourse and those which do not; and though they regularly have the future infinitive, the present and aorist are allowed.'

threatened (with the loss of masculinity). Despite appearances, the mode if not the mood of the future is negative in both cases, not just that of being threatened; indeed it is more, not less so for girls. This is because the hoping sex hopes in vain.

The story that leads, in Freud, to sexual separation has been frequently retold. For both boys and girls, a formative, traumatic moment occurs when they realize the meaning of sexual difference in relation to the presence or absence of a penis. Immediately prior to that point, the 'phallic' phase does not distinguish between the value of the sexes. The 'discovery' or 'recognition' (both words are used) of castration—that the boy has something the girl does not, or that the girl lacks what the boy has—does away for ever with this imagined homogeneity. From now on, two sexes will be marked out by their dissymmetrical relationships to the phenomenon of castration. One hopes to remedy it as something that has happened to her; the other is threatened by the possibility that it could happen to him, as it visibly has to her. This mood, grammatical and emotional, then governs their different futures; for her in particular it becomes what can only be called a life-sentence—one that Freud repeats many times in the course of his writings on female sexuality:

When the little girl discovers her own deficiency [*Defekt*], from seeing a male genital, it is only with hesitation and reluctance that she accepts the unwelcome [*unerwünschte*] knowledge. As we have seen, she *clings* obstinately to the *expectation* of one day having a genital of the same kind too, and her *wish* for it survives long after her *hope* has expired.[2]

The *hope* of some day obtaining a penis in spite of everything and so of becoming like a man may persist to an incredibly [*unwahrscheinlich*] late age and may become a motive for strange and otherwise unaccountable actions.[3]

The second line leads her to *cling* with defiant self-assertiveness to her *threatened* masculinity. To an incredibly [*unglaublich*] late age she *clings to the hope* of getting a penis some time. That *hope* becomes her life's aim.[4]

The girl's *recognition* of the fact of her being without a penis does not by any means imply that she submits to the fact easily. On the contrary, she continues

[2] Freud, 'Female Sexuality' (1931), *SE* xxi. 233; 'Über die weibliche Sexualität', *GW* xiv. 526.

[3] Freud, 'Some Psychical Consequences of the Anatomical Distinction between the Sexes' (1925), *SE* xix. 253; 'Einige psychische Folgen des anatomischen Geschlechtsunterschieds', *GW* xiv. 24.

[4] Freud, 'Female Sexuality', *SE* xxi. 229–30; 'Über die weibliche Sexualität', *GW* xiv. 522.

to *hold on* for a long time to the *wish* to get something like it herself and she believes in that possibility for improbably [*unwahrscheinlich*] long years. ... The wish to get the longed-for penis eventually in spite of everything may contribute to the motives that drive a mature woman to analysis.[5]

The girl appears as the passive protagonist in a distorted fairy tale—one in which wishes, hopes, and tenacity of purpose are not just thwarted, but presented as impossible of fulfilment right from the start. The story is not about a wish that comes true. Instead it begins in mid-wishing with a negative fulfilment, and it tails off without an end into an indefinite future of wishing for what the unwished-for knowledge has rendered unobtainable, unwishable. At the beginning, she gets something defined as that which she does not wish for, the 'unwelcome'—*unerwünschte*, literally 'unwished for'—knowledge. She clings and clings to the hope or wish for what she cannot have; the same verb, *festhalten*—hold tight, hold fast—renders 'cling' all three times as well as 'hold on' in the passages above. She wishes against all the odds that 'in spite of everything [*doch noch einmal*], 'one day [*einmal*]', 'some day ... in spite of everything [*doch noch einmal*]', 'some time [*noch einmal*]', 'eventually [*endlich*]', her penis will come. Continuing in this way 'to an incredibly late age', or for 'improbably long years'—unhappily ever after—the girl lives out a tale that like all fairy tales, good and bad, is unbelievable and unlikely; it does not seem to involve a real, or realistic life. The princess simply grows old in her hopeless hoping and impossible wishing; hope and wish take her place as the active subjects: 'That hope [*Hoffnung*] becomes her life's aim [*Lebenszweck*]'; 'her wish for it survives long after her hope has expired [*der Wunsch danach überlebt die Hoffnung noch um lange Zeit*]'.

This post-castrational story of a woman's life evokes all kinds of features that seem to imply particular kinds of narrative outcome, none of which is actually fulfilled. There are hopes and wishes but no happy ending on the horizon; there are unlikely phenomena leading to 'strange and otherwise unaccountable actions', but no disaster or final revelation ensues. Nothing really happens as life passes the woman by.[6] In *Totem and Taboo* Freud refers to 'the uneventfulness of her emotional life [*die*

[5] Freud, Lecture XXIII, 'Femininity', *New Introductory Lectures on Psycho-Analysis* (1933), *SE* xxii. 125; 'Die Weiblichkeit', *Neue Folge der Vorlesungen zur Einführung in die Psychoanalyse*, *GW* xv. 134.

[6] In Sophocles' *Electra* (ll. 185–6), the heroine laments that she is growing old in a hopeless existence—'most of my life has now left me behind, a life without hope', '*eme men ho polus apoleloipen êdê* | *biotos anelpistos*'. She goes on to name a husband

Ereignislosigkeit in ihrem Gefühlsleben]'.[7] Years later in the development of psychoanalysis, and years earlier in the development of the little girl, this extended eventlessness would acquire a partial counterpart in the pre-Oedipal period of exclusive attachment to the mother, stressed for the first time in the 1931 essay 'Female Sexuality'. This is another time in the girl's life that seems to go on for ever, without significant changes taking place.

THE GIRL'S TRAGEDY

But between the two periods of indeterminacy, the girl is briefly and precipitately at the centre of a dramatic action, what is nothing less than the end-point of a tragedy. The traumatic 'discovery' of her castration involves the fulfilment of a negative destiny; in true Aristotelian style, there is an *anagnôrisis* and a *peripeteia*: recognition and complete reversal. The girl's pride is revealed retrospectively as having been the hubris of a mistakenly confident masculinity on the part of one who was never going to be a hero at all. Castration is her sudden downfall, in wretched realization of a non-future she did not know to be hers.

Unlike the blur of the post-castrational non-story, the tragedy of the girl's castration involves one sharply telescoped event, her seeing herself as lacking. Tragic ideas of fall, destiny, recognition, knowledge, and discovery are regularly associated with this moment as Freud recounts it. They all occur, for instance, in the first passage of the four quoted above, in which 'the little girl discovers her own deficiency', and reluctantly 'accepts the unwelcome knowledge'. What the girl 'learns' (*erfahren* is the discovery verb here) is not in question; it is knowledge. This applies equally to 'the girl's recognition [*anerkennt*] of the fact of her being without a penis',[8] inseparable from the drop in status that accompanies it: 'She acknowledges [*anerkennt*] the fact of her castration and with it, too, the superiority of the male and her own inferiority.'[9] The event is sometimes grandly marked:

> a momentous discovery [*Entdeckung*] which little girls are *destined* [*beschieden*] to make. They notice the penis of a brother or playmate, strikingly visible and

and children as the two elements that would have given life hope. On tragic female hopelessness, see further Ch. 8, pp. 199–200, below.

[7] Freud, *Totem and Taboo* (1913), *SE* xiii. 15; *Totem und Tabu*, *GW* ix. 22.

[8] Freud, 'Femininity', *SE* xxii. 125; 'Die Weiblichkeit', *GW* xv. 134.

[9] Freud, 'Female Sexuality', *SE* xxi. 229; 'Über weibliche Sexualität', *GW* xiv. 522.

of large proportions, at once recognize [*erkennt*] it as the superior counterpart of their own small and inconspicuous organ, and from that time forward fall a victim [*verfallen*] to envy for the penis.[10]

The discovery [*Entdeckung*] of her castration is a turning-point [*Wendepunkt*] in a girl's growth.[11]

But though this critical moment stands out as a tragic event, it is not really an ending or denouement. It does not resolve a pre-existing conflict; instead it creates an indefinitely prolonged and futile struggle for the future. It is as a result of her unfortunate 'discovery' that—and Freud uses the phrase more than once—the girl will 'fall a victim to' penis envy.[12] The verb *verfallen* carries an idea of addiction as well as decline: unheroically, she 'sinks into' penis envy. In classic Greek tragedy, the recognition typically makes explicit to the characters some fact or action of their past, or some aspect of their identity of which up till then they were unaware. Oedipus, in Aristotle's paradigmatic example, is forced to see that he is Jocasta's son and Laius' murderer. That recognition is brought about wholly by the force of words. In other cases, regarded with suspicion by Aristotle, the recognition involves tangible objects: in Euripides' *Ion*, for instance, the visible presence of the identifiable accoutrements of the baby abandoned at birth. The effect of a recognition need not be, as it is in *Oedipus*, destructive. In the *Ion* it produces what is primarily a happy reunion of mother and son, and in all the plays about Electra and Orestes, brother and sister are overjoyed to find one another again at last.[13] In Freud's tragic story, however, the recognition of sexual difference is unequivocally negative; brothers and sisters assuredly do not like what they see in each other. For girls, this recognition does not finish a conflict but starts one: penis envy is a protest, a rebellion, against what is simultaneously 'recognized' as true. All is changed. All that is left is a contradictory future: the tension of a wish that arises out of its being ruled out.

This leads to two further points about recognitions and expectations. Female hopes and hopelessness are a constant theme of Greek tragedy,

[10] Freud, 'Some Psychical Consequences', *SE* xix. 252; 'Einige psychische Folgen', *GW* xiv. 23.

[11] Freud, 'Femininity', *SE* xxii. 126; 'Die Weiblichkeit', *GW* xv. 135.

[12] As well as in the passage quoted above, the verb occurs in this context in Freud, 'Femininity', *SE* xxii. 125; 'Die Weiblichkeit', *GW* xv. 133–4.

[13] On the complexities of the *Ion* recognition, see Ch. 8, below. Recognition scenes between the long-separated Electra and Orestes occur in Aeschylus' *Libation Bearers*, Sophocles' *Electra*, and Euripides' *Electra*; in Euripides' *Orestes*, which is also about them, the recognition is in the past.

and most often in relation to children—losing them to war or sacrifice, or not being able to have them at all. Children and childlessness are not, however, a central concern for Freud, perhaps because women's desire for maternity is not a given in his theory.[14] In Freud's own thinking, the sequence of a tragic recognition (by a woman) followed by the creation of an unconscious conflict, rather than by a resolution, goes back to the *Studies on Hysteria*. In the case of Fräulein Elisabeth von R., Freud postulates a moment when she did realize her illicit love for her sister's husband:

[O]n certain occasions, though only for the moment [*flüchtig*], the patient recognized her love for her brother-in-law consciously. As an example of this we may recall the moment when she was standing by her sister's bed and the thought flashed through her mind [*der Gedanke durch den Kopf fuhr*]: 'Now he is free and you can be his wife'.[15]

The recognition is both instantaneous and fleeting, *flüchtig*; it is no sooner conscious than it is rejected as unacceptable. These are Elisabeth's moral strictures; but for the general psychoanalytic girl of Freud's later writings on femininity, there is no such personal or ethical contingency in the 'not a boy' realization. That's that.

THE BOY'S *BILDUNGSROMAN*

The Freudian girl is thus caught up in the end of a tragedy that is followed by fragments of an unresolved fairy tale. In the boy's case, though the story likewise centres on the same decisive 'turning-point' of seeing the girl as castrated, the sequence of events and the genres in which they take place are very different. Being under threat provokes a radical change; instead of being condemned to 'cling' to previous attachments, the boy is able to leave the mythical sphere of family and childhood and move on out into a wider, modern world. For girls, it is the recognition of castration that pushes them into the Oedipal situation. In search of the penis, they turn from the mother to the father; from this no subsequent life-changing event will ever definitively release them. For boys the possibility of castration—the existence of defective

[14] On childlessness in tragedy, see further Ch. 8, below. Two of Euripides' plays, *Iphigenia in Aulis* and *Hecuba*, focus their protests against the injustices of war on a mother's rage at the required sacrifice of a beloved daughter.

[15] Freud, *Studies on Hysteria* (1895), *SE* ii. 167; *Studien über Hysterie*, *GW* i. 234.

'girls'—is just as traumatic a realization as it is for girls, but it resolves, rather than instigating, the Oedipus complex: in deference to the threat they give up their erotic wishes in relation to the loved mother and their rivalry with the father.

Freud stresses the sharpness and neatness of the boy's Oedipal situation as a point of distinction between the sexes. In several ways, his is a much more classic tragedy than the girl's. First, there is a clear conflict that arises from the realization of the possibility of castration: 'If the satisfaction of love in the field of the Oedipus complex is to cost the child his penis [through the threatened punishment of castration], a *conflict* [*Konflikt*] is bound to arise.'[16] This conflict is seconded by the force of the passionate love triangle:

> It is only in the male child that we find the fateful combination [*schicksalhafte Beziehung*] of love for the one parent and simultaneous hatred for the other as a rival. In his case it is the discovery [*Entdeckung*] of the possibility of castration, as proved by the sight of the female genitals, which forces on him the transformation [*Umbildung*] of his Oedipus complex, and which leads to the creation of his super-ego and thus initiates all the processes that are designed to make the individual find a place in the cultural community [*Kulturgemeinschaft*].[17]

The characters of this drama are clearly differentiated according to the motives and emotions that structure the conflict. Love and hate and the disposition of roles produce the 'fateful combination' that can be identified as such. There is a radical and forced upheaval (*Umbildung*). A hero is brought down to a human level.

This passage also brings out the teleological and reformulating aspects of the boy's post-Oedipal development: 'all the processes that are designed to ...'. In the German, the aspects of purpose and placement come out more strongly. The processes directly 'aim [*abzielen*]'. Finding a place in the cultural community is '*Einreihung*': the man is not merely put somewhere, but is subject to a 'classification' in which his individuality is irrelevant. It is a movement from uniqueness and exclusivity to equality and the sharing of 'community': a social revolution following a shake-up of the existing autocratic regime. 'His Majesty the Baby', in Freud's immortal characterization of infantile omnipotence, was the

[16] Freud, 'The Dissolution of the Oedipus Complex' (1924), *SE* xix. 176; 'Der Untergang des Ödipuscomplexes', *GW* xiii. 398.

[17] Freud, 'Female Sexuality', *SE* xxi. 229; 'Über die weibliche Sexualität', *GW* xiv. 521; on this passage see also Ch. 5, above, pp. 141–2.

centre of his kingdom and the invulnerable source of royal commands and wishes.[18] He has to give up his unique position and give way to a community of citizens in which each person, himself among them, has a place. The boy is from now on involved in a very different kind of subjective universe from the one that sustained his Oedipal wishes—one in which there are contracts and conditions, promises and oaths.[19]

Emotionally, the same motive forces are present for both sexes but they too are reversed in the temporal order, contributing to the very different stories. The boy starts off, Oedipally, in a situation of 'hopeless longing [*hoffnungslosen Neigung*]'[20] in relation to his mother, but he gets away from it; reversing the order, this state of longing is where the girl arrives as she belatedly enters her own version of the Oedipus complex after the traumatic recognition of her castration. Then the girl too is subject to threats of various kinds, but these are presented as being of a lesser order than those that apply to the boy: they do not have the same determining force. The girl's 'threatened masculinity [*bedrohten Männlichkeit*]'[21] appears at the point at which she has just found out that she is without masculinity in any case: when the difference of masculine and feminine has just arisen, for the first time giving masculinity, for both sexes, the quality of threatenedness. In boys, crucially, the threat is combined with fear. But the girl has nothing to lose and hence nothing to fear, so again the threat appears as relatively small:

The fear of castration being thus excluded in the little girl, a powerful motive also drops out for the setting-up of a super-ego and for the breaking-off of the

[18] Freud, 'On Narcissism: An Introduction', *SE* xiv. 91; 'Zur Einführung des Narzißmus', *GW* x. 157. The phrase 'His Majesty the Baby' is in English in Freud's text; in a footnote Strachey suggests that Freud may have been familiar with a recent English painting of that title, showing the London traffic held up by policemen to allow a pram and nursery-maid to cross the road. Freud's own point is not about the public deference and nanny responsibility shown in such a scene, but about parents, who, he says, transfer their own grandiose ambitions onto their baby: 'Parental love, which is so moving and at bottom so childish, is nothing but the parents' narcissism born again [*der wiedergeborene Narzißmus der Eltern*]' (*SE* xiv. 91; *GW* x. 158). If Freud is alluding to the picture, then perhaps he is suggesting the complicity of the wider world in the fantasies of the (absent) parents.

[19] The 'Family Romances' scenario discussed in Ch. 5, p. 130 n. 6, is a little different, in that the child is not himself the prince, but must gain his freedom from parents initially regarded as godlike, 'the sole authority and the source of all belief' (*SE* ix. 237; 'Der Familienroman der Neurotiker', *GW* vii. 227). What the two situations have in common, however, is a clear move away from a monarchical and mythical world, to one of relative independence and rationality.

[20] Freud, 'Dissolution', *SE* xix. 173; 'Der Untergang', *GW* xiii. 395.

[21] Freud, 'Female Sexuality', *SE* xxi. 229; 'Über die weibliche Sexualität', *GW* xiv. 522.

infantile genital organization. In her, far more than in the boy, these changes seem to be the result of upbringing and of intimidation from outside which threatens her with a loss of love.[22]

There is no big story, and no elementary emotions: 'a powerful motive ... drops out [*entfällt*]', is missing from the plot. You cannot have a proper tragedy without the force of fear or dread (Aristotle's *phobos*). As a threat, 'loss of love' is much vaguer than castration. The girl's Oedipal situation, implicitly, lacks the sharp outline and hence the certainty of a 'fateful combination' that will bring about the *Umbildung*, an unbuilding followed by reconstruction, to which the boy is subject. Thus during the early phase of her attachment to her mother, the girl's father does represent 'a troublesome rival', '*ein lästiger Rivale*', but still 'her hostility towards him never reaches the pitch which is characteristic of boys' in their Oedipus complex.[23] For the girl, the story whose traumatic turning point is the realization of castration is in other respects, before and after that crisis, a domestic tale. In the passage above, 'changes' come about as 'the result of upbringing' and their outcome will be her staying indefinitely at home. Instead of forcing her beyond the Oedipal wishes that stay in the family, the discovery of her castration encourages them. Thus there are 'women who cling [*festhalten*] with especial intensity and tenacity [*Zähigkeit*] to the bond with their father [*Vaterbindung*] and to the wish in which it culminates of having a child by him'.[24] As in the previous examples of the girl's later orientations, clinging and wishing seem to be ends in themselves; the women 'cling', over-cling ('with especial intensity and tenacity') to the father-bond: they clingingly cling to clinging.

THE MYTH OF CASTRATION

In the outline story of male development, the boy is able to move forward from a pre-civilized, mythmaking state, into a reasonable world of social responsibility in which infantile expectations of heroic centrality have been abandoned and forgotten. Mythical, ancient thinking is superseded by modern, rational thinking. Fear of castration is the

[22] Freud, 'Dissolution', *SE* xix. 178; 'Der Untergang', *GW* xiii. 401.

[23] Freud, 'Female Sexuality', *SE* xxi. 226; 'Über die weibliche Sexualität', *GW* xiv. 518–19.

[24] Freud, 'Some Psychical Consequences', *SE* xix. 251; 'Einige psychische Folgen', *GW* xiv. 22–3.

plot-clinching device that makes the break between the early and mature phases, between mythological and social orientations: the prince is forced to become a citizen, held in place from now on by the understanding that his masculinity is not invulnerable. Thus the boy is pushed beyond the familial scene of passionate struggle, and into a new order of rules and measures. The threat of castration is the precondition for his post-mythological subjectivity; it is a marked turning point. But it also remains as the back-up to a newly circumscribed masculinity: it does not altogether disappear from the psychological scene once its catalytic role has been fulfilled.

In this respect, the castration complex differs sharply from the explicitly mythological scenario of the boy's development, the Oedipus complex. This, Freud says in 1924, should ideally be seen no more once the aftermath of the castration complex has done away with it; 'the process ... is equivalent, if it is ideally carried out, to a destruction [*Zerstörung*] and an abolition [*Aufhebung*] of the complex.'[25] In the following year this is put even more forcefully, making *Zerstörung* and *Aufhebung* sound like calm philosophical abstractions by comparison: 'the complex is not simply repressed, it is literally smashed to pieces [*er zerschellt förmlich*] by the shock of threatened castration.' The complex goes out with a bang; and Freud concludes that 'in ideal cases, the Oedipus complex exists no longer, even in the unconscious'. This dramatic destruction radically re-forms the grounds of the boy's existence: 'the catastrophe [*Katastrophe*] to the Oedipus complex (the abandonment of incest and the institution of conscience and morality) may be regarded as a victory of the race over the individual.'[26] What is explicitly derived from myth, the Oedipus complex, is dramatically surmounted. By contrast, the castration complex survives as basic to the possible paths and the impasses of adult subjectivity.

For the most part, the episode of the castration complex in children's development is presented without reference to any stories or facts that might independently suggest or support it. There is no equivalent to the overtly mythological scaffolding, built up and destroyed after use, that is attached to the idea of the Oedipus complex. In that connection Freud many times reminds his readers of the 'legend' represented in Sophocles' play. His claim for the universality of the experience is based

[25] Freud, 'Dissolution', *SE* xix. 177; 'Der Untergang', *GW* xiii. 399.

[26] Freud, 'Some Psychical Consequences', *SE* xix. 257; 'Einige psychische Folge', *GW* xiv. 29.

directly on an appeal to the power of the Oedipal themes of incest and parricide to move an audience.[27] The castration complex, on the other hand, appears to be independent of mythical or ancient roots.

Yet castration does have its Greek myth, and Freud does refer to it on a number of occasions. Behind the more developed mythology from which the story of Oedipus is derived lurk the gods Uranus and Cronus, father and son; Cronus is the father of Zeus. Freud brings them up as a pair or trio several times. Their paternal and filial exploits, sometimes involving Zeus and sometimes not, include multiple infanticide and father-castration: Zeus may have castrated his father Cronus, and Cronus did the same to *his* father, Uranus. The Freudian Oedipus wishes to murder his father, and the mythical Oedipus does so by accident; a Cronus, mythical or Freudian, simply gets on and does it, and not for any secondary motive such as gaining possession of a mother.

Zeus provides the pivot or dividing point between different orders of legend. Cronus and Uranus, his father and grandfather, are not the subjects of multifarious or elaborate narratives but are confined to some pretty elementary pre-human acts: eating their children and castrating their fathers. As fathers, they don't exactly do the family thing. Freud's statement that the supersession of the Oedipus complex implies the victory of the 'race' over the individual applies, *a fortiori*, to the movement of mythology beyond these monstrous fathers, absolute and obsolete individuals who seek to annihilate both their offspring and their own fathers. Tellingly, the word translated by 'race' is '*Generation*'. Zeus, at first sight, does not quite seem to fit in these connections; his other links, beyond his progenitors, make him an unlikely pater-emasculator. Yet his position is always to some extent that of one situated ambiguously 'between' different orders of divine existence. He mostly belongs to the newer world of gods who have relationships and enter into the plots and affairs of both the immortal and the mortal worlds. Zeus is both a participant and an arbiter; he has the ruling power, and is supposed to be aloof and neutral in his role as judge; and yet he is one among other gods, and not indifferent to mortal attractions and issues. He takes sides, although he also stands apart from strife, divine and human.[28] Thus Zeus' normal transitional or straddling place, between two incommensurable orders, is further confused by his alleged perpetuation of his father's and grandfather's anti-legacy: unfathering.

[27] See Ch. 1, above.

[28] On Zeus' different roles, see further Ch. 3, pp. 83, 85, above.

Freud himself hesitated between the legend which made Zeus a father-castrator like Cronus himself, and the one which reported no such thing, and thus clarified Zeus' separation from those old gods. It was the second of these that Freud usually took to be the more authentic, but he hesitates and checks himself. Almost every time that Cronus comes up in his writings, the issue is raised, and once specifically in relation to the possible significance of making a mistake about the story in this charged father–son connection. In the chapter on 'errors' (*Irrtümer*) in *The Psychopathology of Everyday Life*, Freud considers two passages from *The Interpretation of Dreams* in which—as he would also do many years later, as we shall see—he had made Zeus a father-castrator too, like his own father Cronus: 'I state that Zeus emasculated [*entmannt*] his father Kronos and dethroned him. I was, however, erroneously carrying this atrocity a generation [*Generation*] forward; according to Greek mythology it was Kronos who committed it on his father Uranus.'[29] Freud assumes, in identifying his mistake, that the event of castration was necessarily a unique one—not, for instance, the son repeating what the father had done.

Freud then asks how it was that he came to get this wrong—why, as he strikingly puts it, 'my memory provided me at these points with what was incorrect [*mein Gedächtnis in diesen Punkten Ungetreues lieferte*]', a formulation which makes the error into something like a useful resource. He explains it in connection with his own family history. He was the son of his father's second marriage; a much older half-brother, son of the first marriage, himself had a son, Freud's (half-)nephew, who was Freud's own age. After getting to know this brother on a visit to his home in England, 'my relationship [*Verhältnis*] with my father was changed' because the meeting with the brother had prompted 'phantasies of how different things would have been if I had been born the son not of my father but of my brother'. This then Freud sees as the source of 'my error in advancing by a generation the mythological atrocities [*Greuel*] of the Greek pantheon'.[30]

Freud's 'correct' version of the myth keeps Zeus apart from the sins of his fathers, and thus more clearly confirms Zeus' place as inaugurating a civilized order—one anchored in both the separation and the continuity of 'generation'.[31] In fantasy, Freud's own difference

[29] Freud, *The Psychopathology of Everyday Life* (1901), *SE* vi. 218; *Zur Psychopathologie des Alltagslebens*, *GW* iv. 243.

[30] Freud, *Psychopathology*, *SE* vi. 218–20; *Zur Psychopathologie*, *GW* iv. 243–5.

[31] In Sophocles' *Oedipus the King*, the complete breakdown of the social and familial order is suggested by the blurring of the generations and the associated overlapping

in age from his father (and half-brother) gives realistic support to making the father redundant, or relegating him to the role of grandfather. In his explanation of how he came to make the Cronus mistake, he recalls a significant utterance on the part of his half-brother:

> One of my brother's admonitions lingered long in my memory. 'One thing,' he had said to me, 'that you must not forget is that as far as the conduct of your life is concerned you really belong not to the second but to the third generation in relation to your father.' Our father had married again in later life and was therefore much older than his children by his second marriage.[32]

The solemn, almost oracular tone of the 'admonitions [*Mahnungen*]' links a carefully preserved memory to specific constructions for the future. *Mahnungen* are also reminders; as surely as the brother enjoined the young man 'that you must not forget', so the sayings 'lingered long in my memory', a source of authority and a granting of permission to bypass the father on the part of the one who has himself replaced that father. Freud took his lead, he seems to be saying, from his older brother, in setting himself at a distance from an old-world father; and also, as he doesn't quite say, in making himself analogous to Zeus. This Zeus represents justice, leadership, and the beginning of a new era. But the stretching out of generations, enabling Freud to appear in the place of Zeus, has also, so it is implied, caused a muddle of another kind: if three is really two, then 'Zeus' is not so far apart after all, and is seen like his father as a perpetrator of mythological 'atrocities'.

Everything that has to do with the castration myths seems to be subject to this kind of blur and indistinction. Even Freud's self-correction turns out to need recorrection, or at least qualification. Having stated that he was wrong to include Zeus among the unfilial sons, he puts in a footnote that begins, self-mockingly, '*Kein voller Irrtum!*', 'Not entirely a mistake!', and goes on to cite the Orphic version 'which has Zeus repeat the process of emasculation on his father Kronos'.[33] A further example of indistinction is that fathers and sons in the Cronus story do not stay generationally separate; instead each one is driven only and simply to do away with putative progeny and fathers. In the myth of Uranus whom Freud never mentions other than in connection with the castrating Cronus, the confusions are even more extreme. Uranus (the

of kinship categories like 'mother-wife' or 'sister-daughter' that ought to be mutually exclusive. (See ll. 1406–8.)

[32] Freud, *Psychopathology*, *SE* vi. 220; *Zur Psychopathologie*, *GW* iv. 245.

[33] Freud, *Psychopathology*, *SE* vi. 218; tr. mod.; *Zur Psychopathologie*, *GW* iv. 243.

sky), the son of Gê or Gaia (the earth), has children with his mother but makes her swallow them back; one of them, Cronus, castrates his father, at her instigation—and she is the mother of both parties, father and son.

PSYCHOANALYTIC MYTHOLOGIES

Unlike Oedipus, Cronus and Uranus are rarely mentioned by Freud. But it happens that they, and not Oedipus, appear in a passage where Freud raises general questions about the relationship of psychoanalytic theory to mythology. The passage is worth considering in some detail, as it is fundamental to the issues of knowledge and story presented in relation to castration and sexual difference.

In *The Question of Lay Analysis*, Freud offers his sceptical imaginary interlocutor an analogy with Greek mythology; this is meant as a way of making the extraordinary psychoanalytic description of infant sexuality seem less outlandish. He first appeals to memories of the classical myths taught at school, mentioning as an example the one about the god Cronus swallowing his children: 'How strange this must have sounded to you when you first heard it! But I suppose none of us thought about it at the time.' The strangeness is initially both taken for granted and unexplored, not a matter for thought. But now, Freud goes on, a meaning is clear: 'To-day we can also call to mind a number of fairy tales in which some ravenous animal like a wolf appears, and we shall recognize it as a disguise [*Verkleidung*] of the father.'[34] Thus myths and fairy tales tell the same story, which can be interpreted at another level to which, as 'disguises', they are subordinate. Here the gods of mythology and the animals of fairy tales converge in the same picture of the father. Psychoanalytic theory has provided an explanation: 'it was only through the knowledge of infantile sexuality that it became possible to understand mythology and the world of fairy tales. Here then something has been gained as a by-product [*Nebengewinn*] of analytic studies.'[35]

Freud then moves from a devouring to a castrating father, and makes a slightly different point about the relationship between mythological and analytic understanding. And once more Cronus is brought on as evidence:

[34] Freud, *The Question of Lay Analysis* (1926), *SE* xx. 211; *Die Frage der Laienanalyse*, *GW* xiv. 240.

[35] Ibid.

You will be no less surprised to hear that male children suffer from a fear of being robbed of their sexual organ by their father, so that this fear of being castrated has a most powerful influence on the development of their character and in deciding the direction to be followed by their sexuality. And here again mythology may give you the courage to believe psycho-analysis. The same Kronos who swallowed his children also emasculated his father Uranus, and was afterwards himself emasculated in revenge by his son Zeus, who had been rescued through his mother's cunning [*List*].[36]

Whereas in the first example the myth is strange but can be made comprehensible through psychoanalytic understanding, here the myth is taken as read; its familiarity provides the grounds for believing an otherwise astonishing ('You will be no less surprised') psychoanalytic story. Previously, psychoanalysis gave credence to mythology ('it was only through the knowledge of infantile sexuality that it became possible to understand mythology'); here, it is the other way round: 'mythology may give you the courage to believe psycho-analysis'.[37]

There follow two further hypotheses about the reader's accreditation of psychoanalysis, the second of which is the one presented as preferable. Here is the first:

If you have felt inclined to suppose that all that psycho-analysis reports about the early sexuality of children is derived from the disordered imagination [*der wüsten Phantasie*] of the analysts, you must at least admit that their imagination has created the same product as the imaginative activities of primitive [*primitiven*] man, of which myths and fairy tales are the precipitate.[38]

Here analytic knowledge is identified with the 'primitive'; it does not explain it but is 'the same'. It is wild and chaotic ('*wüsten*') but it is given its low-level validation by the irrefutable identity between the two. Psychoanalytic theory is itself, on *this* theory, a wild story—a fairy tale or myth.

The second hypothesis then raises the stakes by once again situating the analyst of both mythology and infantile sexuality at a distance from the object of study:

The alternative friendlier, and probably also the more pertinent view would be that in the mental life of children to-day we can still detect the same archaic factors which were once dominant generally in the primeval days of human civilization. In his mental development the child would be repeating the history

[36] Freud, *Lay Analysis*, *SE* xx. 211–12; *Laienanalyse*, *GW* xiv. 240.

[37] On belief and disbelief in relation to psychoanalysis, see Ch. 5, above.

[38] Freud, *Lay Analysis*, *SE* xx. 212; *Laienanalyse*, *GW* xiv. 240.

of his race in an abbreviated form, just as embryology has long since recognized was the case with somatic development.[39]

The translation does not speak of 'recapitulation' here, though on other occasions where the combination of repetition ('*wiederholen*') and abbreviation ('*abkürzender*') appears, that is the word that is used.[40] The last clause leaves no doubt that this is a reference to the contemporary scientific theory, and that Freud is endorsing the idea—'long since recognized'—that ontogeny repeats phylogeny. As elsewhere (notably at the end of the 'Wolf Man' case history), Freud transfers this theory to psychological development, positing that the child necessarily passes through a series of incommensurable modes of apprehending its world, each with its own characteristic attached stories or basic outlines; chief among these are the 'primal phantasies', offering and imposing answers to the child's questions about sexuality and the origin of babies.

In recapitulation theory proper, each stage of a recapitulation is superseded by the new form that takes its place. In Freud, on the other hand, no 'stage' of development is ever fully or finally surpassed. There is always the possibility of a detrimental 'return' to a previous one; or, putting this from the other direction, previous dispositions may 'survive' in the present as part of a heterogeneously composed psychical entity. But when Freud directly appeals to recapitulation theory, as in the passage cited, this interference inherent to his own model tends to be unstated. Instead, the stress falls on the succession of stages leading towards adulthood, with the earlier ones associated with a 'primitive' world that the adult will long since have left behind. Thus in this second hypothesis, the adult is not on a par with the mythologizing child or its phylogenetic analogue, the 'primeval days [*Urseitzen*] of human civilization'. This 'friendlier [*freundlichere*]' hypothesis rescues the theorist from the ancient world of the first one; it is also, for good measure, probably 'more accurate [*zutreffendere*]', as well as (in the translation) 'more pertinent'.

The several interlocking hypotheses that Freud puts forward here offer a spectrum of possibilities about the relation between mythology and knowledge for various classes of thinker who are explicitly or implicitly compared. There is the child as opposed to the adult; primitive as

39 Freud, *Lay Analysis*, *SE* xx. 212; *Laienanalyse*, *GW* xiv. 240.

40 For instance Lecture XIII, 'The Archaic Features and Infantilism of Dreams', *Introductory Lectures on Psycho-Analysis* (1915–16), *SE* xv. 199; 'Archaische Züge und Infantilismus des Traumes', *Vorlesungen zur Einführung in die Psychoanalyse*, *GW* xi. 203; here 'abbreviated recapitulation' translates '*abgekürzt wiederholt*'. See Ch. 9, below, for further instances of Freud's direct and indirect uses of the theory of recapitulation.

opposed to civilized human beings; and psychoanalysts as opposed to other people. The discussion comes immediately before a passage in which Freud raises the question of sexual difference specifically in relation to the castration complex, but without naming it as such, despite the proximity of the Cronus myth of '*Entmannung*' and the reference to boys' 'fear of being robbed of their sexual organ by their father': 'Another characteristic of early infantile sexuality is that ... [s]tress falls entirely on the male organ, all the child's interest is directed towards the question of whether it is present or not.'[41] Thus the issues raised are bound to suggest some further considerations in relation to the asymmetrical 'stories' that attach to the different developments of each sex.

It is the Cronus myth that Freud refers to, in *The Question of Lay Analysis*, as implicitly 'disordered' and chaotic: '*wüsten*'. Bodies and body parts are indiscriminately ingested or removed within a caricaturally destructive 'family'. 'How strange [*sonderbar*] this must have sounded to you when you first heard it!' Freud said, referring to the schoolboy understanding of the story that Cronus swallowed his children. Strange, peculiar, weird—but not shocking or shaking. Not a source of disturbance or curiosity, then—'But I suppose none of us thought about it at the time.' And easily assimilated now, intellectually, to an available schema: 'Today ... we shall recognize it as a disguise of the father.' The Titan stories of the old gods are about extreme acts executed without meditation or pause. There is no narrative suspense, no impending fate: no time of delay in which an oracular promise or threat makes its mark on the characters. The response to them, on the part of both children and adults, is not represented by Freud as resembling the fearful effect produced by the tragedy of Oedipus: 'There must be something which makes a voice within us ready to recognize [*anzuerkennen*] the compelling force of destiny in the *Oedipus*.'[42] These myths are outside the complex human time where the present is always steeped in its imaginary futures, whether feared or wished for.

CRONUS' LAST APPEARANCE

There is one occasion in Freud's writing when the Cronus story is given a full symbolic weight. In a brief, incomplete paper written at the

[41] Freud, *Lay Analysis*, *SE* xx. 212; *Laienanalyse*, *GW* xiv. 241.

[42] Freud, *The Interpretation of Dreams* (1900), *SE* iv. 262; *Die Traumdeutung*, *GW* ii–iii. 269.

very end of his life, 'Splitting of the Ego in the Process of Defence', the mechanism of disavowal is described in similar terms to those that Freud had used in 1927 in his essay on 'Fetishism'. In most cases—'the usual result of the fright of castration [*Kastrationsschrecks*]'—the boy's response is to 'obey the prohibition' (of masturbation) as he 'gives way to the threat'; this is the trade-off that will lead to his incorporation into the social world.[43] But in other instances recognition both does and does not take place and the boy finds a means of having it both ways. He acknowledges, but also fails to acknowledge, the 'castration' he sees in the girl, by creating a fetish or substitute for the missing penis; in relation to her (it does not affect his perception of his own penis) he has then 'transferred the importance of the penis to another part of the body'. This 'ingenious [*geschickte*]' or 'artful [*kniffig*]'[44] solution to the problem leaves the boy with a double orientation: on the one hand, the 'apparent boldness or indifference' that defies and ignores the threat, but on the other, 'a symptom which showed that he nevertheless did recognize [*anerkennt*] the danger'.[45] At this juncture the following passage appears:

> [H]e developed an intense fear of his father punishing him, which it required the whole force of his masculinity to master and overcompensate. This fear of his father, too, was silent on the subject of castration: by the help of regression to an oral phase, it assumed the form of a fear of being eaten by his father. At this point it is impossible to forget a primitive fragment of Greek mythology which tells how Kronos, the old Father God, swallowed his children and sought to swallow his youngest son Zeus like the rest, and how Zeus was saved by the craft [*List*] of his mother and later on castrated his father.[46]

First castration is named as what is either elided or out of the picture here: 'silent on the subject'. Then, in connection with this silence, there enters none other than the arch-castrator, Cronus, here only in connection with his other violent deed, the eating of his children. Zeus, on the other hand, whom Freud had long ago sought to exempt, at least probably, from his father's crime, now appears as the first and only father-castrator.

The example concerns a blurring of the usual psychical developments in relation to the negotiation of the castration complex, and the mixture of myth and theory, Cronus and castrastion, echoes that same confusion. Cronus, even though he is its primary mythological agent, is dissociated

[43] Freud, 'Splitting of the Ego in the Process of Defence' (1940), *SE* xxiii. 277; 'Die Ichspaltung im Abwehrvorgang', *GW* xvii. 61.

[44] Freud, 'Splitting', *SE* xxiii. 275, 277; 'Die Ichspaltung', *GW* xvii. 60, 61 .

[45] Freud, 'Splitting', *SE* xxiii. 277; 'Die Ichspaltung', *GW* xvii. 62.

[46] Freud, 'Splitting', *SE* xxiii. 277–8; 'Die Ichspaltung', *GW* xvii. 62.

from castration. But then Zeus, who may not have done the deed at all, comes in as if to compensate for the silence. There and not there, recognized and not recognized: the passage moves back and forth in precisely the same way as in the structure of splitting which it is describing. And almost immediately after this passage, the essay fades away (it was unfinished at the time of Freud's death), mentioning another small symptom, this time the boy's aversion to his toes being touched—'as though', says Freud, 'in all the to and fro between disavowal and acknowledgement [*Anerkennung*], it was nevertheless castration that found the clearer expression ...'.[47]

This oscillating exposition in the 'Splitting' essay echoes the ambiguities in Freud's theory of castration as that which for boys enables the surpassing of myth. The 'castration complex' is made to play a decisive explanatory role in the psychoanalytic theory of children's development. It traumatically divides boys from girls and launches each sex, now in their respectively wanting or threatened states, on the path of a particular orientation towards the future. For the boy, castration postdates and ideally draws a line under the mythical familial involvements of the Oedipus complex. He is able to make the move denied to the girl, from family to culture—or from myth to *logos*. From this perspective, 'castration' is part of Freud's own theoretical myth of human development.

But castration, as much as Oedipus, has Greek mythological sources, sometimes evoked by Freud, which form the underside of its structuring, humanizing role through the recognition of unpleasant but necessary sexual fact. Uranus and Cronus belong to a different age and world from that of Oedipus and Laius, who are themselves superseded in the movement initiated by the castration complex. Far from being to do with clarification or with an admission into sexual and social maturity, the Cronus-related myths are pre-pre-social. There is no narrative or temporal complexity; deeds are done without thought for a future, hoped or feared; progenitors and progeny are destroyed without any sense of generation on the part of the solely self-assertive perpetrator, free of all relations. Castration is embroiled in ur-myths of confusion; what it threatens is the collapse of all 'generational', historical, human distinctions.

The possible exception to the pre-Zeus order is the figure of Zeus' rescuing mother, whom Freud twice alludes to, both times to mention her *List* (the same word is behind both 'craft' and 'cunning' in the

[47] Freud, 'Splitting', *SE* xxiii. 278; 'Die Ichspaltung', *GW* xvii. 62; points of suspension in original.

English) in outwitting Cronus' son-swallowing enterprise. No further details are given, either by Freud or in reported versions of the myth. Rhea does not save her other offspring. From this it could possibly be argued, *ex post facto*, that her forethought and attachment apply appropriately to the one who is destined for a post-Titanic future in a newer mythic world where the gods intervene in human matters of justice and fate; she would thus be in the vanguard of a civilizing process, her 'cunning' standing out against the gross destructiveness of her Titan husband. But it could also be argued that she is simply a mother, Freudian or otherwise, devoted to her baby son as a part of her self, and over and above her devotion to her husband. Her maternal instincts are useful and even indispensable to the move into culture and generation represented by Zeus, but culture is not her invention. Here the woman/mother is ambiguously placed, on the threshold between old and new orders, and identified with neither.

THE MAN AND WOMAN OF 30

In another late essay, 'Analysis Terminable and Interminable', the refusal to accept castration becomes the ultimate impasse, for both sexes. Freud speaks of 'The paramount importance of these two themes—in females the wish for a penis and in males the struggle against passivity'; this is also described as the masculine protest (following Adler) and (Freud's expression) the repudiation of femininity.[48] They may be immutable: 'We often have the impression that with the wish for a penis and the masculine protest we have penetrated through all the psychological strata and have reached bedrock [*zum 'gewachsenen Fels' durchgedrungen*], and that thus our activities are at an end.'[49]

Prior to this, at the end of the 'Femininity' lecture of 1933, the contrast of men's and women's futures that the castration complex installs had

[48] Freud, 'Analysis Terminable and Interminable' (1937), *SE* xxiii. 251; 'Die endliche und die unendliche Analyse', *GW* xvi. 98. On the relationship of repudiation and femininity in Freud, see Rachel Bowlby, 'Still Crazy after All These Years', in *Still Crazy after All These Years: Women, Writing and Psychoanalysis* (London: Routledge, 1992), 131–56.

[49] Freud, 'Analysis Terminable and Interminable', *SE* xxiii. 252; 'Die endliche und die unendliche Analyse', *GW* xvi. 99. The English translation removes the quotation marks that make '*gewachsenen Fels*' (literally, 'evolved rock') a conspicuous metaphor in the German.

been vividly evoked in a picture of modern types. Freud appeals to the same 'impression' as in 'Analysis Terminable and Interminable' as being a commonplace therapeutic perception:

I cannot help mentioning an impression that we are constantly receiving during analytic practice. A man of about thirty strikes us as a youthful, somewhat unformed individual, whom we expect to make powerful use of the possibilities for development opened up to him by analysis. A woman of the same age, however, often frightens [*erschreckt*] us by her psychical rigidity and unchangeability. Her libido has taken up final positions and seems incapable of exchanging them for others. There are no paths open to further development; it is as though the whole process had already run its course and remains thenceforward insusceptible to influence—as though, indeed, the difficult development to femininity had exhausted the possibilities of the person concerned. As therapists we lament this state of things.[50]

At first sight, this passage seems to lend support to the view that the masculine bias of psychoanalytic theory is simply misogynistic. 'Frightens us' recalls the use of the same word in the context of fetishism for the reaction of the male to the sight of the female genitals.[51] In both cases, a shortcoming seen in the woman is a source of alarm to the man. At the same time, in this passage, the woman's inflexibility—her stiffness (*Starrheit*) and unchangeability (*Unveränderlichkeit*)—is set alongside the patently appealing and attractive figure of the blooming young man, 'youthful, somewhat unformed', who is going to make vigorous, '*kräftig*' use of the 'possibilities of development' that analysis 'opens up [*eröffnet*]' to him through therapy. For the woman, in contrast, '*Wege zu weiterer Entwicklung ergeben sich nicht*'. 'Paths for wider development do not arise', or 'paths for wider development are there none': in the German, the emphasis falls on the concluding negative, the *nicht* that immediately cancels the ways forward that the sentence has postulated. Here, in real life, as a kind of sad professional secret ('I cannot help mentioning ...') we are presented with the no-hope, prematurely aged women of the theoretical account.

But this is not all that is suggested. The spectacular, stark contrast also prompts regret that the path to femininity has been so draining as to have left the woman in this undesirable state. For the passage clearly deploys

[50] Freud, 'Femininity', *SE* xxii. 134–5; 'Die Weiblichkeit', *GW* xv. 144–5.

[51] Freud, 'Splitting', *SE* xxiii. 277; 'Die Ichspaltung', *GW* xvii. 61, quoted above. Cf. 'Probably no man is spared the fright of castration [*Kastrationsschreck*] at the sight of a female genital', 'Fetishism' (1927), *SE* xxi. 154; 'Fetischismus', *GW* xiv. 314.

a notion of personal development linked in its positive form to change, openness, movement. Freud assumes that change is desirable for persons of either sex; persons are individuals who may or may not be able to go in new directions, to take up different 'possibilities'. From a historical point of view, the surprising assumption in this connection may be that it is regrettable for a woman of 30 to be settled, to have found a final character. Would that the woman, too, he implies, could have the freedom to go on developing—that the woman, too, could be open to change.

Freud granted women one possible sphere of perfect happiness, in mothering a son: 'A mother can transfer to her son the ambition [*Ehrgeiz*] which she has been obliged to suppress in herself, and she can expect [*erwarten*] from him the satisfaction of all that has been left over in her of her masculinity complex.'[52] For once, the hope or expectation is not unreasonable even though it is compromised by its vicariousness and its dependence on a lost and recovered masculinity. But still the reference to 'the ambition which she has been obliged to suppress in herself' carries the same recognition as noted in the passage about the man and woman of 30. The ambition was rightfully there; it is regrettable that she 'had to suppress it [*bei sich unterdrücken müßte*]'. As before, and even though the ending is a happier one here, there is an assumption of female potential that is undeveloped or thwarted, both psychically and socially.

Since Freud's lifetime, paths of development that were previously closed have been opened up to women in social life, in principle and in practice. This may not have made any difference to the relative states of psychic flexibility or rigidity affecting either sex, as individuals or collectively. Both sexes, though not necessarily in identical ways, are subject to the limitations as well as the opportunities of their place in the 'cultural community', including the obligation to identify as one of two sexes, but not the other; this is what the recognition of 'castration' implies.[53] But 'castration' is no neutral word for limitation; its masculine privilege assumes that the difference of the sexes takes a particular, asymmetrical form. Given the obsolescence of the social correlates of the Freudian complex—there is no longer so sharp a distinction between the paths available to men and women—it seems

[52] Freud, 'Femininity', *SE* xxii. 133; 'Die Weiblichkeit', *GW* xv. 143.

[53] Sylviane Agacinski revises the masculine bias of the theory by equalizing the lack: 'So each sex is "mutilated", each sex knows the castration of not being the other. There really is an *essential lack at the heart of every human being*, which is not the lack of a penis or of some other attribute of the man or the woman, but is that of being only a man or only a woman' (*Politique des sexes* (1998; Paris: Seuil, 2001), 78.

anachronistic and needlessly hopeless now to cling to a myth in which women's most fundamental conflicts are determined by the realization that they are women, not men.[54] Like others, the myth of masculine pre-eminence is ceasing to seem immutable and inevitable.

[54] In 2005 I heard a new version of the myth from a girl of 3. 'I used to be a boy', she began. 'So did you have a big willy?' an older girl prompted. 'Yes, and it came away from me.' A few hours later she revised her story, this time to say that the willy the big girl had added was 'on the end of my nose', and 'I had to cut it off with some scissors.'

7

Oedipal Origins

THE NUCLEAR FAMILY

In the middle of *Oedipus the King*, Oedipus is moved to tell his life story from the beginning—or from what he believes to be the beginning. He is prompted by the fear that the prophet Tiresias, in accusing him of having been the murderer of Laius, many years before, could possibly be right. His wife Jocasta has mentioned a detail about that event: that it took place at a crossing of three roads (l. 730). Oedipus' narrative explains how it came about that just before his arrival in Thebes himself, he killed a man at a place of that description:

My father was Polybus, a Corinthian, my mother Merope, a Dorian. I was raised as the most important man among the townspeople there, until something happened to me [*prin moi tychê toiad' epestê*]—something that was surprising, yes, but which I shouldn't have taken as seriously as I did. At a dinner a man who had had a lot to drink said, with the wine, that I was not my father's real son [*kalei par' oinôi plastos hôs eiên patri*]. I took this hard and contained myself with difficulty for the rest of the day; the next day I went to my parents and interrogated them. They were angry at the slur—at the one who had let fly the utterance. And I was happy with the two of them, but all the same the thing still bugged me. It got to me. Without telling my mother and father I set off for the Pythian oracle, and Apollo sent me away without the honour of an answer in relation to what I had come about, but to my despair he prophesied terrible and awful things to me—that I had to sleep with my mother, and would present a family unbearable for human eyes to look upon, and would be the murderer of my father who engendered me.

And when I heard that, I fled the land of Corinth, for the future measuring its distance by the stars, so as never to see the fulfilment of the slurs of my bad oracles. On my way I came to the region where you say that this king was murdered. (ll. 774–99)

Oedipus characterizes a simple childhood—two parents, their two origins, and an education for a future role—broken apart by an upsetting event; it is in these general terms that he puts it before going into details. The disruptive *tychê*, a fateful 'chance', has the force of an enemy breaking in. From this time forward he is, by his own account, unbalanced (he overreacts, he says)—and divided. He is in two minds, separated by the two days—first he did nothing, then he did something—and by the double reaction to his parents' response: of pleasure or relief on the one hand, and continued disturbance on the other. He both does and does not trust them. He is 'happy', even 'delighted' ('*eterpomên keinoin*', l. 785) at their combined anger and reassurance, but then he acts as if he does not trust them after all.[1] The use of the dual form, *keinoin*, suggests their solidarity as a couple at a moment when that united front is both comforting and something from which he senses his exclusion (they are in fact keeping a secret). Separating himself off from them, he goes to ask another authority; the word '*lathrai*' ('in secret', 'hidden from', l. 787), placed at the start of the line, draws attention to the furtiveness of the initiative. There will be no going back to what he recalls or recounts as the untroubled first stage of a simple trio of father, mother, and son.

When Oedipus reaches the oracle a further division occurs. Apollo gives a response that is apparently unrelated to the question. The horror of his predictions then catapults Oedipus into flight. He never looks back—either to Corinth, from which he resolves to keep far away, or to reconsider the possible application of the oracle's words. The uncertainty about his beginnings is as if forgotten:[2] it does not occur to Oedipus that the father and mother designated by Apollo may not be the parents he has left behind in Corinth, even though it was a questioning of his paternity that had precipitated the sequence of events that took him to the oracle.

In *The Interpretation of Dreams*, summarizing Sophocles' version of the legend, Freud singles out Oedipus' newfound uncertainty about his beginnings as the initial turning point: 'The child was rescued, and grew up as a prince in an alien court, until, in doubts as to his origin [*seiner Herkunft unsicher*], he too questioned the oracle'.[3] Freud also gets this

[1] Loss of belief in what the parents say is a significant moment in the development of the Freudian child. See further Ch. 5, above.

[2] I borrow this phrase from Barbara Melosh. In *Strangers and Kin: The American Way of Adoption* (Cambridge, MA: Harvard University Press, 2002), she describes the prevailing ideology of the mid-twentieth century according to which adoptive families should be as far as possible 'as if begotten', without visible racial difference from the child. The corollary to this, Melosh suggests, was that the birth mother and the out-of-wedlock pregnancy should be 'as if forgotten' (p. 136).

[3] Freud, *The Interpretation of Dreams*, *SE* iv. 261; *Die Traumdeutung*, *GW* ii–iii. 267–8.

bit slightly wrong, saying next that Oedipus 'questioned the oracle and was warned to avoid his home since he was destined to murder his father and take his mother in marriage' (in German, this 'warning' is more neutrally a piece of 'advice' ('*Rat*')).[4] The avoidance of home is actually Oedipus' own idea. The oracle gave him a prophecy, not a suggestion for dealing with it: it is not in the nature of oracles to give advice for how to avoid the fates that they intimate.

For Sophocles' Oedipus, the words of the anonymous man who starts it, a sort of malicious double to the truth-speaking Tiresias, are like a missile ('*methenti*', l. 784) which, once it has found a target, cannot be dislodged. Initially the man is '*hyperplêstheis methêi*' (l. 779), 'topped up with alcohol' and, as if to overcharge the language too with too much of the same, Oedipus also says that he lets out his taunting utterance '*par' oinôi*' (l. 780)—'in his cups', 'with the wine'. Something is spilt. Oedipus is literally 'made heavy' ('*baryntheis*', l. 781), depressed and oppressed, by the remark. It takes him over, gets inside him, weighs him down—a pressure, or force, pressing on him like the drink in the over-filled man, that takes on a life of its own. It hangs over him. The phrase '*hypheirpe gar poly*' (l. 786), 'it got to me'—literally, 'it crept about a lot'—leaves it open whether the movement is internal or external or both: getting under his skin, or growing publicly as a nasty rumour. The oracle then puts this first insult out of Oedipus' mind, since what is prophesied operates as a far more fearful 'slur'. The same word, *oneidos*, is used of both utterances, the drunk's and the oracle's. The oracle is received as an insult but conversely the insult functions like an oracle; it is an utterance that has far-reaching and disturbing effects.

At the point in the play where he offers this capsule autobiography,[5] Oedipus still has no evident thought that he is not the child of Polybus

[4] Freud, *Interpretation*, *SE* iv. 261; *Die Traumdeutung*, *GW* ii–iii. 268.

[5] Perhaps a little late in the day to the wife he has been married to for long enough to have had four children with her. There are other instances in the play of implausible gaps in local knowledge, as when Oedipus is told by his brother-in-law Creon that 'we once had a king called Laius' (l. 103) and Oedipus proceeds to question him about what steps were taken to investigate his death. Commentators have generally had to explain these peculiarities as a matter of 'dramatic necessity', uncertainly backed by Aristotle's allowance, citing this very instance, that what happens 'outside the tragedy' (*Poetics* 1454b) does not fall under the same strictures of verisimilitude as does the action of the time of the play; see e.g. R. D. Dawe, Introduction, *Sophocles 'Oedipus Rex'* (Cambridge: Cambridge University Press, 1982), 8–17. In his late nineteenth-century edition, R. C. Jebb conjectured that sixteen years must have elapsed since the murder of Laius, and therefore since Jocasta's marriage to Oedipus (*The Oedipus Tyrannus of Sophocles* (1885; 3rd edn. abridged 1897; Cambridge: Cambridge University Press, 1927), 67, note to l. 561). The question of the temporal distance of the murder from the wedding (or from

and Merope, nor that he does not originally come from Corinth, even though the story he tells itself concerns a questioning of that certainty long ago. If anything, he is all the more their son in his resistance to the taunt of being only *plastos* ('moulded' or 'fabricated') as his father's son. Oedipus assumes he knows who his parents are and where he comes from; he is exceptional only in that his relation to his imagined origins of place and parenthood is the reverse of the normal, since Corinth and, by extension, Polybus and Merope are now the place and the pair of people that he must at all costs, he believes, keep well away.[6] When the comfortable assumption of knowing his parents is challenged—when the challenge to it reveals it as such—Oedipus seeks reassurance. And then when he is threatened with the prospect of parricide and incestuous fathering, he runs away altogether. It is as if he imagines he would be passive to the perpetration of the dreaded acts; only to be in the same place as his parents would bring closer their possible happening. He represents himself as a helpless onlooker who would have no choice but to witness these things; he flees 'so as never to see the fulfilment of the slurs' (ll. 796–7). So he would be in the same position as other people who, he says, would be confronted with an 'unbearable' spectacle, in the form of the family that he himself would present or 'show forth'; he assumes he would be without power to have prevented these horrible sights even though he would be their principal agent. The oracle has the effect of cutting off Oedipus' sense of his own initiative in relation to his personal life, his power of choosing what he does to or with those to whom he is closest.

Oedipus initially evokes a harmonious, uncomplicated period of growing up with his parents, being educated to understand his place in society. But still, as we know, his parents have kept quiet about his adoption, and they do not reveal it either when Oedipus questions them after the taunt at the dinner has disturbed him. Oedipus then unwittingly follows his parents' own secretive lead by himself going off without telling them to consult the oracle. What did his adoptive parents fear? Or why did they not tell their son that he was not born to them? The insult at the

Oedipus' arrival in Thebes) is not explored or even mentioned within the play. Perhaps the reasoning is that Oedipus, at that point, must have been at least 16 himself, in order to be taken into Thebes as a king (and new husband for the queen), so that that event took place some sixteen years after the baby's exposure. There would then be a temporal symmetry in the repeated cycle of crisis and (temporary) cure that has afflicted the city of Thebes.

[6] As Jean Bollack says: 'In the logic of the intrigue, for Oedipus the fear the oracle inspires makes Polybus and Merope definitely his real parents' (*La naissance d'Œdipe* (Paris: Gallimard, 1997), 138).

party suggests a stigma and seems to hint at something like illegitimacy or adultery, both of which would be compatible with adoption although neither is actually the case. Literally, Oedipus says that the man 'calls me ... that I was faked to my father' (l. 780); 'calls me' half prompts a missing noun meaning 'bastard' in place of the adjective *plastos*, and the syntax gets twisted in a way that merges the man's drunken slurring with its confusing effect as a slur on the young man and his parents.

Oedipus goes to both parents jointly for enlightenment, and he does not say if he asks them only about who his father is, or whether he imagines or raises the possibility that he was the birth son of neither of them. Within the social reality of the drama, adoption is evidently not in itself a stigma because it is no obstacle to Oedipus assuming the role of his father's successor: during the course of the play, a Corinthian messenger turns up in Thebes to inform Oedipus that Polybus is dead and he is expected to take his place as the new king. The messenger knows quite well that Oedipus was adopted, innocently bringing the matter up as a way, he thinks, of laying to rest his remaining fears about the oracle now that Polybus' death has removed the possibility of accidentally murdering him. No need to fear marrying your mother Merope, the man reassures him: 'Polybus was no relation to you' (l. 1016) and nor, by implication, is his wife.

Had he not been ignorant of his adoption (or had his parents told him the truth when he came to ask them), the insult would have been, in both senses, of little consequence to Oedipus. It would not have hit home; and he would never have left—temporarily to begin with, to consult the oracle, and then definitively, once he had been told his fate. The adoptive parents' silence and active withholding of the truth ultimately contributes to the fulfilment of the oracle of which they know nothing and which is not about them. Closer to home, it deprives them forever of the son they had longed for and to whom they had given a happy childhood. In an extreme version of the 'empty nest' syndrome, Oedipus disappears from his parents' lives when he has just grown up, and they never set eyes on him again.

In an influential essay of the 1960s, 'Œdipe sans complexe' ('Oedipus without the complex'), Jean-Pierre Vernant pointed out that Freud's reading of the play ignores the fact that Oedipus is an adopted child.[7]

[7] Jean-Pierre Vernant, 'Œdipe sans complexe' (1967), in Vernant and Pierre Vidal-Naquet, *Mythe et tragédie en Grèce ancienne* (1972; Paris: La Découverte, 1991), i. 77–98.

Not knowing his birth parents, Oedipus cannot have wished to do what he did, and the play gives no support to the idea of unconscious 'Oedipal' impulses in relation to parent figures. Oedipus has no emotional history with the father he kills or the mother he marries, nor does he know their relationship to him when he encounters them in later life. Freud's theory is not tied to blood relationships; it concerns the child's first passionate attachments and rivalries in relation to the adults who are present in his life. Ergo, Oedipus has no complex. Writing in the context of a French classical culture much more imbued with psychoanalytic thinking than has been the case in English-speaking countries, Vernant is further critical of psychoanalytic readers who tend to find the same story of 'Oedipal' rivalry wherever they look in Greek mythology. It is not, he insists, the only story; and he is also concerned to keep *Oedipus* open for readings other than psychoanalytic ones.

More recently, Charles Segal has also drawn attention to the significance of Oedipus' adoptive parents, in particular his father.[8] Segal's emphasis is meant partly as a way of lessening the distance between the detractors and the advocates of Freud's interpretation of the tragedy. He proposes for instance that the brutal Laius and gentle Polybus can be seen as personifying the child's division of parental images; a similar split between the nurturing and the rejecting mother separates Merope and Jocasta. Against Vernant's reading it can also be said, by a Freudian logic, that Oedipus' terror of the oracle does after all indicate, to use Freud's phrasing, that something in him must be 'ready to recognize', '*anzuerkennen bereit*',[9] what he so desperately flees all possibility of doing in relation to the parents he knows. From a contemporary perspective, the multiplication of parents and origins, known and unknown, in this play may add to its forcefulness; Oedipus' fateful error, at the point when he consults the oracle, may have been his continuing assumption that his parental background is only and simply the one he is aware of.

[8] See Charles Segal, 'Sophocles' *Oedipus Tyrannus*: Freud, Language, and the Unconscious', in Peter L. Rudnytsky and Ellen Handler Spitz (eds.), *Freud and Forbidden Knowledge* (New York: New York University Press, 1994), 72–95. In particular, Segal contrasts the benign, consciously known father, Polybus, with the brutal, primitive Laius. There is thus a suggestion within the play of what Freud, and more emphatically later analysts such as Melanie Klein, would propose as the normal splitting of parental images into 'good' and 'bad'.

[9] Freud, *Interpretation*, *SE* iv. 262; *Die Traumdeutung*, *GW* ii–iii. 269. Freud is here speaking of the reason why the play can still appal its audiences, unlike modern 'tragedies of destiny' that attempt to replicate the Greek sense of a divinely ordained fate. On Freud's use several times in this passage of the Aristotelian notion of 'recognition' to describe the reaction of the spectator to the play, see Ch. 1, above.

POLYBUS

There is a moment when, having just learned that his father Polybus is dead, and thus that there is no fear now of his murdering him, Oedipus wonders in passing whether after all his father may have died 'out of longing for me [*tômôi pothôi*]' (l. 969). 'That way,' he goes on, 'he *would* have died because of me' (l. 970). The general sense of the passage is to dismiss the thought as far-fetched. Oedipus starts by saying he was in this case nowhere near a weapon, '*apsaustos enchous*' (l. 969: literally, 'untouching a sword') at the time of his supposed father's death, and concludes with two lines that, Jocasta-like, as we shall see, turn the event into a proof that oracles are worthless. But the mention of loving *pothos* adjacent to the sword points up the severe emotional contrast that is made between Oedipus' two fathers. When the Corinthian shepherd is telling Oedipus how he came to be brought up as the child of Polybus and Merope, Oedipus asks, as if doubting the likelihood, and not quite mentioning the child that was himself: 'And even then, from another's hands, he [Polybus] loved very much [*esterxen mega*]?' The Corinthian replies, simply: 'His former childlessness persuaded him' (ll. 1023–4).[10] *Apaidia*, childlessness, might be thought to imply primarily a source of concern for the preservation of the family or the kingdom. But here, and speaking of the father not the mother, it is love that is mentioned. Polybus big-loves his child all the more for having waited so long, or for having given up hope; the surprising statement is all the more moving for leaving unspoken the recommencement, after the adored son's abrupt departure, of this childless time—now freighted additionally with loss and anxiety. This waiting and declining hope is what Oedipus himself then imagines with the possibility that his father died of missing him.

In contrast to this father, the first father, Laius, tried to bring about the death of his baby son, himself injuring the baby's ankles to increase the chances of his dying once exposed. Nothing is said in the play of any feelings of regret or wishes and disappointments in relation to children, whether as heirs or as objects of love. Laius is represented only as punitive and fearful; he is both alarming and himself afraid (of the

[10] In *The Road to Delphi: The Life and Afterlife of Oracles* (London: Chatto & Windus, 2003), Michael Wood astutely suggests that the oracle's negative prophecy about what a son would do may have served as a consolation to Laius for the childlessness he went to consult it about, 'a good reason for not having the son he thought he wanted' (p. 69).

son who may murder him), and his violence against his newborn child is repeated in the fight on the road when Oedipus ends up killing him.

Oedipus fleetingly alludes to a sadness of his own in leaving his parents, when he tells the Corinthian messenger about the oracle that has kept him away from his home city: 'This is why Corinth has for ages been a very distant place to me. And fortunately. But still the nicest thing is to see your parents face to face' (ll. 998–9). Oedipus makes an oblique reference ('fortunately') to his success in becoming king of Thebes: his leaving had some secondary advantages. But he places himself passively and distances the language from himself or his parents, saying literally that Corinth has been 'living away' from him ('*apôikeito*') all this time; the place is the active subject, as if he has no part himself in the matter. The lines thus echo Oedipus' earlier account of his response to the prophecy: it had the effect of taking away his sense or power of active choice.

JOCASTA

The audience of the tragedy knows all the time that Oedipus is not the birth son of Polybus and Merope and that there is a back-story, before the beginning of his autobiographical narrative, of which he knows nothing. Jocasta, only a few lines earlier, has just described it without having any notion of its reference to the husband she is speaking to. Unlike Oedipus' summary of his upbringing, her own autobiographical narrative presents a nuclear family that is violently broken from the beginning, or from before the beginning. The potential child does not represent the promise of a completion or continuation of the couple, but a threat. Her harrowing story is told briefly and obliquely, not for itself but as would-be proof of the worthlessness of soothsaying. It is meant to reassure Oedipus that he need take no notice of Tiresias' allegation that he was Laius' murderer:

> There was an oracle given to Laius once, I won't say from Apollo himself but from one of his assistants, that it would be his fate to die because of his child, one born to me and him. And Laius, so the story goes, was murdered by foreign [*xenoi*] robbers at a place where three roads cross. As for the child—it was not three days after his birth when that man [Laius] riveted its ankles together and threw it out, by others' hands, onto the untrodden mountainside. So here Apollo did not bring it about that he should be his father's murderer or that Laius should die because of his child—the dreadful thing that he feared. (ll. 711–22)

It is from this testimony, meant as Jocasta's refutation of the validity of oracles, that Oedipus picks up on the detail of the three roads and proceeds to the different story of his own beginnings. He ignores the other coincidence of the father-murdering prophecy which echoes the one he will soon report in relation to himself. There are other overlaps. Oedipus tells of a further repetition of a three. It was on the third day that the baby was put out to die, and on the third day after the drunken insult that, years later, he secretly left his Corinthian home, never to return. It was fear of an oracle that had caused the baby to be thrown out of Thebes and fear of an oracle that led Oedipus as a young man into voluntary exile from Corinth. The parallels hover over the two fragmentary stories as they are presented by speakers unconscious of their connection, each one being brought up not as personal confession or confidential utterance, but as part of a larger argument. Jocasta wants to stop Oedipus worrying about oracles; Oedipus wants to account for his happening to have been in the vicinity of the place where three roads meet. But what he also does is to tell the story of how his own life has been determined by taking an oracle seriously. Without overtly doing so, he is continuing Jocasta's argument although he has seemingly ignored it, going off on a track of his own. He is also quite unaware that he is telling one part of the sequel to Jocasta's story: the baby whose exposure she describes was himself. And he will go on unknowingly to refute her anti-oracular argument, describing how he murdered that baby's father on the road.

Jocasta's snippet of her own autobiography is pregnant with all that it does not say. Seemingly, she is crisply rhetorical in her deployment of information to prove a point. She neither solicits nor receives any sympathy from her interlocutor, who responds to his wife's narrative not feelingly but only as it bears on the present issue of Laius' murder and the value of oracles. She is hardly present herself as an agent in the events she recounts. The oracle she mentions is only half, or less, of the one that Oedipus was later told. Jocasta speaks of parricide (or at least of the son as the cause of the father's death) but not of marrying the mother and having children with her. But it is the maternal elements that dominate in Oedipus' dread of what he might 'see' at Corinth as the oracle's fulfilment: not a murdered father but an incestuous family.

Jocasta, on the other hand, keeps the mother aspect right out of the oracular picture. It is true that it is not part of her immediate argument (that the circumstances of Laius' murder disproved the prophecy of parricide); it could also be that that part of the oracle did not figure in the decision to get rid of the baby. In Jocasta's narrative, it is the fear of his own death that motivates the father's maiming and ejecting of his baby son. The events are narrated anti-chronologically and elliptically in the account of the infant's exposure, as though paring away all detail or naturalism for the sake of the logical argument. Point one: Laius was murdered by non-Thebans, hence not by his son. Point two, long antedating that occurrence: the child was exposed (and thus could not have done it). Jocasta omits to say 'there was a child born to me and Laius'. And she concludes with a symmetrical round-up, describing the same event in two different ways: no, the child did not kill the father; yes, the father was killed, but not by his child.

Because she says nothing directly about them, Jocasta's feelings can only be imagined or conjectured. Depending on how the lines are spoken, there may be bitterness in the specification of 'not three days'. Ostensibly the short time reinforces the point of the baby's incapacity to do any damage to his father, but it may also hint at the grief or anger of a mother whose baby was snatched away so soon or her anger at a father whose precautionary measures were so ruthless. When she says it was Laius who pierced his ankles, the use of the emphatic word *keinos*, 'that man' (l. 718), may carry an accusation, as well as making it clear who is meant. While she specifies that the oracle spoke of the child of both her and Laius, not just Laius' son, Jocasta says nothing of her own thoughts about what should be done if or when a baby son was born. She says nothing about other children born or prevented from living between the time of this baby's exposure and the arrival of Oedipus in Thebes as a young man, a period which must otherwise, and presumably, represent many more years of marriage and childlessness.[11] In particular, she does

[11] Right after the passage on *Oedipus* and *Hamlet* in *The Interpretation of Dreams*, Freud pursues another connection: 'It is known, too, that Shakespeare's own son who died at an early age bore the name of "Hamnet", which is identical with "Hamlet". Just as *Hamlet* deals with the relation of a son to his parents, so *Macbeth* (written at approximately the same period) is concerned with the subject of childlessness [*dem Thema der Kinderlosigkeit*]' (*Interpretation*, iv. 265–6; *Die Traumdeutung*, *GW* ii–iii. 272). This is not a theme that Freud ever develops, although, as we have seen, it is present in Sophocles' *Oedipus* in relation to Polybus and Merope, the Corinthian adoptive parents, childless before Oedipus is given to them and childless once more after he leaves forever. The longing for a child to love is the counterpart to and reverse of the fear of what a child will do (to its parents). But while it addresses the same 'nucleus' of parent–child relationships as the Oedipus complex, the issue of childlessness differs from it in taking adult, not infantile feelings as its starting point. Euripides' *Ion*, discussed in Ch. 8, below, is concerned with both childlessness *and* a child's search for and confusion over his origins.

not make another inference from her claim that the oracle was worthless: that there would have been no reason to do away with the child. She does not say either that Laius' death and her remarriage to another man made it possible for her to have children after all.

Of Oedipus' four parents, Jocasta is the only one to take part in the action of the play, but she does not appear as a mother except in the miserable glimpse of her first baby's first days. It is Oedipus who, after Jocasta's suicide and his own self-blinding, clings to their two daughters and laments the girls' likely fate as subjects of social stigma; once again the word *oneidos*, 'slur' or 'insult', is used (l. 1494), continuing the effects of the drunk Corinthian's fateful utterance. Jocasta's attachments are unspoken, in keeping with the pragmatic and even cynical attitude she publicly promotes. Before she disappears to kill herself, just one hint of suffering appears, when she tries for a last time to deter Oedipus from pursuing his inquiry to the concluding revelation she can now see—that he, her husband, is her baby: 'Please, in the name of the gods, if you care for your own life, don't enquire about that. I have suffered enough' (ll. 1060–1).

Before this, it is she who once again provides the striking, conclusive answer to Oedipus' fears of incest, after the death of Polybus has apparently relieved him of his other anxiety:

JOCASTA Isn't that what I have been telling you all along?

OEDIPUS You did say that. But I was led astray by fear.

JOCASTA Don't now any longer trouble your mind with any of these things.

OEDIPUS And how can it be that I don't have to be afraid of the marrying of the mother?

JOCASTA Why would anyone be afraid who thought that chance controls things, and that there is no clear future knowledge of anything? It is best to live casually [*eikê*: at random], as far as anyone can. Don't you have fears about mother-marrying! Lots of people have slept with their mothers in their dreams. But life is easiest to cope with for someone who thinks nothing of it. (ll. 973–83)

The generalization is at once matter-of-fact and true to Freud, who singled out the passage for quotation in his short discussion of *Oedipus* in *The Interpretation of Dreams*.[12] For everyone but Oedipus himself, dreams of mother-marrying are harmless and inconsequential; psychoanalytically, Jocasta is spot-on, but it is unfortunate that she is faced

[12] Freud, *Interpretation*, *SE* iv. 264; *Die Traumdeutung*, *GW* ii–iii. 270.

with the one exception to the bizarre normal rule. Like Freud, Jocasta universalizes and thereby depersonalizes a peculiar piece of psychology: a son's incestuous dream is only natural. Because it is only a dream and everyone's dream at that, Oedipus can simply put it out of his mind. Literally, she tells him not to 'cast into your mind' ('*es thymon balês*', l. 975), the troublesome thoughts he has seen as being his own individual misfortune, rather than ordinary and trivial disturbances. Jocasta herself throws out what is potentially disturbing.

MEROPE

Oedipus' adoptive mother Merope, who took him in, is barely mentioned in the play, even though at the end she is the only one of his four parents who is still, presumably, alive. She is an even more shadowy figure than Jocasta; indeed it is striking that parental emotions are attributed to fathers alone in this play. Jocasta admits to none, and Merope's are never mentioned. At the start of his autobiographical account, Oedipus distinguishes Merope from her Corinthian husband as being Dorian in origin (l. 775), but in his report of his anxious interrogations after the allegation about his paternity she has no separate identity, just as Oedipus does not mention the possible separation between his two parents that might be implied by the allegation that he is not his father's real son (l. 780). The Corinthian messenger says that he gave baby Oedipus to Laius, and does not mention his wife (l. 1022). Her feelings at the time of the play, in the context of Polybus' death and the decision of the city to send for their son to take his place, are not mentioned by the messenger. It is Polybus' emotional ties to his son, his strong love for a long-awaited child and his likely 'longing' for him after his departure, which are evoked both by the messenger and by Oedipus. Merope emerges only as an almost abstracted source of fear: that while she is alive, there is still that business with the mother to worry about: 'How can it be that I don't have to be afraid of the marrying of the mother [*to mêtros ... lechos*]?' (l. 976). After Jocasta's would-be reassuring speech about incestuous dreams, Oedipus comes back to the same point, unconvinced: because the mother ('*hê tekousa*', 'the woman who gave birth' to him), is still alive—he means Merope—there is every reason, even if Jocasta is right, to be afraid. Jocasta attempts again to allay his anxiety, by pointing out in a logical and emotionless way: 'Even so, the burial of your father is a big relief' (l. 987).[13] Oedipus does not disagree but still reiterates the same unchanging point in four sparse words, '*alla tês zôsês phobos*': 'But the living woman is a source of fear' (l. 988). It is at this point that the messenger comes in with an innocent question that suggests the enigmatic sound of Oedipus' remarks to an outsider:

MESSENGER Who is this woman [literally: 'what manner of woman is it'] who makes you fearful?
OEDIPUS Merope, old man, Polybus' wife.
MESSENGER What is there about her that leads you into fear?
OEDIPUS A dreadful divine oracle, stranger. (ll. 989–92)

It is this messenger who asks for human detail in place of mysterious abstractions, just as he now goes on, with the best will in the world, to seek to calm Oedipus' remaining fear by letting him know that he is adopted. Oedipus has told him about the content of the oracle, which the messenger now understands as being the explanation for his extended absence from home:

MESSENGER Do you know that rightfully you have nothing to be scared of?
OEDIPUS How could I not have, if I was born the child of those parents?
MESSENGER Because Polybus was no relation to you [*ouden en genei*].
OEDIPUS What do you mean? Didn't Polybus beget me?
MESSENGER No more or less than I did. (ll. 1014–18)

Here once more, Merope has disappeared; it is now only the father–son relationship which is present to the two men.

FOSTER-FATHERS

The idea that the servant might have been his father is as ludicrous to Oedipus at this point as the idea that Polybus might not have been. Yet this man, along with the Theban servant who shortly appears, has in fact occupied the role of foster-parent to Oedipus. Between them, they

13 'Relief' translates *ophthalmos*, literally 'eye', and by extension a 'light' or comfort. Jebb remarks that 'A certain hardness of feeling appears in the phrase: Iocasta was softened by fear for Oedipus and the State: she is now elated' (*Oedipus Tyrannus*, 107, note to l. 987). The new 'eye' also appears as a false hope in the context of Oedipus' subsequent self-blinding.

prevented the child of Laius and Jocasta from dying; on the uplands of Mount Cithaeron he was passed from one to the other and then handed on to Polybus—and Merope—to be raised as their own child. The two of them each reappear in the time of the play for reasons that have nothing to do with this history—an embarrassing one for the Theban, who disobeyed the king's instructions by not leaving the child to die. The Theban is summoned in another connection, as the only witness of the murder of Laius and his men. Here too he has guilty knowledge, since he subsequently saw something else: the man he recognized as Laius' killer installed as the new king of Thebes and as the husband of Jocasta. This was a connection that he alone was in a position to make, as the only survivor among Laius' people of the road-rage incident.

The Corinthian turns up at Thebes on quite other business, nothing to do with the murder inquiry in progress. He comes to inform Oedipus of his election as king. It is these two men's coincidental presence together and their conversation at the end of the investigation which finally brings out the truth of the oracle's fulfilment and Oedipus' real history. This exchange between them then echoes and reverses the one so long ago when together they gave the baby a second chance of life; now, unknowingly in the one case and knowingly but wholly reluctantly in the other, they are bringing about his downfall.

Both men separately describe, under questioning from Oedipus, their involvement with him as a baby. In contrast to the 'fear' attributed over and over again to Oedipus and his parents—his birth parents' fear of what he would do to them, his own fear of what he would do to his parents—different motivations lay behind the actions of these men. There is reference instead, at many points, to pitying, rescuing, giving. Here is the Theban servant answering Oedipus' aggressive questions. He has got to the point of establishing that the baby given to the other man was said to be a child of Laius himself:

SERVANT Her inside, your wife, would be best able to tell you, how it was.
OEDIPUS She gave the child to you?
SERVANT She did, sir.
OEDIPUS For what purpose?
SERVANT For me to destroy him.
OEDIPUS And she was its mother [*tekousa*], poor woman?
SERVANT It was out of fear of bad oracles.
OEDIPUS What were they?
SERVANT He was going to kill his father—that was the story.
OEDIPUS And how come you gave it away to this old man here?

SERVANT Out of pity [*katoiktisas*], sir. Thinking he would take it away into another land, whereas I was from round here. (ll. 1171–9)

The servant's pity takes over from the mother's (and father's) fear.

The later handing of the baby from the Theban to the Corinthian has already been evoked, in equally gentle terms. The Corinthian does not realize the Theban's reasons for embarrassment at what he did, and prods him: 'Come on, say it now, you know that in those days you gave me a child, for me to raise it for myself, the little creature?' (ll. 1142–3). The words used here are tautologically both endearing and down-to-earth, '*hôs emautôi thremma threpsaimên egô*'—literally, 'for me to raise it for myself as a young-creature-for-raising'. The noun *thremma* is commonly used of the young of animals, not humans. The baby was to be tended with the care that any living thing deserves, without royal privileges or royal abuses, in this world that is out of the city.

The Corinthian is twice referred to as having 'saved' or 'rescued' Oedipus. First by the Theban servant, after he has explained the need to have the baby taken abroad: 'But he rescued him for the worst of futures [*kak' es megist' esôsen*]' (l. 1180). And secondly, by himself when he chides Oedipus for seemingly suspecting him of having done what he did for money:

OEDIPUS Had you bought [the child], or just come across it when you gave it to him [Polybus]?
MESSENGER I had found [you] among the twists and turns of Cithaeron's valleys.
OEDIPUS What were you doing wandering about in those parts?
MESSENGER That was where I was stationed as an upland shepherd.
OEDIPUS So you were a shepherd and a hired labourer?
MESSENGER Child, I was your rescuer [*sôtêr*] at that time. (ll. 1025–30)

Exasperated, or gently corrective, the shepherd ends by putting Oedipus in his original, helpless place. He restores priorities of life and death that Oedipus, both in his assumed superiority over the man he is speaking to, and in his concern for his personal status, ignores. Oedipus cannot bear the idea of low-born origins that might even have made him an object of purchase as a future slave. Later on, now talking to Jocasta, he also baulks at the thought that he might have come from a line of slaves (ll. 1062–3).

The theme of rescue also has the effect of identifying the Theban foster-father with his 'son'. At the beginning of the play, the Theban suppliants seeking respite from the plague afflicting their city address Oedipus as its former rescuer or saviour ('*sôtêr*', l. 48). As we have seen, the Theban servant gives 'pity' as his reason for disobeying Laius' orders and instead letting the baby be saved (ll. 1178–80). Oedipus speaks of 'pitying [*katoiktirôn*]' (l. 13) the people's predicament and later addresses them, father-like, as 'pitiful [*oiktroi*] children' (l. 58). Later, in his argument with Tiresias, he describes himself as putting the city's interests above the personal accusations that Tiresias is bringing in: 'But as long as I saved [*exesôsa*] the city, [my own fate] does not matter to me' (l. 443). After the fight in which Laius and most of his entourage are killed by Oedipus on the road, the same man who had first saved Oedipus by failing to expose him was, he says, '*eksôtheis monos*', 'the only one saved' (l. 756) or sole survivor. Then he too, like Oedipus, survived only for the worst of futures. Returning home, he cannot bear to stay, as Jocasta reports it: 'As soon as he came from there and saw you were king and Laius had been killed, he begged me, touching my hand, to send him into the fields to be a shepherd on the hills, so that he would be as far away as possible from the sight of this town' (ll. 758–62). In one of Sophocles' piercing ironic touches, Jocasta explains very well the reasons whose background she does not yet understand herself. The servant knows that the man he sees as the new king is the one who killed Laius, and that is why he begs to be allowed to go. As would fit the logic of his realization, the order of events is reversed. The man already knows (and Jocasta knew that he knew) that Laius is dead, and that is not something new that he 'sees'; but seeing Oedipus king is seeing Laius' murder in a different light, the killer now having taken his place. This isolation of the one survivor now burdened with guilty knowledge is exactly like that of Oedipus himself. Jocasta refers to the Theban's need to be 'as far away as possible from the sight of this town' in the same way that Oedipus, recalling the effect that Apollo's oracle had on him, speaks of needing to get away from Corinth: 'And when I heard that, I fled the land of Corinth, for the future measuring its distance by the stars, so as never to see the fulfilment of the slurs of my bad oracles' (ll. 794–7).[14]

Like Oedipus, the Theban servant who was 'raised in the [royal] household [*oikoi trapheis*]' (l. 1123) is forced to leave home. Oedipus flees a future he fears to bring about unintentionally; the servant flees a present reality that has come about through no fault of his own. And the Theban will be brought back home at the end, against his will, to be tortured into

[14] In *The Women of Trachis*, Sophocles' chorus uses the same combination of distant exile and aversion to an intolerable sight in the wish they express for a wind that might 'take them away from home [*apoikiseien*]' (l. 955) so that they need not die 'looking upon' (l. 958) the sight of Heracles in his agony.

imparting the truth of his kindly role in Oedipus' early story. His crime is that he saved him; like his foster-son, he is himself later rescued, 'the only one saved', and—again like Oedipus—saved only to have to abandon his home forever. Like 'father', like 'son' in this respect; but in every other, the distance between them relegates the servant to insignificance. The servant's story is a sub-plot that is there to be found in the lines of *Oedipus* but has to be extricated piece by piece. It is the marginal tragedy of one who does not count among the major players either in Oedipus' complex personal history or in the political upheavals at Thebes.

MOUNT CITHAERON

At the point when he has learned the whole truth of his birth, Oedipus appeals to Cithaeron, the mountainside where he was meant to have died: 'Cithaeron, why did you take me in? Why did you not get hold of me and kill me on the spot, so that I might never have shown [*edeixa*] people where I came from [*enthen ê gegôs*]?' (ll. 1391–3). Cithaeron is another of Oedipus' partial parents, embodied in the fixity of a place. Cithaeron is personified as a halfway home-giver, between the birth and the adoptive parents, and between the two nurturing shepherds through and with whom the mountain 'took him in'. Its protection in infancy has only made inevitable a worse exposure as Oedipus now reveals to the world his origins, where and who he 'came from'. In the Greek, place and parents are linguistically indistinguishable kinds of origin; the child 'comes from' a city or region or parent. At this final, hopeless point in the denouement, Oedipus settles on Cithaeron as the intermediate site, getting away from his real birthplace and birth parents; Cithaeron is in between his bad and his comfortable origins. He then turns to Polybus and Merope and Corinth (again, place and parents are on the same footing): 'Polybus and Merope, and my old home country, in theory, you raised me [*exethrepsate*] as a beautiful thing [*kallos*] when I was a festering sore of evils [*kakôn*]. For now I am found to be bad [*kakos*] and the son of bad [*kakôn*] parents' (ll. 1395–7).

TYCHÊ

There is one more passing parent. When he has learned that he was a foundling before being adopted and thus, he thinks, likely to be of low birth, Oedipus suggests he might be the child of *Tychê* or Chance, 'the generously giving [*tês eu didousês*]' (l. 1080-1), and he amplifies this idea in an image of alternating good and bad fortune allocated by the varying months of the year who would be accompanying the time of his life (ll. 1082–3). There is an ominous echo of Jocasta's words, not long before: 'Why would anyone be afraid who thought that *Tychê* controls things, and that there is no clear future knowledge of anything? It is best to live casually, as far as anyone can' (ll. 977–9). Jocasta has not herself always lived according to this rubric (her son was exposed), and in the meantime, she has left the stage, never to return. For Oedipus, now, *Tychê* is a desperate fantasy of escape from consequential actions, a dream of a life of passive fluctuation, ups and downs. His words are spoken at a crucial point, between two declarations of resolve to find out his real origins. As transitional carers, the nurturing and the giving, Cithaeron and *Tychê* have features in common with the two foster-fathers who actively brought about Oedipus' rescue, and they add to the burden of one of the play's implicit questions: What are a child's real origins? And concomitantly, what or who is a parent?

ORIGINS

> It shall be my wish to know my origin [*sperma*: seed]. (ll. 1076–7)
>
> [But] it is in my born nature and I couldn't turn out different, not finding out where I come from [*toumon genos*: my race or family]. (ll. 1084–5)

These lines, spoken by Oedipus on either side of the lines about being the son of *Tychê* or Chance, make a strong claim about an inborn, as if original, need to know origins, as being specific to himself and not to others for whom the same urgency may not apply. Oedipus is one who needs to know, to find out; he must ask and answer the question of his own origin or family. But despite the linking of the 'born nature' (literally, 'being born this kind of person [*toiosde ekphys*]') to the search for origins, his determination in this endeavour is in reality newfound; it has been forced upon him in the course of the investigation that he is undertaking into the murder of Laius.

The quest for knowledge of his own birth and beginnings only emerges in the play as an offshoot of what started as a different kind of inquiry, undertaken on behalf of a city state, not a family or an individual. For this Oedipus is qualified for the very reason that he is presumed to be an outsider, as he precisely states: he is (or believes he is) 'a stranger [*xenos*] to the story, and a stranger to what happened' (ll. 219–20). It is civic not private concerns that ultimately drive him to seek, or rather to wonder about, his origins, and to discover that he is anything but a foreigner to either the personal or the public aspects of Laius' murder.[15] The beginning of the personal questioning is signalled when Oedipus pauses, troubled by the seer's allegations, and asks Tiresias: 'Who was my father? [*tis de m' ekphyei brotôn*?]'—or literally, 'Who among mortals engendered me?' (l. 437). Tiresias replies enigmatically or evasively, worried at what he has said himself: 'This day will both engender you and destroy you' (l. 438). Earlier he had himself asked Oedipus sharply, 'Do you know who your parents are?' (l. 415). Oedipus' personal story *is* the story of how Laius was killed and, years before that, the story of Laius' and Jocasta's response to the oracle that led them to put out their baby to die; and the two reconstructions of a past history prove to be wholly enmeshed with one another. What began as a political crisis has become, additionally, a personal one.

Charles Segal wrote that Oedipus' problem is that he lacks 'the basic information about his origins that gives man his human identity'.[16] In other words, his Corinthian parents have not told him that he was adopted. What the play further suggests, I think, is that in this matter the 'basic information', in either a historical or a psychological sense, is never single or straightforward, even if there are no errors or concealments. The parental unit, of whatever form, into which the child is born, appears to him or her as a timeless given. It *is* the 'basic information' for him or her, but from the point of view of the social world or the parents or caregivers themselves it is contingent and open to question, however enduring or stable it may really be. A child's parents were always something else, individually or as a couple, before they were that unit or combination, short-lived or continuing, that 'had' him or her; and

[15] Oedipus' position as *xenos* is differently ambiguous in *Oedipus at Colonus*, where he is given asylum by Theseus, the king of Athens, before his death. In *Oedipus the King* he is (until shown otherwise) a '*xenos* ... *metoikos*' (l. 452), a resident alien 'living amongst' the community: *metoikos*—'metic'—is the standard term. In *Oedipus at Colonus* the *xenos* as visitor or non-citizen is a *xenos* who is subject to special consideration. See Jacques Derrida, *Of Hospitality* (1997), trans. Rachel Bowlby (Stanford, CA: Stanford University Press, 2000), 35–43, 87–121. On the position of the suppliant-foreigner seeking protection from a host country, see also the discussion of Aeschylus' *Suppliants* in Ch. 3, above.

[16] Charles Segal, *Tragedy and Civilization: An Interpretation of Sophocles* (1981; Norman: University of Oklahoma Press, 1999), 207.

in that sense, through that unknown prehistory, the child has 'origins' that are unknown, and more or less significant still for the mother and father, separately or together, consciously or unconsciously, however harmonious and foreseeably permanent the present family unit.[17]

Oedipus' particular history of infant migration from Thebes to Corinth, where well-off childless parents awaited him, also resonates with a specific phenomenon in changing contemporary kinship and reproductive practices: transnational adoption. This has been developing at a rapid rate since the 1990s, with babies typically moving from Third World or former East European countries to the (established) West. Contemporary transnational adoption may, as with Oedipus, begin with a baby's abandonment, in which case there is likely to be an interim period of fostering, whether in private or institutional homes. As with Oedipus, the foster-parents are indispensable but commonly forgotten helpers and sometimes life-savers.

As with almost every other kind of international communication, the internet now facilitates the process of long-distance adoption. But there are also long-term social changes which have contributed to the expansion of the demand. The number of babies available for adoption in most Western countries has greatly decreased—because of contraception and access to abortion when a pregnancy is unwanted, but also, perhaps even more significantly, because of the all but complete disappearance, in the space of a generation, of the stigma attached to illegitimacy, whether for mother or child. Previously, and often accompanied by many kinds of pressure, the assumption was that a child born out of wedlock would quickly be 'given up' for adoption; now it is that mothers of whatever age or circumstances will want to keep their baby. The figure of the 'unmarried' or 'unwed' mother is no longer a meaningful social, let alone moral category, when both single parenthood and joint but non-married parenthood are common family conditions.[18] On the other, adoptive

[17] Derrida makes a related point in Derrida and Elisabeth Roudinesco, *De quoi demain ...: Dialogue* (Paris: Fayard, 2002): 'I think I know my father and my mother. Beyond that, I don't know the origins of my parents. And I would never know, with what we call certain knowledge, what went on between my assumed father and mother "around" my birth' (p. 80).

[18] The decline of the 'unmarried mother' has been matched by the rise of the 'single parent', and the difference between them is indicative of the ideological change that has taken place. Unlike the stigmatized unmarried mother, the neutral 'single parent' suggests only a household situation and refers to parents of either sex; it covers an indefinite number of possible reproductive and relationship histories, often including a former marriage or partnership.

side, changing norms of relationship are equally significant. The fall in the local supply of babies for adoption particularly impacts upon the new kinds of prospective parent: single people or gay couples, among others.

Narratives of the modern experience stress the sense of doubled origins, for the child but also, equally significantly, for the adoptive parent or parents. These may seek to establish a bond with the birth country that reinforces their own tie to the child, as well as offering children a connection with their beginnings. But it is emphasized that there is never a simple story of final reuniting, even though a sense of completion is what is most desired and sometimes experienced.[19] Transnational adoption doubles the already twofold origins inherent in any adoption by adding the dimension of place. The child comes from more than one culture, more than one land, as well as from more than two parents. But this extreme case points to something that is true of all families, even the most straightforwardly nuclear. Oedipus shows this himself when he begins his autobiographical narrative by separating his parents, not just as two individuals but according to their different country of origin: 'My father was Polybus, a Corinthian, my mother Merope, a Dorian' (ll. 774–5).

SILENCES

How far might Oedipus' exposure and rescue have echoed actual experience at the time of the play's first performance? Because the practice is almost inevitably secret and unrecorded, it is not possible to measure the real historical incidence of infant abandonment in fifth-century Greece (or indeed in any culture). In *The Family in Classical Greece*, W. K. Lacey proposes that exposure would have taken place primarily on economic grounds, but that the economic motives are themselves debatable. For instance, against the thought that girls were more likely to be treated as superfluous, it can be argued that girls required only a small dowry, whereas having more than one son meant that the estate might have to be divided on the death of the parents. Lacey states that 'there can be no doubt whatever that the exposure of surplus children was practised

[19] On contemporary transnational adoption see *The Adoption Issue*, *Tulsa Studies in Women's Literature*, 21: 2 (Fall 2002); *Transnational Adoption*, ed. Toby Alice Volkman and Cindi Katz, *Social Text*, 74 (Spring 2003), esp. Barbara Yngevesson, 'Going "Home": Adoption, Loss of Bearings, and the Mythology of Roots', pp. 7–27.

throughout antiquity'.[20] But he also says that 'if exposure was freely practised [in classical Athens], it seems odd that the disposal of her children in this way does not form part of any of the women's tirades against men in the literary sources such as those of Euripides' *Medea*, or Aristophanes' *Lysistrata* and other female spokesmen.'[21] Creusa's speeches in the *Ion*, discussed in the next chapter, are a possible exception to this, and Jocasta's understated protest at her baby's wounding and exposure, discussed above, could be another, vestigial one. Yet the counter-examples may be less important here than the likelihood that silence, or relative silence, does not necessarily imply that there is nothing to be said, or nothing felt; it may be just the opposite. Alongside its homing in on Oedipus' fateful history, Sophocles' play offers many other glimpses, as if from a far-off distance, of origins and parents and babies found and lost.

20 W. K. Lacey, *The Family in Classical Greece* (London: Thames and Hudson, 1968), 164.

21 Ibid. 165–6. Lacey's resort to this argument *a contrario* by reference to two plays is all the more telling in that for the book as a whole he explicitly excludes literary in favour of legal evidence, equally absent on this matter.

8

Playing God: Reproductive Realism in Euripides' *Ion*

In 1920 Gilbert Norwood pointed out an area of feeling left unmarked in Sophocles' *Oedipus the King*, as well as in the commentary on the play. At the end, after the revelations about Oedipus' identity, Jocasta is a mother meeting the son who she thought had died in infancy. But this experience, overwhelming on its own, cannot be separately lived or spoken apart from the other, simultaneous revelations:

> To have lost her child at birth, then after mourning his death for many years at length to find that he lives, that he stands before her, mature, strong, and kingly, but her own husband; then to realize that not now but long ago did she recover him, yet did not know him but loved him otherwise—this even Sophocles has not put into speech.[1]

In the *Ion*, Euripides did put into words the extremes of pain and joy attending both the separation and the reuniting of a mother and son. Here there has been no incest or murder. But the child was the result of a rape, and both infanticide and matricide are reciprocally and unknowingly attempted during the time of the play, before the mutual recognitions. The *Ion* features the story of a mother who, like Jocasta, exposed her child at birth and finds him again when he is grown up. Norwood wrote of this play, in an extraordinary sentence, that 'were it not that the basis of the story is so painfully sexual, the *Ion* would be perhaps the most popular of Greek plays.'[2] Yet in a twentieth century preoccupied with the sexual, and the painfully sexual, it was Sophocles' *Oedipus*—or rather Freud's Oedipus—that occupied centre-stage.

For Freud, Oedipus' story is the extreme case that shows the dark potential underlying normal lives. *Ion*, on the other hand, is closer to the

[1] Gilbert Norwood, *Greek Tragedy* (London: Methuen, 1920), 153.
[2] Ibid. 237.

emotions and experiences of possible lived realities, exploring the secrets and yearnings of men, women, and children in search of family. Its mixture of celebrity sensation and ordinary unhappiness includes a queen who speaks out publicly for the first time many years after being sexually abused; an adopted adolescent's wish to know his birth mother; a woman's search for the baby she had in her teens; and a couple's consultation about their infertility problem. Some of the specific issues raised seem uncannily contemporary, as Margaret Rustin and Michael Rustin succinctly suggest: '*Ion* is a remarkably modern play, nearly 2,500 years old.'[3]

The starting point of the *Ion* is not, as in the *Oedipus*, a pressing, immediate crisis of state, but a long-standing problem that is at once personal, familial, and political. A husband and wife, Creusa and Xuthus, have come to consult the oracle at Delphi, Apollo's shrine, about their childlessness. Creusa is queen of Athens; the succession depends on her offspring. Years ago, before her marriage, she had a baby, as a result of being raped by Apollo, and exposed it to die, having kept both pregnancy and labour secret. Unknown to her, the baby was rescued by Apollo's design and taken to Delphi where he was raised by its priestess, the Pythia, as a temple assistant; this baby is Ion, now grown up. Subsequently Creusa was married to Xuthus, not a native Athenian, but with divine connections (son of Aeolus and grandson of Zeus), as a reward for his aid to Athens in a war. This complicated background is laid out quite fully for the audience in a prologue delivered by Apollo's brother Hermes, together with the god's plans for what is to happen now. Xuthus is to be told (falsely) that Ion is his son, so that Ion

[3] Margaret Rustin and Michael Rustin, *Mirror to Nature: Drama, Psychoanalysis and Society* (London: Karnac, 2002), 49. Given its resonance with contemporary issues, it is fitting that this relatively neglected play has recently been revived. On the two London productions in 1994, see Ruth Padel, '*Ion*: Lost and Found', *Arion*, 4 (1996), 216–24. The *Ion* was also performed in Colchester in 2004. The play had an earlier moment of modern cultural significance when William Whitehead's mid-eighteenth-century adaptation, *Creusa, Queen of Athens,* contributed to two burning issues of family politics at the time—foundling children and legal marriage. The Foundling Hospital, recently established in Bloomsbury by Thomas Coram, was based on the principle that children could thrive, and should be given the chance to, outside a family. Whitehead's Ion figure does not fully vindicate this, partly because, unlike Euripides' Ion, he unequivocally has a mortal father who had a relationship with his mother and who has contributed to his nurturing. The play also speaks to the intentions of the Marriage Act, which formalized the conditions of legal marriage and favoured the choosing of spouses for love; this came into effect in 1754, the same year as *Creusa*'s first performance. See Edith Hall and Fiona Macintosh, *Greek Tragedy and the British Theatre 1660–1914* (Oxford: Oxford University Press, 2005), 128–51.

can be taken into the family and adopted by Creusa as the Athenian royal heir; Creusa is to find out subsequently that her supposed stepson is really her own after all. This is indeed the ambiguous situation at the end of the play, with the establishment of the Athenian succession backed by separate, incompatible parental beliefs; but through Creusa's unanticipated protests, it has come about sooner than planned.

At the beginning, Creusa strikes up an immediate intimacy with Ion. She is waiting for her consultation with the oracle and he is bustling about his temple duties, taking an interest, as presumably he does every day, in the problems that the morning's visitors have brought for the god's attention. Without saying she is speaking about herself, Creusa tells Ion about a woman she knows who is seeking for news of a long-lost baby; Ion, in return, tells what he knows of his own history as a foundling, one who longs to know his birth mother. But subsequently Creusa and Ion almost murder one another before happily, on both sides, finding each other as mother and son. The hitch occurs because Xuthus is told by the oracle that he already has a child of his own; Creusa finds out, and the news that this natural son of her husband is none other than the nice young lad in the temple turns her against him. She is furious at Apollo's inferred forgetting of her and of their child, and also at the plan that Xuthus' child, non-Athenian as well as extra-marital, should be adopted as her family's. At the instigation of her old servant, she attempts to have the usurper murdered. The plan backfires and Ion, at this point believing himself to be Xuthus' son, then turns against his would-be murderer and jealous stepmother. It is when Creusa is taking refuge at Apollo's altar that the priestess brings in the cradle in which the baby Ion was found at the temple, and the recognition and reconciliation of mother and son take place (now, to calm the situation, rather than later, following the return to Athens, as Hermes had stated the plan). Athena, another sibling standing in for Apollo, is then brought on as a *dea ex machina* to explain the future, which includes Ion's 'Ionian' descendants in parts of Asia Minor, and children of both of them to be born at last to the previously childless couple of Xuthus and Creusa.[4]

[4] Freud read the *Ion* at the very end of his life, in the newly published English translation by the poet H.D., which she had sent him (she had been his patient). On 26 February 1937 he wrote in thanks to her: 'Deeply moved by the play (which I had not known before) and no less by your comments, especially those referring to the end, where you extol the victory of reason over passions' (trans. Annemarie Holborn, in H.D., *Tribute to Freud* (Manchester: Carcanet, 1970), 194).

ION AND OEDIPUS

The plot and preoccupations of *Ion* have many points in common with those of *Oedipus*, and the comparison may help to highlight the different issues raised by each of them.[5] In both, a baby boy born to a royal mother and now grown to young manhood was abandoned but, unknown to the birth mother, subsequently adopted. In both, the mother and her husband have been childless ever since (explicitly in the *Ion*, presumably in *Oedipus*). For both Oedipus and Ion there are four, not two principal parents (Apollo, Creusa, Xuthus, and the priestess in the *Ion*). Both young men take on the role of investigator, questioning witnesses to try to establish the truth. Both plays involve a retracing of the old story of the baby's birth and exposure, leading to what is new knowledge for the grown man about his origins. In both, there is violence between parent and child.[6]

There is also a comparison in terms of the politics of royal kinship. Both plays involve the arrival from elsewhere of a new heir or ruler whose legitimacy turns out to be additionally justifiable on grounds of blood relationship. Ion initially seems to be the son of the queen's foreign husband, and not of her. Oedipus is made king and given the queen in marriage because he defeats the Sphinx. Both men are revealed—Ion almost immediately, Oedipus much later—as being in reality natural sons of the two ruling families.

There is a further likeness. As Freud pointed out himself, the urgent conversational unravelling that makes up the action of *Oedipus* can be 'likened to the work of a psycho-analysis', leading towards a dramatic, final ending.[7] The *Ion* also is reminiscent of therapeutic processes, and directly so, since Delphi is an ancient equivalent. As Margaret and Michael Rustin put it, 'It is as if the temple were trying to practise a

[5] Charles Segal has also explored this comparison, in 'Euripides' *Ion*: Generational Passage and Civic Myth', *Bucknell Review*, 43: 1 (1999), 100–2, and *Oedipus Tyrannus: Tragic Heroism and the Limits of Knowledge* (1993; 2nd edn. New York: Oxford University Press, 2001), 29–30, 66. *Oedipus the King* was almost certainly the earlier of the two plays, though neither is securely dated. Various historical or stylistic criteria have been used to argue that *Oedipus* was probably performed between 429 and 425, and *Ion* between 415 and 410.

[6] In one case (Creusa and Ion), between mother and son, during the time of the play, and intended on both sides as murder; in the other between father and son (Oedipus and Laius), a long time ago. Murder was the intention of Laius' manacling of his baby's legs prior to its exposure, and the unintended result of the son's defensive assault on the road, many years later.

[7] Freud, *The Interpretation of Dreams*, *SE* iv. 262; *Die Traumdeutung*, *GW* ii–iii. 268.

sort of psychotherapy with each member of this family separately and is finding great difficulty in bringing together all the narratives constructed in this process.'[8]

These similarities can serve point by point to show up radical differences between the two plays. Sophocles' Jocasta was married when she had her baby; pregnancy was not as such a source of shame. Creusa was a virgin, raped (she claims or believes) by a god. Until the time of the present action, Oedipus never knew of his adoptive history, whereas Ion is fully aware of having been a foundling and hence of not knowing who his birth parents were. In fact he longs to be reunited with his mother, whereas Oedipus has removed himself deliberately from his supposed origins.[9] Oedipus goes back over his personal history only to aid the public inquiry in progress; Ion is curious about his personal history from the start. In the *Ion*, Creusa comes out with a protesting narrative of her rape and motherhood that she has known and kept secret for years; in *Oedipus*, Jocasta's brief story of her lost baby is not given a personal colouring, but meant to prove a point about the futility of oracles. Another point of divergence concerns the plurality of parents in the two plays. In *Oedipus*, leaving aside the role of the shepherd foster-fathers, the four parents—Jocasta and Laius, Polybus and Merope—pair off normally into two married couples. But in the *Ion*, there is muddle. Mutually incompatible revelations and parent–child recognitions take place, and none of the various possible pairs of natural or fostering parents has ever been publicly coupled.[10] This is true even though this play ends with the supposedly secure constitution of a nuclear family of two parents plus their son, and *Oedipus* with the opposite, a family broken up by the unbearable disclosure of its unknown histories. In the *Oedipus*, an inextricable confusion and conflation of relationships is too clearly revealed, and Oedipus' own imagined nuclear origins as the one child of his Corinthian parents are shown up as masking the truth; in the *Ion*, parental origins and family futures are not really sorted out at all, even if on the surface they may appear to be.

In political terms, the contrast is of a different kind. The discovery that Oedipus was in fact Laius' son is catastrophic, but Ion turning out to be the son of Creusa, not just her foreign husband's illegitimate son, will positively establish the dynastic future of Athens. At this level the play

[8] Rustin and Rustin, *Mirror to Nature*, 62.

[9] Sophocles, *Oedipus the King*, ll. 794–6. See further Ch. 7, above.

[10] These couples are (by birth) Apollo and Creusa, or Xuthus and a young woman from Delphi; and (by upbringing) Apollo and the priestess.

can function as patriotically satisfying for its first audience. Beginning with Hermes' prologue, there are references to the grand mythological past of Athens and its future destiny throughout. The Athenian women accompanying their queen to Delphi are tourists gratified to recognize a picture of their civic deity Athena on the walls of the famous temple. Ion is able to flatter Creusa and thence the audience by showing his detailed knowledge of Athenian historical mythology when he speaks to her for the first time. But the allusions to myth are not straightforward at the level of the personal story of the play, since the distinction between human and divine is a live issue. Creusa claims to have had a child with a god; her forebears only a couple of generations back were supposedly born directly from the earth. This play actively engages the status of the mythical as an open question, and one that is crucial to the characters' understanding of their situations in the present time. Parenthood and sexuality, as central issues, are explored through the different kinds of story through which they are narrated and experienced.

HER STORY

Secrets of parenthood run through the *Ion*, providing the motivations of action and the subject of present talk and ancient silence. There are things known and not spoken (Creusa's early baby), or things known as unknown (Ion's parentage, a mystery both to himself and to the Pythia, his foster-mother). Creusa's pregnancy and birth are mentioned by Hermes in the prologue as 'unknown to her father [*agnôs de patri*]' (l. 14) at the time, just as the origin of the baby that is dropped off at the Delphic temple is unknown to the woman who brings him up and therefore to the child himself: 'She [the priestess] didn't know the father was Phoebus, nor did she know who the birth mother was, and the boy was not aware of who his parents were' (ll. 49–51). Apollo being the father would signify for the Pythia, while Creusa, who is nothing to her individually but matters in her first relation to Ion (which the Pythia will later recognize as that of a prior claim), is referenced only as the hypothetical mother. Ion, as the ignorant child, would like simply to know the identities of his parents, though it is his mother about whom he speculates most often. Creusa, up to the time of the play, has told no one her secret during the many years that have elapsed since her baby was born. Talking to Ion, she tells the story of the god's violation and the loss of the baby indirectly, as that of someone else, '*tis emôn philôn*', 'one of my friends' (l. 338).

Commentators generally refer to Creusa's third-person character in quotation marks, as her 'friend';[11] the device is like a screen-name alias, suggestive of a modern consciousness of the uses of anonymity and the disguise of personal identities. Quite different from pretending to be someone else, a type of disguise that occurs in many Greek tragedies,[12] this is a strategy that involves telling your own story as that of another: pretending *not* to be the subject of the story. At the same time, the absence of a name—not just not 'my' story, but the story of an unidentified 'friend of mine'—works something like the modern 'urban myth': the likely story verging on the incredible, but authenticated by the relative closeness of the source (typically given as a friend of the friend who told the present narrator). Creusa's anonymous personal story is all the more pointed since Ion himself, at this stage, is without a name. It is Xuthus, in his own new, belated role of father, who names him Ion—'going'—because the oracle tells him that the first person he encounters when he is 'going out [*exionti*]', (l. 662) will be his son. Officially, the name points to the 'Ionian' future of the descendants of Creusa and Xuthus.[13] But it might also suggest the lack of fixity in the personal and familial identities assigned and adopted in this play. Ion is a present participle, 'ongoing' in both grammar and meaning—a mobile subject.

In the *Ion* the situation and feelings of both the birth mother and the adopted child are dominant concerns; Ion, unlike Oedipus, knows that there is a mystery about his origin, and knows that the Pythian priestess is not his birth mother. Hence his interest in Creusa's initial story about her friend, and his repeated expression of longing to know who his mother was. He enters sympathetically into the thought of her predicament, as involving a loss they share, and tells her that he was not breast-fed (l. 319). Later, when their real relationship has been revealed, there is a sensual evocation of the baby pleasures that both have missed: 'During the time when I should have been wallowing in my mother's arms and finding some joy in life, I was deprived of the nurture of my dearest mother. But she who gave birth to me was miserable too.

[11] As long ago as the late nineteenth century: A. W. Verrall referred to 'a pretended "friend"', in *Euripides the Rationalist* (1895; New York: Russell & Russell, 1967), 142.

[12] Examples include Sophocles' *Philoctetes* and *Electra*, and Euripides' *Helen*.

[13] The name was previously announced by Hermes in the prologue (ll. 74–5) as linking Ion with the founding of eponymous settlements in Asia. In *Converging Truths: Euripides' 'Ion' and the Athenian Quest for Self-Definition* (Leiden: Brill, 2003), Katerina Zacharia argues that the play skilfully joins this myth of an Ionian future with its flattering allusions to the myth of Athenian authochthony.

Because her suffering was the same, having lost the delights of a child' (ll. 1375–9). The reciprocity here includes Ion's grown-up imagining of what it would have been like to enjoy being both mother and baby.[14] He never blames his mother for abandoning him, and instantly forgives his would-be murderer turned long-lost mother at the end.

Creusa too asks many questions of the boy who must be about the same age as her own son would have been; the dialogue between them goes to and fro with each in turn taking the initiative. Ion first shows his familiarity with the typical topics of oracular enquiry:

ION Is it about harvests or about children that you have come?
CREUSA We have no children, although we have been married for a long time.
ION So you have never given birth but you are childless?
CREUSA Apollo knows about my childlessness.
ION Poor woman! Although you are fortunate in other ways, yet you are so unfortunate.
CREUSA And you—who are you? I consider your mother a very lucky woman.
ION I am called the god's, his slave, and I am.
CREUSA Given by a city or sold by someone?
ION I only know one thing: I am called Apollo's.
CREUSA Then I pity you in my turn.
ION Because I don't know who was the woman who gave birth to me or who my father was. (ll. 303–14)

The exchange is steeped in the irony of double reference, with Creusa unknowingly pointing to her 'lucky' self as Ion's mother, and knowingly but covertly (Ion is not meant to get it) pointing the finger at Apollo as an answer to the question about whether she has ever had a child. Ion is quick off the mark in spotting the possible discrepancy between childlessness and giving birth. But as far as he himself is concerned, double meanings need not be mysterious. To be 'the god's' or 'Apollo's' is to be his slave but also, in another sense, his son. He has yet to acquire the name Ion, and for the time being he has neither a name nor a fixed abode or space of his own: though he lives in the temple, he kips down, as he tells Creusa in answer to a further question, 'wherever sleep takes hold of me' (l. 315). So the effect of the irony here is not so much to

[14] Euripides also evokes the pleasures of babyhood in *Hecuba*, where Philoxena, about to be sacrificed on the command of the Greeks, speaks to her mother of 'your breast, where I had such sweet suckling' (l. 424).

prefigure a dark truth that will later emerge (as in *Oedipus*) as to add to the sense of the provisionality of all identities in the play.

Later, we will turn to the singular complexities of Ion's subjective predicament. But the 'modernizing' of the *Ion* in recent decades began, in the wake of 1960s feminism, with a concentration not on him but on the sexual politics of his mother's history. Her story is an old story—not just because it is a commonplace tale of cruel seduction and abandonment, but because, in the time of the play, it has stayed with Creusa as her secret all these years.

Initially, Creusa is drawn to telling her story, but only indirectly, to the young man serving at the shrine of the god who ruined her life but from whom she has come to seek help. Then she becomes outraged by Apollo's injustice in allocating a child to Xuthus but not to her, whom he wronged both in seducing her and in depriving her of her motherhood. It is at this point that she decides to tell her long-suppressed narrative of the rape itself to the chorus and the old servant:

> Oh, how shall I be silent? But how shall I bring to light my dark 'marriage' and leave behind my shame? Yet what is stopping me now? Who am I fighting in a contest for virtue? Hasn't my husband become my betrayer? I am deprived of my home, I am deprived of children. My hopes are gone; I was unable to bring them to fulfilment as I wished, decently keeping silent about my union and my lamentable giving birth. (ll. 859–69)

It is at this moment when she feels that all her hopes have vanished or fled—'*phroudai d' elpides*' (l. 866), as children might leave home—that Creusa gives up or gives way, no longer keeping her secret and her complaint to herself. In her conversation with Ion she had explained how she (or rather her friend) had hoped that Apollo might make amends for his former wrongs (ll. 425–7) or else give her information about the fate of their baby (ll. 346, 388–9).[15] Now, taking Xuthus' newly affirmed paternity as the final answer, she has nothing to lose (or gain), so no more 'shame' ('*aidous*', l. 861). The loss of hopes is the loss of the possible future stories to which she has clung as a chance of putting the past behind her. The secret, source of shame, had also sustained her—kept her hoping.[16]

[15] In a late Victorian edition for schoolboys, M. A. Bayfield sensitively remarks, in his note to Creusa's confessional monody, that 'Two hopes made it possible to live. She thought she might some day find the baby she had lost, or if not that, that at least she might have another child. ... In a moment this last hope is rudely torn from her, and with insult' (*The 'Ion' of Euripides* (London: Macmillan, 1889), 117).

[16] Female hoping and hopelessness in relation to lost children also appear in Sophocles' *Electra*. In that play, Electra bemoans her *biotos anelpistos*, 'a life without hope' (l. 185),

The confession and protest that follow dwell on the moment before the seizure of innocence, as Creusa seems to look back at the picture of herself as a young girl gathering flowers, when the god came and snatched her away:

You came to me with your hair shimmering gold when I was gathering yellow flowers in my lap, a golden light of flowers. Gripping me by my pale wrists you took me without shame and laid me down in a cave crying out *Oh mother*, a god, a lover, gratifying Aphrodite. (ll. 887–96)

It is the agonized '*Oh mother*' in mid-flow which cries out that this was a forceful encounter. But while the passage makes sexual initiation a cruel incursion, it also includes Creusa's image of her own girlish beauty and pleasure, eroticized in retrospect. Adele Scafuro has argued persuasively that this is 'Euripides's creation of a female voice that tries to articulate her experience from her own perspective'.[17] She insists, however, that Creusa's utterances do not therefore imply a broader indictment of a god's crime–both because that is not how the (male) spectators would have seen it, and because gods are not subject to the same strictures as humans—or men.[18]

Scafuro is extending Anne Pippin Burnett's insistence, twenty years before, on one side of the same point: that Apollo is not to be criticized because that would imply a moralizing and anachronistic—or timebound—rejection of sexuality. Burnett had derided the 'Victorian attitudes' according to which 'the first requisite for a god, in any society, is that he shall be a gentleman' and in this case 'Apollo has undeniably

and now half gone by, without husband or children. The brother who was to have avenged their mother's murder of their father is blamed for destroying all her hopes by his failure to do the deed (ll. 305–6), and when she is misinformed (by Orestes himself, in disguise) that that brother is dead, she urges her sister to violence (the murder of their stepfather) because now all hopes have collapsed (ll. 958–9). After being reunited with Orestes, Electra also represents herself as having been more than a mother to him: 'You were more loved by me than by your mother, and it was not the servants at home who nursed you but me' (ll. 1145–6). On female hopelessness in Freud, see Ch. 6, pp. 147–51, above.

17 Adele Scafuro, 'Discourses of Sexual Violation in Mythic Accounts and Dramatic Versions of "The Girl's Tragedy" ', *differences*, 2: 1 (1990), 148.

18 'In revivifying Kreousa's charge against Apollo's forced union ... I am *not* revivifying the view that Euripides created Apollo as "a lecher and a seducer" to be castigated by his audience. ... [T]he Athenian male's response to rape is perhaps not precisely of the same order of outrage that it is in some modern societies. But this is not to say that a woman would not feel outraged, and Euripides has in fact created a voice to express precisely that' (ibid. 155).

seduced a young lady in a cave'.[19] She downplays the force of the scene between Apollo and Creusa, highlighting details she regards as mitigating Creusa's complaint on the different occasions in the play when she utters it.[20] In 1990 Scafuro's argument added to Burnett's a component that allowed for Creusa's public declaration of her traumatic experience to coexist with an acceptance that that is what a god must do. Incommensurable registers of value and emotional response are thus admitted into a feminist interpretation; no general critique is made of the kind which Creusa suggests herself at one point, in legal language: 'Where shall we apply for justice if we are destroyed by the injustices of those in authority?' (ll. 253–4).

Burnett speaks of Creusa's 'unconscious tendency to praise [of Apollo]' and claims, dramatically, that Creusa 'is perhaps the only figure of ancient tragedy whose unconscious motives are a matter of legitimate concern'.[21] This seems to mean that only with Creusa are unconscious motives there to be identified, legitimately, as such—perhaps because she is presented as something like a psychologically complex 'case'. Burnett goes on to elaborate on the unconscious features of Creusa's motivations, as versions of ambivalence: both awe and protest in relation to Apollo; both attraction and murderous rage in relation to Ion. But she also, before that, describes other kinds of mental division that are initially characterized as conscious. Here is the passage at length:

> Creusa's passions are contradictory, and beneath those she recognizes are others which she does not. She is perhaps the only figure of ancient tragedy whose unconscious motives are a matter of legitimate concern. In the first scene written for her, the poet has skilfully flayed his heroine, and he asks us, from our amphitheatre, to admire both his hand and the separated sinew and flesh, the mixture of health and disease, that he has revealed. He shows us a Creusa consciously torn between her public and her private purposes, torn between her husband and the god, between the sons she hopes to bear in the future and the one she abandoned in the past. In her private purpose she is still torn, between the fiction she has prepared and the truth that almost insists upon being spoken. ... She is unconsciously torn between her rebellion and her awe,

[19] Anne Pippin Burnett (trans. with commentary), *Ion by Euripides* (Englewood Cliffs, NJ: Prentice-Hall, 1970), 9–10.

[20] See e.g. ibid. 86. Burnett's understanding of Creusa's reference to the nightingale at the scene of her seduction as 'a romantic and lovely epithet' (p. 122) is criticized by Nicole Loraux on the grounds that 'throughout the Greek tradition, the nightingale's song speaks the pain of a mother who has killed her child' (*Les enfants d'Athéna: Idées athéniennes sur la citoyenneté et la division des sexes* (Paris: La Découverte, 1984), 238).

[21] Burnett, *Ion*, 83, 12.

as she finds herself on Apollo's ground, and unconsciously torn, too, between the instinct that draws her close to Ion and the appearance that makes him a stranger, even a threat, to her.[22]

Creusa 'torn', as Burnett puts it five times here, is matched by a writer said to have 'skillfully flayed his heroine', making her a spectacle which we are asked 'to admire' from the comfort of our armchair/amphitheatre—a spectacle of a torn female body equated with a 'mixture of health and disease'. From this point of view, the play's action plausibly effects the cure of what is diagnosed as Creusa's psychological stasis. Burnett continues:

Creusa has spent her life in contemplation of two moments in her past—the moment when the god came to her and the moment when she turned her back on her child. This contemplation has not made her reflective, however; it has simply made her a creature wholly given over to simultaneous love and hate. And this is why we can believe in her reorientation in the end. Long ago she loved her newborn child; from this love she has made a hatred for Apollo, a hatred that, on this stage, leads easily to hatred for her husband and for her unrecognized son. As soon as her blood has been instructed in what it has already felt, as soon as the recognition tokens have commanded her to love Ion again instead of hating him, it is almost a chemical necessity that she shall love her husband once again, and the god.[23]

Harmony with all three significant males in Creusa's life—the son, the husband, and the god—is thus enabled, through a process that seems, like her own magical potion, to involve an irresistible effect: 'blood' is 'instructed' by means of what is then, in modern terms, 'almost a chemical necessity'. Taken as a whole, Burnett's analysis—chemical, psychological, surgical—is itself both subtle and simplifying, both sympathetic and judgemental: in each case torn between the two, perhaps.

In Burnett's reading of Creusa and her complaint, both a diagnosis and a cure are seen as accessible and attainable. The 'recognition' she at last enjoys enables and precedes an attachment that is after all based on nature. But this focus on Creusa's wrongs and righting leaves out of consideration many other questions to do with the politics of family secrets. To begin with, as with the silence about Jocasta's feelings in *Oedipus*, there is someone in this play—the least significant of the four parental figures—whose story is not told. A second maternal secret emerges, towards the end of the play, when the priestess who has fostered Ion brings out the tokens by which he and his birth mother

[22] Burnett, *Ion*, 83, 12–13.

[23] Ibid. 13.

will recognize one another. Ion calls the priestess 'mother'; Hermes' opening speech describes her change of heart from disapproval of a girl depositing her unwanted burden on sacred ground, to 'pity' (l. 46) for the baby whom she then took in. And her possession of the cot and its contents has been a secret as solitary as Creusa's untold story: 'No mortal human being knew that I had these things or where they were hidden away' (ll. 1361–2). The Pythian priestess does not hesitate to produce the objects that will lead to the end of her maternal role. But her predicament and action are given no attention.

The question is raised, by the ever-querying Ion, as to why the evidence has been kept hidden up till now. The priestess's response is contradictory: that Apollo directed it; that she doesn't know; that Apollo was waiting for the time when he would name Ion's father. Ion momentarily takes the decision to look no further, not to trace his mother as the priestess suggests (l. 1355), but to leave well alone: he does not want to discover that his mother was a slave (l. 1382).[24] But he has second thoughts. It is this that then leads to Creusa's cry of 'What then is this appearance of things unhoped-for [*phasma tôn anelpistôn*] that I see?' (l. 1395). The public confession of her seduction and thwarted maternity had marked the end of her hoping, maintained along with the secrecy of the memories; now the showing of this material secret means renewed and fulfilled hope. The foster-mother's son is restored to the birth mother as her own. And no words are given to the priestess's feelings about what is now her own relinquishment of Ion.

The happier outcome for Creusa might seem to point towards a future of harmony and transparency, with sexual secrets abolished, parents and children reunited, and children's origins known to all. The priestess's minor story of secondary secrets is one indication that this is not the case. And other secrets, or confusions, underpin the establishment of the new family. The ostensible truth, as given in both the prologue and the epilogue, is that Ion is the son of Apollo and Creusa, but this is not what Xuthus has been told by the oracle; he continues to believe that Ion is his son and he does not know that in reality (at least in the dominant, divine reality of the play's framing statements) he is Creusa's.

[24] There is another echo of *Oedipus* here. At the point where Jocasta is desperately trying to prevent him from pursuing his inquiry further, because she has realized the truth, Oedipus takes her to be concerned only that he might find out that he has lowborn origins: 'Don't worry,' he sarcastically says; 'even if I turned out to be a slave three times over, my mother a slave and the daughter and granddaughter of slaves, *you* will not turn out to be low-born' (ll. 1062–3).

To her Athena says: 'Be silent now about this boy being your own, | So that Xuthus may be happily deluded' (ll. 1601–2)—'sweetly held by his belief [*dokêsis*]'. Another secret is being positively enjoined, even in the official plan.

Thus though the play appears to end with a successfully constructed threesome of mother, father, and son, this unit is sustained by contradictory beliefs about the boy's parenthood, with the existence of the contradiction known to two but not all three of them. The childless husband and wife have been endowed with a son whom each believes to be his or her own, when in fact he is the child of only one of them. Mother and son are in the know, a couple united by their secret knowledge that must be kept for his own protection from the unknowingly adoptive (not actual) father. The father, meanwhile, believes himself to be bringing back his natural son, and the son is to help him to maintain that fiction, his sweet delusion.[25] Lastly, Ion himself is subject to the conflicting beliefs and wishes of his two parents, each separately thinking of themselves as the one real parent out of the two of them. In a travesty of normality, Ion acquires on the same day both a biological mother and a biological father, who are married to one another but who in fact cannot possibly both be his parents. Each has a claim to him that excludes the other; each thinks it is they, and they alone of the two, who is his true parent. Margaret and Michael Rustin are hopeful that the play may be pointing to ways of coping constructively with its difficult issues. But ending as it does with a picture of a newly established parents-and-child trio founded on mutually contradictory secrets, the play may also look like an exposé of the nuclear family as a mere illusion—a sweet delusion—of psychological stability and security. Writing about the sexual and political implications of the *Ion*, Nicole Loraux sharply put the question: 'Might the parental couple be a fiction, a civic way of smoothing over the inevitable disjunction between the paternal and the maternal? Seeing the omnipresence of this disjunction in the tragedy, we might well think that that is the lesson of the *Ion*.'[26]

[25] Kevin Lee's view is that Xuthus' 'simple-minded and shallow attitudes ensure that we treat him principally as a legal necessity in Apollo's ordering of Ion's destiny. We should waste no time wondering about his future' ('Shifts of Mood and Concepts of Time in Euripides' *Ion*', in M. S. Silk (ed.), *Tragedy and the Tragic: Greek Theatre and Beyond* (Oxford: Clarendon Press, 1998), 95). But leaving aside Xuthus' personal destiny or qualities, the existence of the secret would be likely to have effects on the family, not only on him.

[26] Loraux, *Les enfants*, 234.

REPRODUCTION AND REALISM

Burnett's analysis of the play implicitly acknowledges that natural processes—'blood' or chemistry—have to be catalysed by human beliefs: she says that the blood needs to be 'instructed' or 'commanded' by the meanings supplied through the tokens of recognition. This brings in a further issue, one that underlies all the questions of identity and experience that the play evokes. What is the level of reality that is meant to be attributed, by characters or by the audience, to its various stories of origin and parenthood? This issue is highlighted through the specific problem that faces Ion himself of who really *is* to be taken as his father. In 1890 A. W. Verrall notoriously contended that the Athenian audience would have understood the alleged divine paternity as part of a Delphic scam: the oracle's activities (and the god's existence) were exposed as 'fraudulent' and another story, 'realistic' and exclusively human, was there to be gleaned between Hermes' prologue and Athena's epilogue.[27] This story of Verrall's includes such features as Xuthus being, after all, the real father and the Pythian priestess the mother: she must have got her job after her pregnancy, and would have concealed the fact of the child being really hers. The recognition of Ion's baby things by Creusa would be down to some quickly cobbled-together 'evidence' on the part of the priests at Delphi keen to see the Athenian succession assured; and Creusa would be naturally disposed to see what she wanted to see in the cradle.

[27] Verrall, *Euripides*, e.g. 'What we propose to show is that according to the story the oracle is *a fraud*' (p. 140); 'The story of the *Ion* is intensely, powerfully realistic' (p. 137). In *Ironic Drama: A Study of Euripides' Method and Meaning* (Cambridge: Cambridge University Press, 1975), Philip Vellacott saw a 'contrast between realism and ancient fable' in the play (p. 121); in it there are 'two worlds [that] face each other—the ancient world of miraculous legend which offers shelter to an ill-used woman, the realistic world of an honest young man' (p. 123); Ion is 'matter-of-fact' (p. 121) in his talk. The sacred precincts of Delphi with their tableaux of mythical scenes provide a backdrop that fits with Creusa's legendary past. Verrall's emphasis on realism *contra*, as opposed to alongside, myth is echoed more recently by a different but related approach in W. Geoffrey Arnott's 'Realism in the *Ion*', in Silk (ed.), *Tragedy and the Tragic*, 110–18. Arnott is interested in the multitude of accurate details in the descriptions of Delphi which would have functioned for the audience as a mode of familiarization and as an implicit challenge to myth as superstition. I would add that the contentious issue about the plausibility of the various reproductive stories, some realistic and some mythical, is a crucial aspect of this division, and the point at which its stability gives way, in that reproductive stories, however 'matter-of-fact' in their culture's terms, are inherently fabulous. (See further Ch. 5, pp. 134–7 above, on children's inventions of explanatory stories to account for the strange phenomenon of a new baby's appearance.)

Verrall's would-be detective work and no-nonsense hypotheses (his book was called *Euripides the Rationalist*) have provoked counter-arguments that bring out the local rationalities of critics' own assumptions about sexual relations. A. S. Owen, for instance, whose edition of the play appeared in 1939, rejected the 'priestess's baby' story on the grounds that 'the type of woman who would have been a Maenad [whom he might have slept with] on the occasion of Xuthus' visit would have been little likely to secure such promotion'.[28] Owen argues, too, that the sympathy between Ion and Creusa at the beginning ('singularly drawn to one another when they meet') loses its force if they are not really mother and son; and he takes the initial hostility between Xuthus and Ion as evidence reinforcing the theory that they are *not* really father and son.[29] On this view, *contra* Freud for instance, the parent–son couple is naturally and neutrally harmonious, while conversely, a spontaneous attraction between two people may be evidence of a blood relationship. The contingent appeals of mutually meshing stories, as between Creusa and Ion, mother-without-son and son-without-mother, have no weight unless they correspond to the truth.

[28] A. S. Owen (ed.), *Euripides Ion* (Oxford: Clarendon Press, 1939), p. xxxv. T. S. Eliot's play *The Confidential Clerk* (1953), loosely based on the *Ion*, avoids this issue by having its priestess-figure a widow, one Mrs Guzzard, who did indeed have a (legitimate) child of her own. She passed him off, however, as the illegitimate son of Sir Claude Mulhammer, for whose fostering he was paying, but who in fact had died. In this farcical but also religious play, there are no fewer than three adult children whose beginnings are confused. Apart from Mrs Guzzard's son Colby, seemingly Sir Claude's, Sir Claude and Lady Elizabeth Mulhammer, the middle-aged childless couple who are the equivalents of Xuthus and Creusa, each had another illegitimate child before they were married. On the parallels with Euripides' play, see David E. Jones, *The Plays of T. S. Eliot* (1960; Toronto: University of Toronto Press, 1965), 156–8; Carol H. Smith, *T. S. Eliot's Dramatic Theory and Practice: From 'Sweeney Agonistes' to 'The Elder Statesman'* (1963; New York: Gordian Press, 1977), 204–8; Grover Smith, *T. S. Eliot's Poetry and Plays: A Study in Sources and Meaning* (1956; Chicago: University of Chicago Press, 1968), 237–43. Grover Smith argues that the play is not just Euripidean but '"Verrallian"' (p. 242) because, he thinks, it leaves uncertain its 'real' story—the question of who are the birth parents in the case of all three children; the point is the affirmative freedom of Colby/Ion's future calling which, like Ion's beginning but not his end, will be religious and obscure. But Eliot's interest in Colby's spiritual vocation has the effect of highlighting the parodic treatment of other plot elements, including those that are furthest from comedy or irony in the *Ion*. Lady Elizabeth resembles Creusa in little more than social class; she is tormented neither by her past nor by her present childlessness. She was not raped, and seems to have lost touch with her son out of simple scattiness. Euripides' exploration of female suffering in the history and the emotional complexity of Creusa is quite absent from Eliot's Elizabeth, who remains weakly Wildean in her superficiality.

[29] Owen (ed.), *Ion*, p. xxv.

But what is the truth here? Is Ion meant to be seen as 'really' Creusa's son—or Apollo's or Xuthus'? And does it matter, so long as all the human characters are satisfied with their respective stories at the end, taking them for real? The principal characters in the *Ion* themselves entertain a number of different theories of reproductive origins. 'The ground does not give birth to babies'—'*ou pedon tiktei tekna*' (l. 542)—says Xuthus to Ion, putative father to son, during the conversation in which, after initial disbelief, Ion will come round to the view that Xuthus may well be his father. As he will later do with Creusa when she claims to be his mother, it is the child, Ion, who takes the initiative in questioning the 'parent' in order to ascertain the plausibility of their story. But in Xuthus' case, as we learn, the story is not so much doubtful as non-existent in his memory:[30] Ion's interview gradually pieces together the likely circumstances of a drunken sexual encounter. Xuthus' scorn for earth-birth comes as a response to a riposte by Ion, exasperated by his failure to have considered the issue that most concerns him:

ION Of what mother was I born your son?
XUTHUS I couldn't say.
ION Didn't Phoebus say?
XUTHUS I was so happy about this news [of being a father] that I didn't ask about that.
ION Was earth the mother who bore me then?
XUTHUS The ground does not give birth to babies. (ll. 540–4)

At first sight, the last two lines would seem to confirm a blunt agreement between two sparring men of common sense. Ion is irritated by his supposed father's indifference to the identity of the woman who was his mother; the tone might verge on 'Oh, I suppose I'm a child of the earth, then?', with an impatience to which Xuthus responds with his own statement of the obvious. He could be trying to soften the sharpness of Ion's remark by literalizing it—bringing it down to earth. Or perhaps he is humbly accepting that Ion has a point: there must have been a woman who should have been thought about too.

But there is another level to the exchange. The conclusion crudely dismisses the myth of Athenian genealogy dear to Creusa (and probably to the contemporary audience) according to which her grandfather Erichthonius was indeed born from the earth. In the first scene between

30 As Kevin Lee puts it, 'Xouthos entered the play desiring nothing more than a son. Once he thinks that his wish has been granted, he shows little concern for its explanation' (Lee, 'Shifts of Mood', 94).

them, Ion had taken the opportunity to interview his royal visitor on the subject of her family's idiosyncratic reproductive history, including the grandfather's alleged autochthony and Creusa's own survival as a babe in arms when her father was sacrificing his older daughters for the sake of the city (ll. 276–80). It is not possible to tell whether Ion's question to Xuthus about whether the earth bore him (he does not yet know he is meant to be Creusa's child too) is sarcastic or sincere; if the first, then his earlier conversation with Creusa reveals a young man pandering to celebrities' self-aggrandizing fantasies, but at the same time, as he will later be, nobody's fool. Xuthus' quick response, however, seems to be a straightforward rejection of the reality of the founding identity-story of his family and country by marriage.

It might further follow that if the ground does not give birth to babies, then neither are mortals made pregnant by gods. This is the point of Ion's later gentle interrogation of the woman who has just recognized him as her son, and told him a version of her story of his conception, birth, and abandonment:

> Come here. I want to say these words in your ears and throw a cover of darkness around these matters [*perikalupsai toisi pragmasi skoton*]. Do consider, mother, whether you fell, with the kinds of malady that afflict young girls, into a secret sexual relationship, and then you are ascribing the cause to the god, and trying to run away from the shame of me you are saying you had Apollo's child when you had me. (ll. 1521–7)

Ion introduces his question as itself hidden and intimate, something that will make or 'cover' a 'dark' secret as much as reveal it. The next sentence comes out as disjointed, mixing its tenses and thus its times as it puts together an elaborate hypothesis about Creusa's possible retrospective reconstruction of what happened. Here the general and the personal are interleaved so that it is not possible to see where one shades into the other. The suggestion that this is what young girls do, both in having sex and in blaming gods for their pregnancies, is given the force of a typical story. As such it is both a pattern of experience to which Creusa might naturally have been subject and, at the same time, an explanation for and exculpation of what she did. 'The kinds of malady that afflict young girls [*ha parthenois engignetai nosêmata*]', evokes both sexual attraction and a pregnancy—literally, the sickness 'gets inside' them—and the clause is difficult to situate precisely. It belongs either with the sexual relationship (as translated above) or with the blaming of the god, just as much a female fallibility. The vagueness of the phrase in both placement and meaning crosses the very different times and events of sexual experience, pregnancy, birth, and the subsequent telling or hiding or flaunting of any of them. It poignantly enacts the way that very disparate elements of experience and meaning come to be welded into the stuff of normal or plausible stories.

This first part of the sentence makes its sympathetic case by carefully suggesting common and understandable sequences of experience and narrative. Creusa's stories—both what really happened to her and what she tells and conceals about those events—were typical; she is not, as she felt she was, alone. 'The shame of me' then strikes another note because Ion, the considerate interlocutor, now identifies himself with the baby of long ago—both blameless and, unavoidably, implicated, in being subject to the story of his origins and birth. This is a long way from the generalizing statements of the first part of the sentence in that unlike the gentle distancing just before, it hurtfully marks the point where the story's narratability does not soothe but shames. The imputation involves them both in the guilty shared secret re-marked as such by the framing of this conversation, to be covered in darkness.

In response to Ion's questions and suggestions, Creusa does not flinch; instead, she musters all the authority of her royal and mythological history to declare once more that Ion is Apollo's and no one else's: 'Your father is no mortal man, child, but the one who raised you, the lord Loxias [Apollo]' (ll. 1530–1). Ion then reasonably asks why his actual father should be handing him over to another man, whereupon Creusa—who has evidently worked it all out with some speed since her recent rediscovery of Ion—provides him with a perfectly credible account, based on regular Athenian adoption practices for the purpose of securing an heir:

ION How come then that he gave his own son to another father and says I was born the child of Xuthus?

CREUSA He doesn't say you are Xuthus' by birth, but he is making a gift of you who came from him. After all, a friend might give a friend his own child to be the master of his household. (ll. 1532–6)

Apollo's motives are being likened to those of any man, in a possible transaction between male friends—though in this case without the knowledge of one of them. Fatherhood is a matter of practical arrangements to do with property inheritance, and it is something negotiated between men, '*philos philôi*', 'friend to friend'.[31] But Ion persists with his

[31] The legal complications of adoption and inheritance partly determine the confused conclusion. Creusa, as a woman, is an *epiklêros*, an heir without testamentary powers. So

logical questioning: either the oracle has been wrong in telling Xuthus that he was Ion's father, or else it was right, making Creusa wrong, so that Xuthus, not Apollo, is his father. 'Understandably [*eikotôs*: 'as is likely'] I can't get my head around this, mother', he says (l. 1538). He then proposes to ask Apollo himself, which shows how far his attitudes have changed since the start of the play. Then, Ion had turned away Creusa's equivalent request (on behalf of her pretended friend), insisting that the god could not be consulted on a question of his own paternity (ll. 365–77). And now, as if to evade this confrontation or ultimate denouement, Athena turns up to present Apollo's closing statement. This reiterates the theory of pragmatic adoption, here said to be for Ion's sake, 'so that you may enter into the most noble of families' (l. 1562), rather than for the benefit of the adoptive father, who is to continue to believe the oracle's statement of his own natural paternity.

There is also a comical side to the paternity question, primarily owing to contrasts of character between Xuthus and the other protagonists, and revealing in this case a disjunction between different degrees of both seriousness and attentiveness in people's relations to their sexual and reproductive histories. Xuthus is the 'guy' to Creusa's suffering victimhood and Ion's sensitivity; he is well-meaning but unreflective. Initially, having been told that the first person he comes across on leaving the oracle will be his own child, he rushes to embrace Ion as his long-lost son, without any thought for how the young man might feel himself.[32] When Ion, to whom she is always his first concern, asks Xuthus who his mother was, Xuthus gormlessly replies that he didn't think of asking the oracle that. Nor, until Ion brings up the problem, does he think about the effect on Creusa of expecting her to accept his son from

is Xuthus, who has been 'adopted' into her family where normally, as a female *epiklêros*, she would be expected to marry a male relative. Children of both Xuthus and Creusa could inherit; a child of one of them would have to be legally adopted by the other. If each separately believes Ion to be his or her own child, then there will be no difficulty in securing the agreement to adopt. See Burnett, *Catastrophe Survived: Euripides' Plays of Mixed Reversal* (Oxford: Clarendon Press, 1971), 106, and Burnett, *Ion*, 28–9; K. H. Lee (ed.), *Euripides Ion* (Warminster: Aris & Phillips, 1997), 166; Zacharia, *Converging Truths*, 75 n. 106.

[32] Since Ulrich von Wilamowitz-Moellendorff first made the suggestion in print, in his 1920s edition of the play, this scene has often been read as the comedy of Ion's increasingly irritated fending off of this older man apparently making a flamboyant pass at him. 'Ion ist Ephebe; wenn ihn ein Herr in seine Arme schließen will, so ist es ein erotischer Überfall, was er befürchten muß', *Euripides Ion* (Berlin: Weidmannsche, 1926), 111, note to l. 517: 'Ion is an ephebe; when a man wants to clasp him in his arms, then that is a sexual advance that he must be wary of.' See also Lee, 'Shifts of Mood', 93.

her very different position. She may turn against him (Ion knows all about vengeful stepmothers); but also, 'I pity your wife, father, growing old without children' (ll. 618–19). And when Ion then proceeds to cross-question his supposed father about the possible identity of his mother, Xuthus is perfectly willing to entertain any plausible theory about his likely sexual behaviour at the relevant times and places, readily admitting, when Ion's questions get as far as a Delphi party around the right period, that yes, of course he would have been plastered (l. 553). Xuthus is unthinking but not unkind; Creusa goes out of her way to spare him from the murder plan being proposed by her servant, on the grounds that 'I respect our marriage in the days when he was decent [*esthlos*]' (l. 977). When presented belatedly with a son, he sets about doing what he takes to be the right things, going through the motions of making appropriate ceremonial sacrifices that should otherwise have happened at the time of the birth. And he is boyishly enthusiastic about becoming a father: as one editor puts it, 'he cannot keep the word *teknon* [child] off his lips'.[33] Unlike either his wife or his 'son', he is not at all preoccupied by questions about origins or past events.

Contrasted to Creusa's tortured emotional history in relation to her early sexual experience and her lost baby, Xuthus' easy-going reproductive disposition is perfectly suited to illustrate one of several kinds of naturally given dissymmetry between the two sexes. Speaking to Xuthus, Creusa voices the Hippocratic theory that babies are made by two parents, rather than the mother being simply a nurse for the seed provided by the father; this latter theory is implied for instance in Aeschylus' *Eumenides* (ll. 57–66), where it is used by Apollo as an argument for the lesser seriousness of matricide as compared to parricide. In Sophocles' *Electra*, Clytaemnestra makes the opposite argument. Speaking to her daughter, she claims that the mother's part in childbearing is greater than the father's, with the quantity of pain the measure. Agamemnon had no right to sacrifice Iphigenia when he 'did not labour an equal amount of suffering [*lypês*], he who sowed her, like the one who bore her, me' (ll. 532–3). Creusa offers the modern perspective of two biological components: she hopes that eventually 'the children-seed from us two will be mixed together' (l. 406). But even if the parts that go to conceive the child come equally—fifty–fifty—from each parent, there remains a discrepancy between the sexes in their relation to becoming parents. No woman can be unaware of giving birth to a baby (although there have

33 Owen, *Ion*, p. xxx.

always been stories attesting to ignorance, or denial, of pregnancy up till the birth itself). A man, on the other hand, may have no suspicion of having fathered a child, just as, until DNA testing, he could have no verifiable certainty of having done so either.[34] Creusa and Xuthus personify this separation in an extreme form. Creusa has unquestionably had a baby and become a mother, an experience that has marked her for life.[35] About his alleged paternity Xuthus, on the other hand, has no idea. For all he knows, he may well have fathered this particular boy; he has no specific memory of a relevant sexual encounter and no connection of either rejection or recognition with any ensuing offspring.

The peculiar situation of the restored or reinvented family in the *Ion* is emphasized by ubiquitous indications in the play of other forms of parenthood, mostly involving more or less recognizable versions of single parenting or adoption (and fostering), or both at once. Starting with the various memorabilia that Creusa wrapped around her baby, this is bound up with the idiosyncratic Athenian mythological history according to which the earthborn Erechthids, lacking human parents, were raised by various divine, mythical, and animal foster-parents; in the first generation Athena herself had set up rather special childcare—two holy snakes and three legendary sisters—for Creusa's grandfather, Erichthonius. The autochthonous status is meant to ground Athens' 'native' rights; but it is a complex mythological and psychological issue, involving the difficulty of getting from single-source, asexual reproduction (from the earth) to the post-mythological point of a clear division of the sexes with combined roles in reproduction.[36]

In the course of the drama, Ion's ignorance of his origins is more than—too much—made up for. At the beginning, he has one (fostering) mother, the Pythian priestess, but knows that somewhere there is or was another one.[37] In a single day he acquires two fathers, Xuthus

[34] Another aspect of reproductive dissymmetry between the sexes is discussed in Ch. 3, p. 85 above.

[35] Early on, following her account of what happened to her long ago, Creusa's old servant asks her how it was that she could bring herself to abandon the baby (l. 958). As Brian Vickers points out in *Towards Greek Tragedy: Drama, Myth, Society* (London: Longman, 1973), 'what the myths take for granted, Euripides exposes to examination and judgement' (p. 333). And very often such verbal exposures have precisely to do with the crises and losses of women's lives.

[36] See Loraux, *Les enfants*, 229–36.

[37] Spiritually at least, Ion begins with a harmonious parental pair. As Lee points out in the Introduction to his commentary on the play, 'Delphi is presented as his home because it is indeed his father's home, and because his surrogate mother, the Priestess,

and Apollo, and two further mothers—Creusa pre-eminently, at the end, but before her, in conversation with Xuthus, the hypothetical girl that Xuthus must have slept with; he meets one of the two out of both possible conceiving couples, but the parental unit he is left with as his future, Creusa and Xuthus, is not one of the two pairs that have each been posited as his original parents. He also thereby learns two (incompatible) stories of his conception and birth, both of them involving sexual details, and both differently painful: in one case (Xuthus) casual obliviousness, and in the other (Apollo) cruelty on the part of his father to his mother. Ion's wish to know where he came from is over-rewarded; the relative simplicity of his initial situation—he is called Apollo's; he calls the priestess mother—is compounded and confused by an embarrassment of possible parents and alternative parental couples, accompanied by profoundly disturbing stories.

It is worth again making the comparison with Oedipus. He too has multiple parents by the end of the drama, but the question about his origins arises only as an apparently secondary issue in connection with the public inquiry into King Laius' death many years before. Growing up in Corinth, Oedipus had no reason to doubt that he was born there or that his birth parents were his parents, Merope and Polybus. As described in Chapter 7, it is the challenging of that certainty, together with its mistaken reinforcement in the wake of his doubts, that precipitates the chain of events that leads to his fatally fulfilling the oracle, given to his birth parents and then to him, that he will murder his father and marry his mother. When he questions his parents about the allegation that he is not really his father's son (l. 780), they do not even then tell him the truth (as far as they know it) about his adoption. Still bothered, Oedipus decides to take independent advice through a visit to the oracle but does this '*lathrai de mêtros kai patros*', 'keeping it secret from my mother and father' (l. 787). The parents' own holding back is replicated by the son's withdrawal from them. Had Oedipus, like Ion, known that he was adopted, he would not have committed the crimes foretold by the oracle because he would not have assumed that it referred to his Corinthian parents and fled his home. But *Ion* disturbs this reassuring indication of the desirability of openness by suggesting that, after all, the offered stories of origin may themselves divide a child who comes to know or is presented with different and mutually jarring stories.

is a woman in an all but physical union with the god who fathered him' (*Euripides Ion*, 22).

Like Oedipus, Ion becomes an investigator, but in his case the inquiry is personal from the beginning rather than becoming so unexpectedly. Ion seeks to get to the truth of private sexual stories that concern himself. He is a grown child cross-questioning adults—his own supposed parents—and he shows himself at once cynical, sensitive, vulnerable, and decisive. He will not stand equivocations or fibs from any of the four of them; he wants and needs to know, and in order to match and make sense of his parents' constructions, he is full of theories of his own. Despite his cloistered life, he speaks as a man of the world. He is ready with his notions of what it is like to be a suspected outsider, at the centre of political intrigue in a city, even though he has no direct experience of any such things: this is his initial reason for not wanting to go to Athens with his new father. Critics have often found this contradictory, taking Ion's diatribe against the conspiracies of Athenian politics as a moment when Euripides crudely and inappropriately uses a character as the mouthpiece for his own views. But in this connection he is not so different from a modern teenager who has heard some things, seen some TV, read some newspapers. He is familiar with the typical personal problems that visitors bring to the shrine and has clearly reflected too on what their stories may sometimes embellish or omit. Creusa is presumably not the first woman, or woman with a 'friend', to tell the nice lad an extract from her personal history while she waits for her appointment; he knows that infertility of body or land are the two most common problems that punters bring: 'Is it about harvests or about children that you have come?' (l. 303). And in relation to his own history, ignorance, known to be ignorance, was the comparative bliss of his daily life at the start, as the busy temple servant who would like to find his real mother but in the meantime is content. Where *Oedipus* ends with truths that are intolerable and manifestly true in their mutual confirmation, the *Ion* ends with a set of contradictory hypotheses, each presented as the truth, but whose collective incoherence is overlaid by the seemingly outstanding and unifying event of a mother and son reunited.

PLAYING GOD

Apollo never appears in person, but delegates his siblings Hermes and Athena at either end of the play to lay out his plans. This is the only surviving Greek tragedy in which a prologue does not present what really then happens in the play, and the discrepancy is one of the criteria by which critics have measured the likelihood of a deliberately anti-theological stance on Euripides' part. More generally, the divine cock-up raises the issue of human beliefs in or hopes for the infallibility and omnicompetence of others. Once again, this makes the *Ion* acutely relevant to contemporary concerns.

Media controversies about new reproductive technologies often make use of the critical cliché of the consultant 'playing god' (by creating 'designer babies'). Among other things the phrase implies a recognition that parents are not autonomous makers of babies. This is clearest in the case of IVF, where others have contributed actively to starting the baby, and the parents are dependent on them for the security of knowing the child is biologically theirs. Clinical conception is necessarily fallible; through a simple mistake, such as mislabelling, it is not impossible for the wrong two gametes to be brought together to conceive an embryo. In 2002 a case of error came to light in Britain, but only because the twins who were born were visibly different in skin colour from their supposed genetic parents. This situation has much in common with older stories of babies accidentally switched in maternity wards, leading to unconscious adoption and the dilemma of what to do if or when the mistake is revealed, given that both children will have been raised from birth in the families they know as their own. In the new case, this confusion is compounded by the children being genetically the offspring of neither real-life parental couple; the radically anti-naturalistic element is that the paired genetic parents would never so much as have met.[38] In a case of accidental confusion there would be no possible choice between birth and adoptive families; instead, in each of two families the child has one biological and one non-biological parent.

This kind of crossover made possible by technology (and human error) is presumably very rare, but it also evokes a comparable contemporary social situation which is in fact extremely common. When a child's parents have both had subsequent children with other partners, the child may then know two homes in each of which the couple consists of one of their natural parents and a step-parent. Ion the son of Creusa and stepson of Xuthus, and/or the son of Xuthus and stepson of Creusa, uncannily highlights very modern predicaments of mixed or muddled parentage—as well as very old predicaments of mixed or muddled fantasies and beliefs about where a child has come from or belongs.

[38] This can also be true of egg or sperm donation; but in that case both genetic parents know they do not know one another.

9

Retranslations, Reproductions, Recapitulations

RETRANSLATIONS

Freud often described the aim of psychoanalytic therapy as being the 'translation' of unconscious thoughts and impulses into conscious ones. Implicitly that second language, the destination language of consciousness, is a better place for these thoughts to be, because in this new setting they can be understood and handled. From the patient's point of view, this translation may be a transformation: Freud uses the verb *verwandeln* interchangeably with 'translate' in this context:

> What we make use of must no doubt be the replacing of what is unconscious by what is conscious, the translation [*Übersetzung*] of what is unconscious into what is conscious. Yes, that is it. By carrying what is unconscious on into what is conscious, we lift the repressions, we remove the preconditions for the formation of symptoms, we transform [*verwandeln*] the pathogenic conflict into a normal one for which it must be possible somehow to find a solution.[1]

But from the analyst's point of view, the synonym for translation is not transformation but interpretation—Freud says, for instance, that it is wrong 'to give the patient a translation of his symptoms as soon as we have guessed it ourselves'.[2] The time is not right: there is no point in making the new text available when the intended reader is not yet ready for it.

Freud's metaphors and analogies link translation very closely to the idea of publication, or rather republication. In this connection, revision

[1] Freud, Lecture XXVII, 'Transference', *Introductory Lectures on Psycho-Analysis* (1915–17), *SE* xvi. 435; 'Die Übertragung', *Vorlesungen zur Einführung in die Psychoanalyse*, *GW* xi. 451.

[2] Freud, 'On Beginning the Treatment' (1913), *SE* xii. 140; 'Zur Einleitung der Behandlung', *GW* viii. 474; the German has the plural, 'translations', 'die Übersetzungen'.

is preferable to reprinting without any alteration, in the same way that translation is preferable to leaving an unreadable text unmodified. What's bad is when there is no translation at all—when you leave an unconscious process, a first version, as it is, and simply make a copy. These metaphors and analogies from printing and publication are again particularly dominant in Freud's essays on analytic practice, where it is often a question of the reissues and re-editions of patterns of behaviour both in a patient's life and in the situation of the transference—the German word for which, *Übertragung*, is the same as one of the words for translation. Transference-love, Freud declares, 'is entirely composed of repetitions and copies [*Abklatschen*] of earlier reactions, including infantile ones.'[3] He goes on to say that this is in fact the condition of any kind of being in love; it is always a question of 'new editions [*Neuauflagen*] of old traits'.[4] There is no alteration.

An intriguing example of such a printing analogy occurs in the essay 'The Dynamics of Transference'. As a preliminary to describing the effects of the transference, Freud is speaking about how people's modes of being in love are both idiosyncratic and consistent: each person does it differently but does it over and over again in their own peculiar way. 'This produces', he says, 'what might be described as a stereotype plate (or several such), which is constantly repeated—constantly reprinted afresh [*neu abgedruckt*]—in the course of the person's life, so far as external circumstances and the nature of the love-objects accessible to him permit'.[5]

What exactly lies behind this stereotype plate, unfamiliar to us today? The German word is *Klischee*. As the French *cliché*, from which it is taken, that nineteenth-century *Klischee* passed into English as primarily a linguistic notion of mechanical repetition. But it has a precise technical meaning, too. The reference is specifically to a printing method that had become widely used in the second half of the nineteenth century. Its significance was in book publishing, in that it enabled the storage of pages of type for future reprints. A stereotype plate—a *cliché* or *Klischee*—is a copy, of one or several typeset pages, made by pressing papier-mâché over the type and then pouring metal over it to solidify

[3] Freud, 'Observations on Transference-Love' (1915), *SE* xii. 167; 'Bemerkungen über die Übertragungsliebe', *GW* x. 316.

[4] Freud, 'Observations', *SE* xii. 168; 'Bemerkungen', *GW* x. 317.

[5] The sentence concludes: 'and which is certainly not entirely insusceptible to change in the face of recent experiences.' Freud, 'The Dynamics of Transference' (1912), *SE*, xii. 99–100; 'Zur Dynamik der Übertragung', *GW* viii. 364–5.

the mould. '*Abklatschen*', the word translated as 'copies' in the passage quoted above, refers to similar equipment. The purpose of therapy, which Freud goes on to discuss, would then be to help us to break the mould of our own private clichés or stereotypical patterns of behaviour. 'Stereotyping', the English term for the printing method, can carry the same double sense of the *Klischee* or *cliché* that is present in both German and French.

In drawing on this modern invention for his description of the mental apparatus, Freud is being up-to-date in his metaphorical thinking. But the stereotype plates are never going to mean to us what they might have done to his first readers: the technology to which they refer no longer carries a connotation of relative modernity, but instead seems to need a footnote. In the early twenty-first century, a writer might look for equivalent or comparable metaphors in the language of computers—in templates, or files saved and stored. In that sense a text that is a century old can never be innocently translated, as though translation were simply a moving over from one set of signs to another; it has to be unbuilt and rebuilt in a way that either conceals or shows up those features that now appear to us as its historical specificity. If a translation updates the terms—for instance, by translating the stereotype plates as templates—it makes the text sound readable and modern, as it was in Freud's day. If it exposes the particular history, it reinforces the sense of the text as belonging to its original times—its bygone modernity.[6] Neither procedure is wrong, but there are different implications in each case.

These issues of metaphorical and practical translation have some bearing on the history of translations of Freud's own works, especially in relation to the essays in which translation and publication are metaphorically most at issue. It happens that like all Freud's papers on analytic technique, the essay in which the *Klischee* appears was omitted

[6] Beginning with a long analysis of Freud's use of the self-erasing writing pad as an analogy for the mind receiving constant new impressions, Jacques Derrida considered how conceptual thinking is shaped or determined through the available linguistic, material, and technological resources that mediate it. See Derrida, 'Freud and the Scene of Writing', in *Writing and Difference* (1967), trans. Alan Bass (Chicago: University of Chicago Press, 1978), 196–231; *Mal d'archive: Une impression freudienne* (Paris: Galilée, 1995), 29–39; '"Paper or Me, You Know...": (New Speculations on a Luxury of the Poor)' (1997), in *Paper Machine*, trans. Rachel Bowlby (Stanford, CA: Stanford University Press, 2005), 41–65. The Freudian starting point is 'A Note upon the "Mystic Writing-Pad"' (1925), *SE* xix. 227–32; 'Notiz über den "Wunderblock"', *GW* xiv. 3–8.

from the first Penguin Freud series, which appeared in the 1970s. As if—or so we might imagine in retrospect—this was not something thought to be appropriate or interesting for ordinary readers; or as if the Penguin Freud was to be regarded as primarily a thinker rather than a practitioner. The inclusion of these essays in the new Penguin venture partly reflects the much greater presence of therapy in British culture than a generation ago, when talking therapies were relatively rare, and commonly regarded—if regarded at all—as the province of an exclusive or eccentric few.

The 'new' Penguin Freud, edited by Adam Phillips, began to be published in 2002. It presents its selection differently from the first (different texts are combined together in single volumes), as well as making a somewhat different overall selection. But the crucial change—which is the reason for its being a new Penguin Freud at all—is that it consists of new translations. James Strachey's classic *Standard Edition* translation, reproduced in the old Penguins, is now if not superseded, then supplemented by these further texts by diverse hands. There is no attempt to standardize the terminology from volume to volume, translator to translator, although some differences are highlighted because translators get an introduction of their own in which to comment on their individual decisions about particular terms in their texts.

Unfixing and renewing both the translation and the selection of texts may have various effects. For one thing, it will reinforce the sense of a Freud always open to rereading and repackaging, a Freud whose meaning is not established or standardized once and for all, whose texts necessarily fulfil and take on different roles at different historical moments. The *Standard Edition* is unlikely to disappear, any more than Freud's German original faded away in the wake of Strachey's English—though Strachey's English Freud certainly took on a defining life of its own, setting the terms for the understanding of Freud in the English-speaking world.[7] New translations, like new readings and interpretations, keep the conversations going and the words alive to the changing questions of a changing cultural environment. In other

[7] The Strachey translation has been immeasurably significant as a resource for translators of Freud into other languages than English as well; some of its footnotes have also been adapted to editions of Freud's work in German. See Darius Gray Ornston, Jr. (ed.), *Translating Freud* (New Haven: Yale University Press, 1992). Bruno Bettelheim's *Freud and Man's Soul* (1982; New York: Vintage, 1984) drew attention to the way that some of Strachey's choices had the effect of making Freud's writing sound more scientific and technical in English than it does in German.

words, with other words, they prevent a text (and, in this case, a doctrine and a practice) from becoming too set in its ways.[8] If the first Penguin Freud volumes went some way to put Freud's writings on the broader cultural map—if they made them familiar and accessible in English—then perhaps the new Penguin Freud, encouraging a return to the texts and presenting them differently, will help to prevent both Freud and psychoanalysis from remaining the same, or even becoming a cliché. Neither a wholly new Freud nor the same old Freud, somewhere between transformation and interpretation, we could call this the translating cure.

REPRODUCTIONS

Such a 'translating cure' is also, more broadly, what occurs every time Freud's writings are called out of their original contexts to speak to a new historical moment or a new kind of personal story or typical experience. In this book, I have tried to indicate how that process can contribute, among other things, to thinking about the changing conditions of modern identity, particularly in relation to sexuality and kinship. Greek tragedy and classical myths may offer analogies with some of our present predicaments in relation to sexual and familial identities, just as Freud used the stuff and the narrative patterns of myth and tragedy to forge his own theories of how such identities shape our possible futures. Some of these Freudian myths, I have been arguing, are now obsolete in the sense that they have lost the explanatory force they might have had a century ago, in a world whose social norms and even biological facts were different. But new myths—new typical patterns of explanation and stories of identity—are emerging all the time, along with the rapid transformations in the forms and practices of sexuality, reproduction, and kinship. Finally, then, I want to start from the other end and consider two recent, related shifts in reproductive ideologies. The shifts are real, but the new ideologies may have more in common with older myths than at first appears. And once again, in these new

[8] Comparable to this revitalization in an interpretative rather than specifically translating mode was Jacques Lacan's mid-twentieth-century rereading of Freud's writings in the light of structuralist linguistics and anthropology. See Samuel Weber, *Return to Freud: Jacques Lacan's Dislocation of Psychoanalysis*, trans. Michael Levine (Cambridge: Cambridge University Press, 1991).

contexts some of Freud's preoccupations and some topics he neglected now stand out as such in the light of the different issues that confront and engage us a century after his time.

The first mythological movement is in relation to the having of babies. In the space of two or three decades, spectacular changes have taken place in the mythologies of motherhood. Consider the implications of this statement in 2005 on the part of a well-meaning male fertility consultant speaking in relation to the legal change that deprives sperm donors in Britain of the right to anonymity; this has led to a steep fall in the number of volunteers. The consultant is concerned that the facility should be available to women, even if it involves going via the internet (which evades the non-anonymity problem), because of cases when women have no male partner. 'Using these services', he said, 'has got to be a step better than asking some half-drunk man to have unprotected sex, which is presumably what happens otherwise.'[9] Poor women! In order to have a baby, they might actually have to have sex—caricatured here in the most binge-unappealing form of the 'half-drunk' pick-up. (Why *half*-drunk, by the way? Perhaps this is no casually vulgarizing adjective, but rather a precisely measured calculation on the part of the imagined damsel—because fully drunk he would be unable to deliver, and without a glass or two he might be unwilling to.) And poor men too!—now to find themselves pursued by women who are literally only interested in them for one thing.

There is a double ideological shift here. First, the attitude (on the part of the consultant) is one of the chivalrous protection of girls and ladies that would formerly have been offered to those in danger from the unwelcome and pregnancy-risking onslaughts of crude male lusts. Male and female sexuality are still what they always were, and why should women have to resort to bodily involvement with a live and present man, rather than one who can arrive hygienically in a sober brown envelope? Second—and this is the crucial change, to which the old idea of protecting the lady has been readjusted—the woman without a partner, whether straight or gay, is deemed not just not unsuitable for motherhood but having a positive right to choose and achieve it, on her own.

In the wake of the destigmatization of illegitimacy, an equivalent right to seek to have children, whether biologically or by adoption, is now

[9] Bill Ledger, quoted in Ian Sample, '"Severe shortage" of sperm donors', *Guardian*, Monday, 15 August 2005, 10.

assumed for many different categories of potential parent—men as well as women, gay as well as straight, and single as well as partnered—who would previously not have been considered (or, by the same token, considered themselves) in this light. The logic of this would seem to lead to mothers who can be single both socially and reproductively. Yet such individual autonomy in the choice to have a child does not produce children with 'single' parental origins, since—until cloning—there must always have been gametes from two different parents. And the loosening of the previously standard tie between parenting and sexuality (both the act of conception and the parents' heterosexual orientation) may ultimately modify the kinds of question that children imagine in relation to the origins of babies—as well as the kinds of answer that grown-ups both give and withhold (see Chapter 5, above). Just how many parents can a child imagine or seek, now that the old, automatic assumption has broken down that in the beginning there must have been two, who once had sex, and to whom the baby was born? Today, it is taken as a matter of course that adopted children should be told of their status (as Oedipus was not), but this is not true yet for those who are partly engendered by disembodied eggs or sperm. As discussed in Chapter 7, transnational adoption entails not just four parents but also (at least) twofold cultural origins. The cross-cultural multiplication of parents and cultures occurs in another form in so-called 'reproductive tourism', when IVF babies are conceived abroad, using eggs and sometimes sperm from local donors, then born in the (future) mother's home country. In this instance there is evidence to suggest that, unlike what happens with transnational adoptions, parents may seek to forget the child's other country, the place of their genetic origin.

Yet what could it ever mean to disclose to a child the complete history of where he or she comes from? Even in the seemingly straightforward situation of two biological parents raising their own child, there are origins unknown to each of them (including most aspects of their own). These new sexual and familial predicaments thus not only start new stories; they also reveal complexities and assumptions that were there all along, unobserved or unquestioned, in the past. Freud drew attention to the strangeness, rather than the obviousness, of the processes that lead to women wanting to become mothers. Yet the question of men wanting or fearing to become fathers was one that he did not examine, even though paternal (and pre-paternal) feelings—of both fear and longing—are considered in Sophocles' *Oedipus*, to the exclusion of those of the mothers. As I have tried to show, if we turn back to the classical tragedy on which Freud set such store in his formulation of the nodal or 'nuclear' pattern of early human relationships, then other kinds of both distance and proximity now emerge. Freud did not notice the strong emphasis in tragedy on situations of female hopelessness, a theme that came to be central to his own conceptualization of the impasses of female subjectivity. Nor, *a fortiori*, did he see the association tragedy usually makes between such hopelessness and childlessness. In his own time, the dominant trouble for women was not infertility but too many pregnancies; and here, Freud's own theoretical indifference matches exactly that of the feminist movement through most of the twentieth century. During that time the characteristic form taken by feminist demands was a refusal of everything that tied women to the place allotted to them within an overarching patriarchal order. The emphasis was on the right for women *not* to have children—on pregnancy and motherhood as burdens, if not the key to all female oppression. This in turn implied the longer-standing feminist claim to the right to a life in some other sphere than the family. Motherhood, at this time, was really not much of an issue in feminist debate other than negatively, as what not to do or to be. Theoretically, it was either the reproduction of patriarchy (just as, in Marxist theory, it had been the reproduction of the proletariat for capitalism); or else, in Freudian terms, it was a compensation for not being a man (and what kind of 'choice' was that?). Now, the right not to have a child has been replaced by the right to have a child—for women of all sorts, and also for men, including men without women. No doubt this change in the mythology has much to do with the broader changes in women's status: raising a child, for men too, is no longer (old-fashioned) 'women's work' (see Chapter 3, above).

My second example of a changing myth starts with a tale of three parents. In a case that was front-paged in the *Daily Mail* in 2005, a baby girl was born to a woman in her fifties, following IVF using an embryo from her son-in-law and adult daughter (who had a condition that meant she could not sustain a pregnancy of her own). The birth mother was thus also a grandmother since the baby was also her older daughter's biological daughter. This baby had been given the (second) name Trinity. Intra-familial scenarios of this kind, blurring and multiplying identities either within or between generations, are not uncommon in surrogacy arrangements or egg or sperm donation. The overt media narrative surrounding them is not about disturbances of identity, but about family generosity: the *Guardian* briefly and positively reported the case in the context of an article on organ donation between family members.[10] At the same time, such stories seem to verge on the fantastic, which is why they can feature prominently in a tabloid newspaper. Yet they probably won't seem sensational for long. IVF, at its inception in the late 1970s (the first baby, Louise Brown, was born in 1979), was regarded in just the same way: the extraordinary sci-fi case of the 'test-tube baby'. But in the space of a single generation, IVF has come to be seen as a routine medical procedure.[11] Such rapid transformations in the norms and possibilities of chosen reproduction may take us back to the forgotten strangeness of any process of conception and birth—a tale of metamorphoses and secret seedings whose myth-like improbability fades away in the light of grown-up and responsible familiarity with 'the facts of life'.

The blurring of identities and generations implicit in the Trinity story is not, however, unique to the opportunities offered by modern reproductive medicine. It is also the stuff of the 'blended' families that result from serial parental relationships and, in particular, second families, in which the older children of the second-time parent (or parents) may be a generation older than the new ones, with children of their own of the same age as their own new (half-)siblings. As with the multiplication of children's seekable origins, there is a proliferation of relationships here (by definition, where there are step-parents there were or are 'parents' as well). I have mentioned Freud's own situation, born to his father's young second wife, who was the same age as her stepsons, Freud's much older half-brothers.[12] The boy who was technically Freud's nephew, or rather half-nephew (and older than baby Sigismund, as he was called), lived nearby and was a regular playmate for the first few years of Freud's life. So the generational conflation was not just some piece of family knowledge that Freud might only have understood at a much later stage; it was there as his own given world from the very beginning. The core intergenerational Oedipal unit was in Freud's own case literally bordered by the evidence of other possibilities

[10] Emma Cook, 'Our Flesh and Blood', *Guardian* 'Family' section, 25 March 2006, 1–2.

[11] This is the case despite IVF's relatively low rate of success and the physical and emotional stresses involved. The story promoted by the media as well as by private clinics themselves is that the procedure offers 'hope' to hopeless—'desperate'—couples (and now single people too). In *Embodied Progress: A Cultural Account of Assisted Conception* (London: Routledge, 1997), Sarah Franklin focuses on this aspect in her critique of IVF as a 'hope technology'.

[12] See Introduction, p. 10, and Ch. 6, pp. 157–8, above.

which, like the presence or arrival of siblings, challenge its stability and complicate the identity of the child.

The confusion of generations and thus of identities is also a significant feature in Sophocles' *Oedipus*; yet not one mentioned by Freud, despite its applicability in his own birth family. Apart from the directly incestuous 'Oedipal' assimilations of son and husband, wife and mother, Oedipus is brother as well as father to his own children, just as Jocasta is their grandmother as well as their mother. Of course, the ordinary scenarios of generational conflation—both today and in Freud's time—do not include the incestuous history which gives the Oedipus story much of its force. Nevertheless, with the chosen—modern—form of second families, which are not the result of a spouse having died, there can be—or could be at first—a lesser but real sense of there being a violation of the natural order of things. In the mid-1980s, when stories of men having second families late in life were not yet common, someone I knew learned that her father, still married to her mother, had a 2-year-old son with a woman who was younger than either her or her sister. She herself had a son of exactly the same age. She said that what had distressed her more than anything else in what had happened was that her father had muddled the generations—'il a brouillé les générations'. Since that time, the 'blended family' has become common and thus common sense, so that it may no longer be seen as either legitimate or natural for an adult child of the first generation of offspring to react negatively at the prospect of a new half-sibling. 'He's a man of 27', one second-time father said of his sullen son in the early 1990s: he should, he meant, be grown-up enough to see a new baby as a baby and not as a threat. If the father, in starting a new family, was doing once more what he had first done when he was the young man's present age, then that was not something for the son to notice, or resent. The 'second family' story was meant, by now, to be second nature, an unremarkable eventuality for any audience, inside or outside the 'blendextended' family. In some cases, for some people, so it is, with the story's naturalization facilitating the process;[13] for others, for whom the complexities remain, the simplification and normalization of the overt story may be part of the difficulty.

[13] 'Sally and Elizabeth have got *every* kind of sister: half-, step-, and whole', complained a 7-year-old girl in 2001 who herself had only the whole sort, recently acquired: the blended family is here the envied and complete variety, with the nuclear one lacking by comparison.

RECAPITULATIONS

Recapitulation has the peculiar quality of being an ending that includes a beginning. To recapitulate is to go over the main points of an argument, at the end, but from the start. A recapitulation is shorter and sharper than the detail and evidence to which it refers back and from which it makes a selection, and it is normally followed by a further statement which is the next point or conclusion that follows after, and follows from, the full argument and the principal points that have been summarized in the recapitulation.

Let me illustrate this from two texts. The first is *The Origin of Species*, whose final chapter is entitled 'Recapitulation and Conclusion'.[14] True to the form, Darwin repeats the main points he has covered in the preceding chapters, before moving on to consider the 'open fields' of future research and discovery. The second text is 'The "Wolf Man"' whose last chapter, in its English translations—both Strachey's and the new Penguin one, published in 2002—is called 'Recapitulations and Problems'.[15] Freud attempts to clarify and focus what he presents as likely to have been a blur.[16] A brief, clearly pointed narrative is duly given, followed by the statement of two 'problems' for further reflection.

Recapitulation, in this first and primary sense, is an old term from classical rhetoric. The Latin word *recapitulatio* is a direct translation of the Greek *anakephalaiôsis*.[17] Common to both is the 'head'—*capitulum* in the Latin and *kephalê* in the Greek. In bullet-point fashion, a recapitulation targets and thereby establishes the main heads or headings of an argument; it gives it an order, literally making head and tail of it.

Consider then the striking departure that takes place in the second half of the nineteenth century, between Darwin and Freud as it were,

[14] Charles Darwin, *The Origin of Species* (1859), ed. Gillian Beer (Oxford: Oxford University Press, World's Classics, 1996), 371.

[15] Freud, 'From the History of an Infantile Neurosis' ('The "Wolf Man"') (1919), *SE* xvii. 104; 'From the History of an Infantile Neurosis' ['The 'Wolfman'], in *The 'Wolfman' and Other Case Histories*, trans. Louise Adey Huish (London: Penguin, 2002), 303; cf. 'Aus der Geschichte einer infantilen Neurose', *GW* xii. 138. The German word translated by 'Recapitulations' is *Zusammenfassungen*.

[16] See Freud, 'Wolf Man', *SE* xvii. 104; 'Aus der Geschichte einer infantilen Neurose', *GW* xii. 138.

[17] The Greek lexicon LSJ cites a single example of the noun, from the first century BCE (the rhetorician and historian Dionysius of Halicarnassus). There are more examples of the associated verb, including one from Aristotle.

when recapitulation enters into a new existence. 'Recapitulation theory', as it came to be called, had nothing to do with words or arguments; it designated a way of thinking about the relations between the evolution of species and the development of individual organisms: 'Ontogeny recapitulates phylogeny', in the slogan put forward by the biologist Ernst Haeckel. That is to say, each organism, in the process of reaching its own distinctive species-form, repeats in series the principal forms through which it has passed in its supposed evolutionary history. Haeckel uses 'ontogeny' interchangeably with 'embryology'. It is the embryo that does the recapitulating, starting from the single cell and passing through what he calls a 'brief, condensed' version of all the hypothetical stages of its species-history.[18] But as these specifications already indicate, recapitulation is in many ways different from the development it is said to repeat. First, because it is predictable where the history was haphazard. Second, because it is speeded up—a few weeks of gestation whizz-forwarding through aeons of evolution. And third, because the repeated forms succeed one another in a sort of secret intra-uterine screening, not in the outside world: their conditions of existence are different.

With the birth of biological recapitulation, the word itself seems to have undergone a metamorphosis. Rhetorical recapitulation—the original sort—engages active choice and selection. It is bound up with the artful use of language and logic; it is a skill to be mastered, a useful technique, designed to move or persuade or educate an audience or readership. Biological recapitulation, on the other hand, is passively undergone. He or she or it that recapitulates does so without agency; its résumé of ancestral stages, its little prenatal curriculum vitae or run-through of life, serves no practical purpose, does no harm or good, either for it or for other individuals or species. In the rhetorical sense, to say that man is a recapitulating animal is to make the Aristotelian point about human distinctiveness: man is an animal with *logos*—with logic, rhetoric, and language. In the biological sense, to say that man is a recapitulating animal is almost tautological; recapitulation, like other evolutionary humiliations, dismisses the human pretension to difference or priority. A pre-eminently discursive word about words seems to have plotted or wormed its way under the microscope, looking for all the

[18] Ernst Haeckel, *The Evolution of Man: A Popular Scientific Study*, i. *Human Embryology or Ontogeny* (1874), 5th edn. trans. Joseph McCabe (London: Watts, 1906), 2–3.

world like a living, ultimately breathing organism: the word made flesh, made actual heads and tails.

Yet in other respects this difference between the two recapitulations is less stark than these contrasts make it sound. The etymological 'head' in the word suggests an animal as well as an argument. Haeckel's favourite way of presenting the stages of evolutionary development is in terms of alphabetical sequence: 'We may designate this uninterrupted series of forms with the letters of the alphabet: A, B, C, D, E, etc., to Z.' But in practice the series is always interrupted. Some letters are missing. Or there has been a mysterious crossing with other alphabets: 'Thus, instead of the Roman B and D, we often have the Greek B and D. In this case the text of the biogenetic law has been corrupted, just as it had been abbreviated in the preceding case [where letters have dropped out].'[19] Letters and organisms seem to vie with one another for the prestige of the primary, the starting points of the story that recapitulation re-enacts. But in fact, as already hinted by Haeckel's acknowledgement that the series is never complete in the first place, the distinction between the letter and the organism of the biological law is blurred throughout. The figure of the corrupt text is elaborated in relation to a distinction between the main line of development and its add-ons, or 'supervening structures'. In an argument about linear development that is nothing if not circular, Haeckel distinguishes between what he calls 'palingenetic' and 'cenogenetic' developments. The palingenetic processes *are* the recapitulatory processes; cenogenetic processes, on the other hand, are any deemed extraneous to the main, palingenetic line. This distinction, says Haeckel, 'is of the same importance to the student of evolution as the careful distinction between genuine and spurious texts in the works of an ancient writer, or the purging of the real text from interpolations and alterations, is for the student of philology.'[20] Textual critic and evolutionary biologist do a similar job.

Haeckel's presentation exemplifies a problem that must beset all recapitulations, be they biological or textual or both. Recapitulations are shortened repeats or replays of organisms or arguments that have been and gone; they go through a development which then has the retroactive effect of separating the features of a first, extended version into the essential and the peripheral. There is a kind of self-fulfilling necessity in the process by which some points are selected out for inclusion in the shortened summary, leaving those omitted to fall,

[19] Haeckel, *Evolution*, 3. [20] Ibid. 4.

inevitably, into the category of the superfluous or secondary. The primary version is established only at a subsequent moment, by the emphases of the recapitulation. In biological recapitulation the first version, the ancient ancestry, may have left no trace; the embryonic development may be the only evidence for that evolution which it hypothetically relives in a speeded-up, virtual form.

Darwin, at the time of *The Origin of Species*, is registering and practically endorsing the biological theory of recapitulation, which is outlined under the heading of 'Embryology'. Haeckel is not yet on the scene; the theory, not yet named recapitulation, itself appears in embryo, so to speak. The persistence of long superseded forms in the embryo can be explained, Darwin thinks, because variations that may then be passed on to subsequent generations occur only at a later stage, when the animal has to fend for itself—to 'gain its own living', as he puts it:[21] 'This process, whilst it leaves the embryo almost unaltered, continually adds, in the course of successive generations, more and more difference to the adult.'[22] Unlike Haeckel's censorious editorial drive, Darwin welcomes 'more and more difference'. It is the positive sign of 'new and improved' variations and species.[23] Recapitulation is the prelude to innovation, the addition of new parts; after recapitulation, the organism becomes itself. Darwin then goes on to describe how 'the embryo comes to be left as a sort of picture, preserved by nature, of the ancient and less modified condition of each animal'.[24] Crucially, Darwin also stresses that this theory may well be unprovable, since fossil evidence is unlikely ever to be found for such deep-down antecedents. The history is seen in the recapitulation alone.

Recapitulation theory is now, by common consensus, more or less extinct (if not necessarily disproved). But as Gillian Beer remarks, it survived or was modified in certain twentieth-century forms, in particular the habit of evoking a 'primitive' man as part of (not distant from) the modern self.[25] And in Freud, one of Beer's examples, recapitulation emerges in a number of different connections and provides a revealing lens through which to look at his thinking about human development—about how people do and don't change in relation to patterns set down in the past.

[21] Darwin, *Origin*, 362. [22] Ibid. 273. [23] Ibid. 85, 256, 279.
[24] Ibid. 273.
[25] Gillian Beer, *Open Fields: Science in Cultural Encounter* (Oxford: Oxford University Press, 1996), 144–5.

Freud directly uses recapitulation theory in two connections: when he is thinking about children's development in terms of a series of more or less separate stages, and when he is considering the relation between what is inherited from a human history of indefinite length and what is unique to individuals as a result of their own experience.[26] In the second connection, the 'Problems' at the end of the 'Wolf Man' case history, like much of Freud's writing at that time, highlight the issue of the relation between heredity and new experiences. How much in the individual life is programmed repetition, and how much is dependent rather on individual factors, whether the person's own 'disposition' or the circumstances and events of their lives? Phylogenetic history becomes not the bodies but the deeds and dispositions of archaic forebears, framing reality in certain pre-ordained ways when compatible real-life experience is lacking:

> [A] child catches hold of [*greift*] this phylogenetic experience where his own experience fails him. He fills in the gaps [*füllt die Lücken*] in individual truth with prehistoric truth; he replaces occurrences in his own life by occurrences in the life of his ancestors.[27]

Two prehistories are operating here, the adult's childhood and human ancestry; part of Freud's polemical purpose, as he goes on to say, is to assert, *contra* Jung, the claims of personal prehistory as equal to those of the larger prehistory of humanity. But still, ancient stories kick in to 'fill in the gaps' when the present experience fails to instantiate or repeat them; the emphasis shifts from present, individual contingency to historical, hereditary inevitability.

At the very end of the 'Wolf Man' case study, the two 'Problems' that follow the formal 'Recapitulation' of the case return to this question of human recapitulation, now introducing the notion of 'phylogenetically inherited schemata [*Schemata*]' which are likened—though Kant's name is not mentioned—to 'the categories of philosophy'. These are concerned with '"placing" the impressions derived from actual experience'.[28]

[26] This has been abundantly documented. See Stephen Jay Gould, *Ontogeny and Phylogeny* (Cambridge, MA: Harvard University Press, 1977); 156–61; Frank J. Sulloway, *Freud, Biologist of the Mind: Beyond the Psychoanalytic Legend* (1979; London: Fontana, 1980), *passim*; and Lucille B. Ritvo, *Darwin's Influence on Freud: A Tale of Two Sciences* (New Haven: Yale University Press, 1990), 74–98.

[27] Freud, 'Wolf Man', *SE* xvii. 97; 'Aus der Geschichte einer infantilen Neurose', *GW* xii. 131.

[28] Freud, 'Wolf Man', *SE* xvii. 119; 'Aus der Geschichte einer infantilen Neurose', *GW* xii. 155. The Kantian '*Kategorien*' are given inverted commas in the German, while

Not only that, but 'wherever experiences fail to fit with the hereditary schema, they become remodelled in the imagination';[29] the Oedipus complex is given pride of place among these hereditary schemata. Here, as with the Wolf Man's revised view of the sex of his would-be castrator, from female to male, pattern is made to prevail over the particular—not only to 'fill in gaps' but also to reject and reshape.

Fatefulness looms over such instances—as if the individual's experience were incidental, as if the changes accomplished or experienced in a life were superficial, both personally and historically, in relation to the unchanging underlying *Schemata.* Here the primeval takes hold of each new arrival into actuality; or rather, Freud says that the child itself, in search of completion, grasps onto—'catches hold of'—the gap-filling ancient truth. In the biological theory, recapitulation leaves no trace: the individual goes through all the successive stages and transformations to emerge as itself, with no residue remaining of this personalized collective prehistory. With Freud, on the contrary, no stage is ever fully superseded; or insofar as it is, there is always the chance that it may be reactivated or returned to in later life, for better or for worse. This is the force of one argument of the *Three Essays on the Theory of Sexuality*: the child's uncoordinated sexual and emotional organization passes through several different phases, beginning with the oral and the anal, but there is no simple sequence, one after the other, still less a simple ending in which they are all surpassed and left behind in favour of the adult formation of heterosexual maturity. The earlier ways of experiencing remain in the background of the adult's reality, disturbingly not harmoniously; modern man is stuck with a primitive past.

But this is not the only way in which a concept of recapitulation is utilized or reworked in Freud. During the same period as he is thinking in recapitulatory terms about the relation between childhood experience and prehistory, with the primal fantasies as ur-stories in human development, Freud is also writing about the workings of psychoanalytic treatment. Here, I would argue, recapitulatory thinking appears again. In one connection it involves an argument about the object of therapeutic change. In the Preface to the 1915 edition of the *Three Essays*, a brief, quite schematic paragraph included the statement that 'Ontogenesis may be regarded as a recapitulation [*Wiederholung*] of

there are none in the phrase about the placing of impressions: '*die Unterbringung der Lebenseindrücke besorgen*'.

29 Ibid.

phylogenesis, in so far as the latter has not been modified by more recent experience'. The general point, however, is that analysis deals principally with 'the accidental [*das Akzidentelle*]' in individual experience, not with the inherited 'dispositional [*das Dispositionelle*]'. It is these accidental and recent additions which are open to influence in the treatment; unlike the residual phenomena, they can be 'almost entirely [*fast restlos*] subject to its influence [*bewältigt*].'[30]

In Freud's papers on analytic technique, elements of recapitulation theory reappear, though it is never named as such. During the course of an analysis, significant past events or situations are redescribed or re-lived in the present. Thus a history is rehearsed or repeated in a shortened form; it occurs in a special environment; it is also the preliminary to a new life or departure. And in a striking return from biology to rhetoric, the primary medium of the analytic recapitulation is words. Freud charmingly calls the transference situation of analysis a *Tummelplatz*: it is for tumbling about in the safety of an area marked off from real relationships.[31] As in biological recapitulation, this is a virtual environment, not real life. Within the security of the playground, childish things are brought out for the last time before being put away.

Recapitulation always distinguishes its different points, whether temporal or rhetorical. Likewise, Freud stresses the separateness of the elements that come up. The operative resistances and symptoms must be gone through one at a time—'bit by bit', 'one by one': '*Stück für Stück*'.[32] That series, passively produced without the conscious selection of the speaker, and listened to with the unfocused receptiveness of 'evenly suspended attention' or '*gleichschwebende Aufmerksamkeit*',[33] rehearses what then—after time—may appear as the hidden headlines in a private history or as established, unconscious habits of relating and behaving. And ideally, the patient learns to see the repeating patterns as such and is able to do something else: 'It is the part of the work which has the most transformative effect on the patient'.[34] To put it in biological

[30] Freud, *Three Essays on the Theory of Sexuality*, *SE* vii. 131; *Drei Abhandlungen zur Sexualtheorie*, *GW* v. 29.

[31] Freud, 'Remembering, Repeating and Working-through' (1914), *SE* xii. 154; 'Erinnern, Wiederholen und Durcharbeiten', *GW* x. 134.

[32] Freud, 'Remembering', *SE* xii. 151, 152; 'Erinnern', *GW* x. 131, 131; the German phrase is the same in both instances.

[33] Freud, 'Recommendations to Physicians Practising Psycho-Analysis' (1912), *SE* xii. 111; 'Ratschläge für den Arzt bei der Psychoanalytischen Behandlung', *GW* viii. 377.

[34] Freud, 'Remembering', *SE* xii. 155; tr. mod.; 'Erinnern', *GW* x. 136. Strachey has: '[I]t is a part of the work which effects the greatest changes in the patient'. The German

terms, the patient comes out of recap ready to be their grown self, or to 'get [their] own living', as Darwin defined the difference between the embryo and the postnatal animal. To put it in rhetorical terms, the patient has become an active not a passive recapitulator: a thinking animal with the power to change and conclude in their own manner.

Another comparison from *The Origin of Species* may be relevant here, in which Darwin makes a case against a tragically overdramatic view of natural history. Aligning himself with contemporary geological theory, he rejects the idea of 'catastrophes' as marking the transitions from one age or one species type to another;[35] instead, variations occur all the time and in infinitesimal ways whose cumulative effects can only be remarked in the longer term, retrospectively. On this view there are no big events, no tragic disasters, but instead 'a slowly changing drama'.[36] This might be a suggestive way of thinking about how modifications might occur in what Freud calls the 'schemata' of human development, said to grip and grasp with a fateful inevitability that abolishes the significance of contingent contemporary events. In small and gradual ways, the schemata are subject to change; for the new child the likely stories and questions about who he is and where he came from will be just that much different, in ways perhaps too tiny to see at the time, from those that affected the previous generation.

The potential openness of a recapitulatory process emerges elsewhere in Freud too, in relation to the early years of life as well as to therapy and its outcomes. In an essay of 1919—the year after the publication of the 'Wolf Man' study—Freud writes of the inevitable end of children's first Oedipal loves:

> Most probably they pass away because their time is over, because the children have entered upon a new phase of development in which they are compelled to recapitulate from the history of mankind the repression of an incestuous object-choice, just as at an earlier stage they were obliged to effect an object-choice of that very sort. (Compare the part played by Fate in the myth of Oedipus.) [(*Siehe das Schicksal in der Ödipusmythe.*)][37]

reads: 'Es ist aber jenes Stück der Arbeit, welches die größte verändernde Einwirkung auf den Patienten hat'.

35 'The old notion of the inhabitants of the earth having been swept away at successive periods by catastophes is very generally given up' (Darwin, *Origin*, 256).

36 Ibid. 254.

37 Freud, '"A Child is Being Beaten"' (1919), *SE* xvii. 188; '"Ein Kind wird geschlagen"', *GW* xii. 208. The word translated as 'recapitulate' is *wiederholen* ('repeat'), which is Haeckel's usual word for the process.

Strachey relegated the last sentence of this passage from a parenthesis in the main text to a footnote; in fact it suggests a crucial further point. The Oedipal children in the passage passively recapitulate—are 'compelled' and 'obliged' first to take and then to drop their subsequently forbidden objects of love. They have no choice in their choices of whom to love, but this is not yet their life. Oedipus, on the other hand, is no recapitulator: the incestuous relationship has been his real, long-term life, in the overlapping relationships of husband and father and brother and son; the father-murder is a past reality, not a distant impulse. Oedipus' 'Fate' made him seek to avoid and unknowingly commit unbearable crimes. The Fate that follows the Oedipal child is an inherited script of early longings, and later prohibitions and forgettings. It refers to desires, not deeds, and it is neither fulfilled nor resisted, what Oedipus did when he stayed away from his home after hearing the oracle's prediction. The oracle's fateful utterance is what starts Oedipus off on his Oedipal course. There is an equivalent to the oracle in the Freudian story, too, but it is not the same. Instead of beginning it, the oracle is what ends the child's 'Oedipal' period: it is the threat of castration that he believes when he has seen, from the evidence of girls, that it might come true. From that point on he can no longer be omnipotent Oedipus—and his life proceeds.

The story of the Oedipus complex, unlike the story of Oedipus, is not, in the end, a tragedy. Where there is recapitulation something else follows—a different conclusion, another version of an old story, a possible new beginning. And one in which women, too, may get a life.

Bibliography

The Adoption Issue. Special issue, *Tulsa Studies in Women's Literature*, 21: 2 (Fall 2002).

Agacinski, Sylviane, *Politique des sexes* (1998; 2nd edn. Paris: Seuil, 2001).

Ahl, Frederick, *Sophocles' Oedipus: Evidence and Self-Conviction* (Ithaca, NY: Cornell University Press, 1991).

Alaux, Jean. *See* Mazon, Paul.

Alford, C. Fred, *The Psychoanalytic Theory of Tragedy* (New Haven: Yale University Press, 1992).

Appignanesi, Lisa, and John Forrester, *Freud's Women* (1992; 2nd edn. London: Penguin, 2000).

Armstrong, Richard H., *A Compulsion for Antiquity: Freud and the Ancient World* (Ithaca, NY: Cornell University Press, 2005).

Arnott, W. Geoffrey, 'Realism in the *Ion*: Response to Lee', in Silk, *Tragedy and the Tragic*, 110–18.

Austin, R. G. (ed.), Virgil, *Aeneid II* (Oxford: Clarendon Press, 1964).

Barthes, Roland, *Mythologies* (1957; Paris: Seuil, coll. 'Points', 1970). Selection trans. Annette Lavers, *Mythologies* (1972; St Albans: Paladin, 1976).

Baudelaire, Charles, *Œuvres complètes*, 2 vols., ed. Claude Pichois (Paris: Gallimard, Pléiade, 1975).

Bayfield, M. A. (ed.), *The Ion of Euripides* (London: Macmillan, 1889).

Beer, Gillian, *Open Fields: Science in Cultural Encounter* (Oxford: Oxford University Press, 1996).

Bell, Michael, *Literature, Modernism and Myth: Belief and Responsibility in the Twentieth Century* (Cambridge: Cambridge University Press, 1997).

Benjamin, Walter, *Illuminationen* (1955; Frankfurt am Main: Suhrkamp, 1977), trans. Harry Zohn, *Illuminations* (1968; New York: Schocken Books, 1969).

Bernays, Jacob, 'Aristotle on the Effect of Tragedy' (1857), trans Jennifer Barnes, in Andrew Laird (ed.), *Ancient Literary Criticism* (Oxford: Oxford University Press, 2006), 159–75.

Bernheimer, Charles, and Claire Kahane (eds.), *In Dora's Case* (London: Virago, 1985).

Bettelheim, Bruno, *Freud and Man's Soul* (1982; New York: Vintage, 1984).

Bollack, Jean, *La naissance d'Œdipe: Traduction et commentaires d' 'Oedipe roi'* (Paris: Gallimard, coll. 'Tel', 1995).

Bollas, Christopher, *Hysteria* (London: Routledge, 2000).

Bonner, Campbell, 'A Study of the Danaid Myth', *Harvard Studies in Classical Philology*, 13 (1902), 129–73.

Bowie, Malcolm, *Freud, Proust and Lacan: Theory as Fiction* (Cambridge: Cambridge University Press, 1987).

—— *Lacan* (Cambridge, MA: Harvard University Press, 1991).

Bowlby, Rachel, 'One Foot in the Grave: Freud on Jensen's *Gradiva*', in *Still Crazy after All These Years: Women, Writing and Psychoanalysis* (London: Routledge, 1992), 157–82.

—— 'Frankenstein's Woman-to-be: Choice and the New Reproductive Technologies', in *Shopping with Freud* (London: Routledge, 1993), 82–93.

—— 'Domestication', in Diane Elam and Robyn Wiegman (eds.), *Feminism Beside Itself* (New York: Routledge, 1995), 71–91.

Bremmer, Jan (ed.), *Interpretations of Greek Mythology* (London: Croom Helm, 1987).

Breuer, Josef. *See* Freud, Sigmund.

Bronfen, Elisabeth, *The Knotted Subject: Hysteria and its Discontents* (Princeton: Princeton University Press, 1988).

Burnett, Anne Pippin (trans. with commentary), *Ion by Euripides* (Englewood Cliffs, NJ: Prentice-Hall, 1970).

—— *Catastrophe Survived: Euripides' Plays of Mixed Reversal* (Oxford: Clarendon Press, 1971).

Butler, Judith, *Antigone's Claim: Kinship between Life and Death* (New York: Columbia University Press, 2000).

Buxton, Richard, *Imaginary Greece: The Contexts of Mythology* (Cambridge: Cambridge University Press, 1994).

—— (ed.), *From Myth to Reason? Studies in the Development of Greek Thought* (Oxford: Oxford University Press. 1999).

Caird, Mona, *The Daughters of Danaus* (1894; New York: Feminist Press, 1989).

Caldwell, Richard, 'The Psychoanalytic Interpretation of Greek Myth', in Edmunds, *Approaches to Greek Myth*, 344–89.

Camus, Albert, 'Le mythe de Sisyphe', in *Le mythe de Sisyphe: Essai sur l'absurde* (1942; Paris: Gallimard, 1961), 159–66. Trans. Justin O'Brien, *The Myth of Sisyphus* (London: Hamish Hamilton, 1955).

Carson, Anne, 'Dirt and Desire: Essay on the Phenomenology of Female Pollution in Antiquity', in *Men in the Off Hours* (New York: Alfred A. Knopf, 2000), 130–57.

Cave, Terence, *Recognitions: A Study in Poetics* (Oxford: Clarendon Press, 1988).

Certeau, Michel de, *Histoire de la psychanalyse entre science et fiction* (Paris: Gallimard, coll. 'Folio', 1987).

Coblence, Françoise, *Sigmund Freud 1886–1897* (Paris: PUF, 2000).

Collier, Mary, *The Woman's Labour*, in *Two Eighteenth Century Poems*, ed. E. P. Thompson and Marian Sugden (London: Merlin Press, 1989), 13–24.

Constans, L., *La légende d'Œdipe, étudiée dans l'Antiquité, au Moyen-Âge et dans les temps modernes, en particulier dans 'Le Roman de Thèbes', texte français du XIIe siècle* (Paris: Maisonneuve, 1881).

Coward, Rosalind, *Patriarchal Precedents: Sexuality and Social Relations* (London: Routledge & Kegan Paul, 1983).

Culler, Jonathan, *The Pursuit of Signs: Semiotics, Literature, Deconstruction* (London: Routledge, 1981).

Darwin, Charles, *The Origin of Species* (1859), ed. Gillian Beer (Oxford: Oxford University Press, World's Classics, 1996).

Daudet, Alphonse, *Le Nabab* (1877), in *Œuvres complètes*, ed. Roger Ripoll, ii (Paris: Gallimard, Pléiade, 1990), 477–859.

Dawe, R. D. (ed.), *Sophocles 'Oedipus Rex'* (Cambridge: Cambridge University Press, 1982).

Derrida, Jacques, *L'écriture et la différence* (1967; Paris: Seuil, coll. 'Points', 1979), trans. Alan Bass, *Writing and Difference* (Chicago: University of Chicago Press, 1978).

____ *Mal d'archive: Une impression freudienne* (Paris: Galilée, 1995), trans. Eric Prenowitz, *Archive Fever: A Freudian Impression* (Chicago: University of Chicago Press, 1997).

____ *De l'hospitalité* (Paris: Calmann-Lévy, 1997), trans. Rachel Bowlby, *Of Hospitality* (Stanford, CA: Stanford University Press, 2000).

____ *Papier machine* (Paris: Galilée, 2001), trans. Rachel Bowlby, *Paper Machine* (Stanford, CA: Stanford University Press, 2005).

____ and Elisabeth Roudinesco, *De quoi demain ... : Dialogue* (Paris: Fayard and Galilée, 2001).

Didi-Huberman, Georges, *Invention de l'hystérie: Charcot et l'iconographie photographique de la Salpêtrière* (Paris: Macula, 1982).

Dodds, E. R., *The Greeks and the Irrational* (1951; Berkeley: University of California Press, 1973).

____ (ed.). *Plato, 'Gorgias'* (1959; Oxford: Clarendon Press, 1990).

duBois, Page, *Sowing the Body: Psychoanalysis and Ancient Representations of Women* (Chicago: University of Chicago Press, 1988).

Duck, Stephen, *The Thresher's Labour*, in *Two Eighteenth Century Poems*, ed. E. P. Thompson and Marian Sugden (London: Merlin Press, 1989), 1–12.

Easterling, P. E., 'Weeping, Witnessing, and the Tragic Audience: Response to Segal', in Silk, *Tragedy and the Tragic*, 173–81.

____ (ed.), *The Cambridge Companion to Greek Tragedy* (Cambridge: Cambridge University Press, 1997).

Edmunds, Lowell (ed.), *Approaches to Greek Myth* (Baltimore: Johns Hopkins University Press, 1990).

Else, Gerald F., *Aristotle's 'Poetics': The Argument* (Cambridge, MA: Harvard University Press, 1957).

Engels, Friedrich, *The Origin of the Family, Private Property and the State* (1884), trans. Alick West and Dona Torr (London: Lawrence and Wishart, 1940).

Ewans, Michael (ed. and trans.), Aischylos, *Suppliants and Other Dramas* (London: J. M. Dent, Everyman, 1996).

Flem, Lydia, *L'homme Freud* (Paris: Seuil, 1991).

Foley, Helene P., *Female Acts in Greek Tragedy* (Princeton: Princeton University Press, 2001).

Forrester, John, *The Seduction of Psychoanalysis: Freud, Lacan, Derrida* (Cambridge: Cambridge University Press, 1990).

—— *See* Appignanesi, Lisa.

Frankland, Graham, *Freud's Literary Culture* (Cambridge: Cambridge University Press, 2000).

Franklin, Sarah, *Embodied Progress: A Cultural Account of Assisted Conception* (London: Routledge, 1997).

Freud, Sigmund, *Gesammelte Werke* (1951–87; Frankfurt am Main: Fischer Taschenbuch Verlag, 1999).

—— *The Standard Edition of the Complete Psychological Works of Sigmund Freud*, trans. James Strachey, 24 vols. (London: Hogarth Press, 1953–74).

—— *Aus den Anfängen der Psychanalyse: Briefe an Wilhelm Fliess. Abhandlungen und Notizen aus den Jahren 1887–1902* (London: Imago, 1950).

—— *The Letters of Sigmund Freud*, ed. Ernst L. Freud, trans. Tania and James Stern (1960; New York: Basic Books, 1975).

—— *The Complete Letters of Sigmund Freud to Wilhelm Fliess, 1887–1904*, trans and ed. Jeffrey Moussaieff Masson (Cambridge, MA: Harvard University Press, 1985).

—— *Wild Analysis*, trans. Alan Bance (London: Penguin, 2002).

—— *The 'Wolfman' and Other Case Histories*, trans. Louise Adey Huish (London: Penguin, 2002).

—— and Josef Breuer, *Studies in Hysteria* (1895), trans. A. A. Brill (Boston: Beacon Press, n.d).

—— —— *Études sur l'hystérie* (1895), trans. Anne Berman (1956; 11th edn. Paris: PUF, 1992).

Gamwell, Lynn, and Richard Wells, *Sigmund Freud and Art: His Personal Collection of Antiquities* (London: Thames and Hudson, 1989).

Garvie, A. F., *Aeschylus' 'Supplices': Play and Trilogy* (Cambridge: Cambridge University Press, 1969).

Genette, Gérard, 'Vraisemblance et motivation', in *Figures II* (1969; Paris: Seuil, coll. 'Points', 1979), 71–99.

Gilman, Sander L., Helen King, Roy Porter, G. S. Rousseau, and Elaine Showalter, *Hysteria Beyond Freud* (Berkeley: University of California Press, 1993).

Goldhill, Simon, *Reading Greek Tragedy* (Cambridge: Cambridge University Press, 1986).

—— 'The Audience of Athenian Tragedy', in Easterling, *Cambridge Companion*, 54–68.

—— *Who Needs Greek? Contests in the Cultural History of Hellenism* (Cambridge: Cambridge University Press, 2002).

Goodwin, William W., *A Greek Grammar* (2nd edn. 1894; London: Macmillan, 1974).

Gould, John, *Myth, Ritual, Memory, and Exchange: Essays in Gree[...] and Culture* (Oxford: Oxford University Press, 2001).

Gould, Stephen Jay, *Ontogeny and Phylogeny* (Cambridge, MA: Harv[...] versity Press, 1977).

Graves, Robert, *The Greek Myths*, 2 vols. (1955; 2nd edn. Harmondsw[...] Penguin, 1960).

Griffin, Jasper (ed.), *Sophocles Revisited: Essays Presented to Sir Hugh Lloyd-Jo[...]* (Oxford: Clarendon Press, 1999).

Guyomard, Patrick, *La jouissance du tragique: Antigone, Lacan et le désir d[...] l'analyste* (1992; Paris: Flammarion, 1998).

Haeckel, Ernst, *The Evolution of Man: A Popular Scientific Study*, i. *Human Embryology or Ontogeny* (1874); 5th edn., trans. Joseph McCabe (London: Watts & Co., 1906).

Hall, Edith, *Inventing the Barbarian: Greek Self-Definition through Tragedy* (Oxford: Clarendon Press, 1989).

____ Fiona Macintosh, and Amanda Wrigley (eds.), *Dionysus since 69: Greek Tragedy at the Dawn of the Third Millennium* (Oxford: Oxford University Press, 2004).

____ and Fiona Macintosh, *Greek Tragedy and the British Theatre 1660–1914* (Oxford: Oxford University Press, 2005).

Hallett, Judith P., and Thomas Van Nortwick (eds.), *Compromising Traditions: The Personal Voice in Classical Scholarship* (New York: Routledge, 1997).

Harrison, Jane Ellen, *Prolegomena to the Study of Greek Religion* (1903; 3rd edn. Cambridge: Cambridge University Press, 1922).

H.D., *Tribute to Freud* (Manchester: Carcanet, 1970).

Heilmann, Ann, *New Woman Strategies: Sarah Grand, Olive Schreiner, Mona Caird* (Manchester: Manchester University Press, 2004).

Hornblower, Simon, and Antony Spawforth (eds.), *The Oxford Classical Dictionary* (3rd edn. Oxford: Oxford University Press, 1996).

James, Henry, *What Maisie Knew* (1897; Harmondsworth: Penguin, 1982).

Jebb, R. C. (ed.), *The Oedipus Tyrannus of Sophocles* (1885; 3rd edn. abridged 1897; Cambridge: Cambridge University Press, 1927).

____ (ed.), *Sophocles: Plays: Oedipus Coloneus* (1900; London: Bristol Classical Press, 2004).

Jones, David E., *The Plays of T. S. Eliot* (1960; Toronto: University of Toronto Press, 1965).

Jones, Ernest, *Sigmund Freud: Life and Work*, 3 vols. (London: Hogarth Press, 1953–7).

Jones, John, *On Aristotle and Greek Tragedy* (1962; London: Chatto & Windus, 1968).

Kahane, Claire. *See* Bernheimer, Charles.

Katz, Cindi. *See* Volkman, Toby Alice.

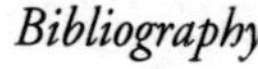

d Philosophy (1968; New York: Doubleday

(Harmondsworth: Penguin, 1974).

ud in High School', *American Imago*, 36:

Classical Greece (London: Thames and Hudson,

hillips (London: Faber and Faber, 2000).

d J.-B. Pontalis, 'Fantasme originaire, fantasmes des origines, antasme', *Les Temps Modernes*, 215 (April 1964), 1833–68.

antasy and the Origins of the Unconscious', in Victor Burgin, Donald, and Cora Kaplan (eds.), *Formations of Fantasy* (London: outledge, 1986), 5–34.

aqueur, Thomas, *Making Sex: Body and Gender from the Greeks to Freud* (Cambridge, MA: Harvard University Press, 1990).

Lattimore, Richard, *The Poetry of Greek Tragedy* (Baltimore: Johns Hopkins Press, 1958).

Lear, Jonathan, *Love and its Place in Nature: A Philosophical Interpretation of Freudian Psychoanalysis* (New York: Farrar, Straus & Giroux, 1990).

Lee, K. H. (ed.), *Euripides Ion* (Warminster: Aris & Phillips, 1997).

—— [Kevin] 'Shifts of Mood and Concepts of Time in Euripides' *Ion*', in Silk, *Tragedy and the Tragic*, 85–109.

Lembke, Janet (trans.), *Aeschylus: Suppliants* (New York: Oxford University Press, 1975).

Le Rider, Jacques, *Freud, de l' Acropole au Sinaï: Le retour à l' Antique des Modernes viennois* (Paris: PUF, 2002).

Lévi-Strauss, Claude, *Structures élémentaires de la parenté* (1949), trans. James Harle Bell and John Richardson Sturmer, ed. Rodney Needham, *The Elementary Structures of Kinship* (Boston: Beacon Press, 1969).

Lloyd-Jones, Hugh, *Blood for the Ghosts: Classical Influences in the Nineteenth and Twentieth Centuries* (1982; Baltimore: Johns Hopkins University Press, 1983).

Loraux, Nicole, *Les enfants d'Athéna: Idées athéniennes sur la citoyenneté et la division des sexes* (Paris: La Découverte, 1984), trans. Caroline Levine, *The Children of Athena: Athenian Ideas About Citizenship and the Division of the Sexes* (Princeton: Princeton University Press, 1994).

Lucas, D. W., *The Greek Tragic Poets* (1950; 2nd edn. London: Cohen & West, 1959).

—— (ed.), *Aristotle's 'Poetics': Introduction, Commentary and Appendices* (Oxford: Clarendon Press, 1968).

Macintosh, Fiona. *See* Hall, Edith.

Mastronarde, Donald J., 'Iconography and Imagery in Euripides' *Ion*', in Mossman, *Euripides*, 295–308.

Mazon, Paul (ed. and trans.), with an Introduction and Notes by Jean Alaux, *Eschyle, Les Suppliantes* (Paris: Les Belles Lettres, 2003).

Melosh, Barbara, *Strangers and Kin: The American Way of Adoption* (Cambridge, MA: Harvard University Press, 2002).

Ménage, Gilles, *Histoire des femmes philosophes* (1690), trans. from Latin by Manuella Vaney (Paris: Arléa, 2003).

Micale, Mark S., *Approaching Hysteria* (Princeton: Princeton University Press, 1994).

Mitchell, Juliet, *Psychoanalysis and Feminism* (1973; Harmondsworth: Penguin, 1974).

____ *Mad Men and Medusas: Reclaiming Hysteria and the Effects of Sibling Relations on the Human Condition* (London: Allen Lane, 2000).

____ *Siblings* (Cambridge: Polity Press, 2003).

Moi, Toril, 'Representation of Patriarchy: Sexuality and Epistemology in Freud's Dora', in Bernheimer and Kahane, *In Dora's Case*, 181–99.

____ *What is a Woman? and Other Essays* (Oxford: Oxford University Press, 1999).

Molière, *Les femmes savantes* (1672), in *Théâtre complet de Molière*, ii, ed. Robert Jouanny (Paris: Garnier, 1958), 677–749.

Morel, Geneviève, *Ambiguïtés sexuelles: Sexuation et psychose* (Paris: Anthropos, 2000).

Mossman, Judith (ed.), *Euripides* (Oxford: Oxford University Press, 2003).

Murray, Gilbert, *Aeschylus: The Creator of Tragedy* (Oxford: Clarendon Press, 1940).

Nietzsche, Friedrich, *Die Geburt der Tragödie* (1872), in *Werke*, ed. Karl Schlechta (Darmstadt: Wissenschaftliche Buchgesellschaft, 1958), i. 57, trans. Shaun Whiteside, *The Birth of Tragedy* (London: Penguin, 1993).

Norwood, Gilbert, *Greek Tragedy* (London: Methuen, 1920).

Nussbaum, Martha C., *The Fragility of Goodness: Luck and Ethics in Greek Tragedy and Philosophy* (Cambridge: Cambridge University Press, 1986).

____ '*Oedipus Rex* and the Ancient Unconscious', in Rudnytsky and Spitz, *Freud and Forbidden Knowledge*, 42–71.

Nuttall, A. D., *Why Does Tragedy Give Pleasure?* (Oxford: Clarendon Press, 1996).

Ornston, Darius Gray, Jr. (ed.), *Translating Freud* (New Haven: Yale University Press, 1992).

Ovid, *Heroides* and *Amores*, trans. Grant Showerman (Loeb Classical Library, 1914; Cambridge, MA: Harvard University Press, 1963).

____ *Metamorphoses*, i, trans. Frank Justus Miller (Loeb Classical Library, 1916; 3rd edn. Cambridge, MA: Harvard University Press, 1984).

Owen, A. S. (ed.), *Euripides Ion* (Oxford: Clarendon Press, 1939).

Padel, Ruth, *In and Out of the Mind: Greek Images of the Tragic Self* (Princeton: Princeton University Press, 1992).

—— *Whom Gods Destroy: Elements of Greek and Tragic Madness* (Princeton: Princeton University Press, 1995).

—— '*Ion*: Lost and Found', *Arion*, 4 (1996), 216–24.

Page, T. E. (ed.), *Q. Horatii Flacci, Carminum, Liber III* [Horace, *Odes*, Book III] (London: Macmillan, 1952).

Phillips, Adam, *The Beast in the Nursery* (London: Faber and Faber, 1998).

Pindar, *Olympian Odes, Pythian Odes*, ed. and trans. William H. Race (Cambridge, MA: Harvard University Press, Loeb Classical Library, 1997).

Platnauer, Maurice (ed.), *Fifty Years of Classical Scholarship* (Oxford: Basil Blackwell, 1954).

Poole, Adrian, *Tragedy: Shakespeare and the Greek Example* (Oxford: Basil Blackwell, 1987).

Porter, Roy. *See* Gilman et al.

Prendergast, Christopher, *The Order of Mimesis: Balzac, Stendhal, Nerval, Flaubert* (Cambridge: Cambridge University Press, 1986).

Ritvo, Lucille B., *Darwin's Influence on Freud: A Tale of Two Sciences* (New Haven: Yale University Press, 1990).

Roudinesco, Elisabeth, *Pourquoi la psychanalyse?* (Paris: Fayard, 1999), trans. Rachel Bowlby, *Why Psychoanalysis?* (New York: Columbia University Press, 2001).

—— *La Famille en désordre* (Paris: Fayard, 2002).

—— and Michel Plon, *Dictionnaire de la psychanalyse* (Paris: Fayard, 1997).

—— *See also* Derrida, Jacques.

Rousseau, G. S. *See* Gilman et al.

Rudnytsky, Peter L., *Freud and Oedipus* (New York: Columbia University Press, 1987).

—— and Ellen Handler Spitz (eds.), *Freud and Forbidden Knowledge* (New York: New York University Press, 1994).

Rustin, Margaret, and Rustin, Michael, *Mirror to Nature: Drama, Psychoanalysis and Society* (London: Karnac, 2002).

Sachs, Murray, *The Career of Alphonse Daudet: A Critical Study* (Cambridge, MA: Harvard University Press, 1965).

Scafuro, Adele, 'Discourses of Sexual Violation in Mythic Accounts and Dramatic Versions of "The Girl's Tragedy"', *differences*, 2: 1 (1990), 126–59.

Schopenhauer, Arthur, *The World as Will and Representation* (1819), trans. E. F. J. Payne, 2 vols. (New York: Dover, 1969).

Seaford, Richard, 'The Tragic Wedding', *Journal of Hellenic Studies*, 107 (1987), 106–30.

Segal, Charles, 'Sophocles' *Oedipus Tyrannus*: Freud, Language, and the Unconscious', in Rudnytsky and Spitz, *Freud and Forbidden Knowledge*, 72–95.

—— 'Catharsis, Audience, and Closure in Greek Tragedy', in Silk, *Tragedy and the Tragic*, 149–72.

—— *Tragedy and Civilization: An Interpretation of Sophocles* (1981; Norman: University of Oklahoma Press, 1999).

—— 'Euripides' *Ion*: Generational Passage and Civic Myth', *Bucknell Review*, 43: 1 (1999), 67–108.

—— *Oedipus Tyrannus: Tragic Heroism and the Limits of Knowledge* (1993; 2nd edn. Oxford: Oxford University Press, 2001).

Showalter, Elaine, *Hystories: Hysterical Epidemics and Modern Culture* (London: Picador, 1997).

—— *See also* Gilman et al.

Silk, M. S. (ed.), *Tragedy and the Tragic: Greek Theatre and Beyond* (Oxford: Clarendon Press, 1998).

—— and J. P. Stern, *Nietzsche on Tragedy* (Cambridge: Cambridge University Press, 1981).

Sissa, Giulia, *Le corps virginal* (Paris: Vrin, 1987), trans. Arthur Goldhammer, *Greek Virginity* (Cambridge, MA: Harvard University Press, 1990).

Smith, Carol H., *T. S. Eliot's Dramatic Theory and Practice: From 'Sweeney Agonistes' to 'The Elder Statesman'* (1963; New York: Gordian Press, 1977).

Smith, Grover, *T. S. Eliot's Poetry and Plays: A Study in Sources and Meaning* (1956; Chicago: University of Chicago Press, 1968).

Steinberg, S. H., *Five Hundred Years of Printing* (1955; 3rd edn. Harmondsworth: Penguin, 1974).

Steiner, George, *Antigones* (Oxford: Clarendon Press, 1984).

Stern, J. P. *See* Silk, M. S.

Strathern, Marilyn, *Reproducing the Future: Essays on Anthropology, Kinship and the New Reproductive Technologies* (Manchester: Manchester University Press, 1992).

Stray, Christopher, *Classics Transformed: Schools, Universities, and Society in England, 1830–1960* (Oxford: Clarendon Press, 1998).

Sullerot, Evelyne, *La vie des femmes* (Paris: Gonthier, 1965).

Sulloway, Frank, *Freud, Biologist of the Mind: Beyond the Psychoanalytic Legend* (1979; London: Fontana, 1980).

Thompson, E. P., and Marian Sugden (eds.), *'The Thresher's Labour' by Stephen Duck and 'The Woman's Labour' by Mary Collier* (London: Merlin Press, 1989).

Thorlby, Anthony (ed.), *The Penguin Companion to Literature*, ii. *European Literature* (Harmondsworth: Penguin, 1969).

Vasunia, Phiroze, *The Gift of the Nile: Hellenizing Egypt from Aeschylus to Alexander* (Berkeley: University of California Press, 2001).

Veith, Ilza, *Hysteria: The History of a Disease* (Chicago: University of Chicago Press, 1965).

Vellacott, Philip, *Ironic Drama: A Study of Euripides' Method and Meaning* (Cambridge: Cambridge University Press, 1975).

Vernant, Jean-Pierre, 'Œdipe sans complexe' (1969), in Vernant and Pierre Vidal-Naquet, *Mythe et tragédie en Grèce ancienne* (Paris: La Découverte, 1991), i. 77–98.

Verrall, A. W., *Euripides the Rationalist* (1895; New York: Russell & Russell, 1967).

Vickers, Brian, *Towards Greek Tragedy: Drama, Myth, Society* (London: Longman, 1973).

Volkman, Toby Alice, and Cindi Katz (eds.), *Transnational Adoption*. Special issue of *Social Text*, 74 (Spring 2003).

Waldock, A. J. A., *Sophocles the Dramatist* (Cambridge: Cambridge University Press, 1951).

Wallace, Jennifer, *Digging the Dirt: The Archaeological Imagination* (London: Duckworth, 2004).

Weber, Samuel, *Return to Freud: Jacques Lacan's Dislocation of Psychoanalysis*, trans. Michael Levine (Cambridge: Cambridge University Press, 1991).

Webster, T. B. L., 'Greek Tragedy', in Platnauer, *Fifty Years*, 71–95.

Wilamowitz-Moellendorff, Ulrich von (ed.), *Euripides Ion* (Berlin: Weidmannsche, 1926).

Williams, R. D. (ed.), *The Aeneid of Virgil: Books VII–XII* (London: Macmillan, 1973).

Winkler, John J., and Froma I. Zeitlin (eds.), *Nothing to Do with Dionysus? Athenian Drama in its Social Context* (Princeton: Princeton University Press, 1992).

Winter, Sarah, *Freud and the Institution of Psychoanalytic Knowledge* (Stanford, CA: Stanford University Press, 1999).

Wood, Michael, *The Road to Delphi: The Life and Afterlife of Oracles* (London: Chatto & Windus, 2003).

Wrigley, Amanda. *See* Hall, Edith.

Yngevesson, Barbara, 'Going "Home": Adoption, Loss of Bearings, and the Mythology of Roots', *Social Text*, 74 (Spring 2003), 7–27.

Zacharia, Katerina, *Converging Truths: Euripides' 'Ion' and the Athenian Quest for Self-Definition* (Leiden: Brill, 2003).

Zeitlin, Froma I., *Playing the Other: Gender and Society in Classical Greek Literature* (Chicago: University of Chicago Press, 1996).

—— *See* Winkler, John J.

Index